* THE MAN IN THE WHITE HOUSE

THE MAN IN THE

White House * * *

HIS POWERS AND DUTIES

BY Wilfred E. Binkley

The Johns Hopkins Press, BALTIMORE AND LONDON

MEIS NURIBUS

Alice

Isabel

Ruth

Martha

Copyright © 1958 by The Johns Hopkins Press
All rights reserved
Manufactured in the United States of America

The Johns Hopkins Press, Baltimore, Maryland 21218
The Johns Hopkins Press Ltd., London

ISBN-0-8018-0071-4 (clothbound edition)
ISBN-0-8018-1195-3 (paperback edition)

Originally published, 1958
Second printing, 1960
Third printing, 1968
Johns Hopkins Paperbacks edition, 1970

Preface

* **THIS TREATISE** on the American presidency has been undertaken in the belief that it is time to take one more comprehensive survey of the institution into which that office has evolved. Nearly half a century ago Woodrow Wilson took exception to the then widely held mechanistic theory of government with the observation that politics responds to the law of Darwin and not of Newton. This analogy of organic development suggests an appropriate pattern of interpretation of the American presidency as an ever evolving institution. No matter what the Constitution of 1787 prescribed for the office of president, deep-seated forces inherent in American society, playing upon the presidency for more than a century and a half, have transformed the office created by the framers into the unique institution the presidency is today.

Laconic indeed is the Constitution in its provisions for the presidency, but these provisions have been magnified, minimized, tortured out of the plain meaning of the Constitution's words, or even serenely ignored, all by way of statute, judicial judgment, or sheer usage and custom. For example, the Founding Fathers envisaged a nation free from national political parties, a nation in which quadrennially assemblies of notables (presidential electors), convening in their respective state capitals with each elector exercising his individual judgment, would vote blindly by ballot for two persons, not knowing which of his two choices might help elect the president and which the vice-president. But natural forces in American society promptly set to work, political parties emerged spontaneously, in due time national party conventions unexpectedly evolved as products of pure custom, which they remain to this very day, sheer usage converted the Electoral College into nothing but the registrar of the popular vote, and the presidency designed by the framers was converted into the authentic organ of American democracy. The would-be partyless president was meanwhile transfigured into the political chieftain of the party that elects him.

The Constitution gave the president the veto power ostensibly to protect his office from potential congressional aggression, but strong presidents utilized the veto to make the presidency indubitably the third house of the national legislature. The Supreme Court has held that, as chief executive, functioning in the field of international relations and as the head of a sovereign nation, the president of the United States possesses inherent plenary powers invisible to the eye of the uninitiated reader of the Constitution. Moreover, as the commander-in-chief of the armed forces the president can constitutionally dispatch troops to the moon just as soon as the wizards of modern mechanics have devised the appropriate apparatus of transportation.

Shifting metaphors from biology to geology, it can be said that the administrations of strong presidents such as Washington, Jefferson, Jackson, Lincoln, and the two Roosevelts each in its turn has deposited an alluvial sediment and thereby contributed to the formation of the strata that constitute the bedrock of the presidency today. Verily the great office like all other institutions has its fascinating natural history.

Wilfred E. Binkley

Ada, Ohio

ACKNOWLEDGMENTS

Incorporated in this book are some parts of articles first published in periodicals: "The Presidency as an Institution" in the *Western Reserve Law Review* (Summer, 1954); "The President as a Symbol" (September, 1952), and "The President as Chief Legislator" (September, 1956) in the *Annals of the American Academy of Political and Social Science*; and "President and Congress" in the *Journal of Politics* (February, 1949). I am grateful to the editors of these periodicals for permission to use parts of these articles in a revised form. The typing was done by two competent secretaries, Mrs. Betty Boyer of Pittsburgh and Miss Sally Allen, a student at Ohio Northern University, both of whom fortunately understood what they were typing.

Contents

The Presidency
as an Institution

* IN ONE OF those exquisite phrases that he so neatly turns, Walton Hamilton characterized the term *institution* as "a verbal symbol which for want of a better describes a cluster of social usages."[1] That phrase, "a cluster of social usages," serves to floodlight the concept "institution." As to the particular institution under consideration, we seem never to have neglected the presidency as a product of Constitution, statute, and judicial interpretation. But if the mythical Man from Mars were to arrive and, by some miraculous means, were to become cognizant of every clause of the Constitution, every statutory provision and every judicial judgment pertaining to the president, he would yet be woefully ignorant of the presidency as an institution.

He would lack that which vitalizes the great office, that is, the "cluster of social usages" that makes it a dynamic institution. He would know nothing of those extralegal organizations, the major political parties, which exist on a national scale, above everything else, for the purpose of electing the president and which consequently determine so largely what the presidency has been, is,

[1] E. R. A. Seligman (ed.), *Encyclopedia of the Social Sciences*, VIII, 84.

and will be. He would know nothing of the national nominating conventions that emerged without preconceived design and the presidential campaigns that follow. He would lack knowledge of the inauguration and the inaugural parade, which are utterly devoid of legal validity but are none the less profoundly significant of the great institution to the nation that views the majestic spectacle from sidelines or as telecast over the national hookups. There is the president's leadership of his party and of Congress, his use of patronage, his personal charm, if any, his tours of the country, his public addresses and fireside chats. Here is but a random sampling of the usages that, in their totality, constitute some essentials of the presidency as an institution.

Walton Hamilton further observed that "institution is the singular of which mores or the folkways are the plural."[2] But these mores frequently make the transition into what the late Franklin H. Giddings denominated "stateways," that is, laws with their inevitable sanctions. This transition is what the philosopher Emerson must have meant when he wrote, "The law is only a memorandum." He might as well have said, "Here are the mores which we have reduced to writing in order that they may not be forgotten." The Constitution and even more the statutes pertaining to the presidency are, as we shall see, by and large political mores that have somehow made the transition into stateways.

It was a shrewd observation of President Grover Cleveland that "Before I can understand a political problem I have got to know how it originated." Now that we are to investigate problems of the presidency let us see how the office came about. We shall discover that it is a peculiarly American institution, that it had its genesis in embryo in the first permanent English settlement in America, the Jamestown colony in 1607.

The settlement of Jamestown was undertaken as a get-rich-quick enterprise. Elizabethan and Jacobean England was fascinated with fantastic tales of gold and silver and other resources in Virginia,

[2] *Ibid.*

where the rich hauls of Cortez and Pizarro were, they believed, about to be repeated. The London Company, a joint-stock corporation, sold stock to eager buyers in England sure of enormous dividends. The charter granted by James I was that of a commercial corporation that, of course, required a business manager, designated by the charter as governor. But since this economic enterprise was to operate in a wilderness utterly devoid of civil government, the manager was, by the terms of the charter, incidentally constituted a magistrate to enforce the laws of England in the Virginia settlement. A similar official functioned also under the later charters of the Plymouth and Massachusetts Bay settlements and indeed in all the thirteen colonies.[3] The American presidency is indeed a lineal descendant of that old colonial office of governor, either a grandchild or a great-grandchild of it.

No dividends were ever declared by the London Company, and King James eventually wound up the venture by annulling the charter when the colony was only seventeen years old. But the King then appointed a royal governor of Virginia and provided him with a commission conveyed in an elaborate document including, among other things, the civil powers of governor quite as in the charter. In other colonies the letters patent, conveying the land title to proprietors such as William Penn and Lord Baltimore in Pennsylvania and Maryland, made the proprietors governors invested with powers similar to those previously mentioned in the charter colonies and the royal provinces.

In due time there were thirteen colonies, with thirteen governors, thirteen governor's councils gradually evolving into upper branches of legislatures, and thirteen popular assemblies elected by the colonists. But the royal agents, the colonial governors, were sometimes practically compelled to come, hat in hand, to the door of the colonial legislature pleading for funds for every purpose, even for their very salaries. The colonial legislature had

---

[3] See these charters in William Macdonald, *Documentary Source Book of American History* (1929), pp. 1–90.

become absolute master of the purse strings.[4] So miserable did they make the life of the governor that one American scholar has declared that the American Revolution was consummated twenty-five years before Lexington.

At any rate, when independence was achieved and the colonies had become states, the state constitutions they framed promptly reduced the governors to the "mere ciphers" that Madison denominated them in the *Federalist* papers.[5] So odious indeed had the colonial experience made the very title *governor* that four revolutionary states, in search of a decent term, designated the chief executives of their states *presidents*,[6] which title the framers of the Philadelphia Constitution serenely appropriated for the chief executive of the United States.

The intense antipathy generated against the executive in colonial times planted a persistent American prejudice against the executive. Repression of the chief executive was virtually a dogma of the Webster-Clay Whigs, and the Republican party is by no means free from it today. It is scarcely an exaggeration to say that the grim specter of the old colonial governor to this very day haunts the chambers of our state legislatures and the halls of our Congress. The Twenty-second Amendment to the Constitution, limiting the president to two terms or sometimes little more than a term and a half, and the proposed Bricker Amendment, designed to limit the president's negotiating power in foreign relations, are only recent incantations designed to lay the ghost. There will be others.

Since the Congress, under the Articles of Confederation, had no delegated power to exact statutes, no national executive as such existed in America prior to the Constitution. It was when the

[4] Charles E. Merriam, *A History of American Political Theories* (1926), pp. 34–37.

[5] *The Federalist*, No. 48

[6] Alexander Johnson, "What the Federal Constitution Owes to the Several States," *New Princeton Review* (1887). Quoted by James Bryce, *The American Commonwealth* (Commonwealth ed., 1908), ii, 719.

framers of the Constitution provided the imposing list of legislative powers for Congress[7] that the creation of a national executive became imperative. This, however, required no stroke of inventive statesmanship but merely the appropriation and adaptation of the native American institution of the executive already 180 years old. The evidence that this is precisely what the framers did is found in one clause after another of the Philadelphia Constitution. There was no need of inventing a title for the new American chief executive when they could merely reach out and appropriate that already used for the chief executive in Delaware, New Hampshire, Pennsylvania, and South Carolina. When the framers made the president commander-in-chief, they only copied precisely what the framers of twelve of the thirteen state constitutions had already done with their chief executives. The president was given the power of pardon in imitation of the governors of nine of the states. Almost all of the states prescribed a form of the executive's oath of office, and apparently Gouverneur Morris only rephrased that of the Pennsylvania Constitution in his own incomparable style. "Not creative genius," wrote the late Professor Alexander Johnson, "but wise and discreet selection was the proper work of the Convention."[8] Verily the president of the United States was created in the image of the state governor, and he is in fact a glorified state governor.

On one item the framers failed to practice the art of statesmanship—on the method of electing the president. One can scarcely do better than quote Alexander Johnson on this matter: "The presidential electoral system was almost the only feature of the Constitution not suggested by State experience, almost the only feature that was purely artificial, not a natural growth, and democracy has ridden right over it."[9] Curiously enough the framers, early in their deliberations, had decided to have the president

---

[7] *U. S. Constitution,* Art. i, sec. 8.
[8] Alexander Johnson, *op. cit.* above, Chap. i, note 6.
[9] *Ibid.*

elected by Congress just as the governor was then elected by the legislature in most states. But this might have made the president only a bigger "cipher" than the governors.

In plain truth the Electoral College was scarcely expected to elect presidents after Washington would no longer be available. The Constitution provided that each state was to choose, in any manner that its legislature might prescribe, a number of electors equal to the total number of its senators and representatives in Congress. These electors, meeting in their respective state capitols, were to vote for any one they personally thought suitable for president and vice-president. Since formal nominations or political parties were not anticipated, the framers expected that the electoral votes would be so widely scattered among the many voted for as not to produce the majority required for election oftener than once in twenty times as delegate George Mason calculated[10] or once in fifty times as he later estimated it. So the framers provided that the real election would take place in the House of Representatives, which would ballot on only the five who stood highest in the scattered balloting of the Electoral College, with each state casting one vote.

It was the unanticipated emergence of political parties as early as the third presidential election that upset the calculations of the framers and converted the presidential electors into the automata or dummies that have transformed the Electoral College into an organ for registering, somewhat inaccurately, the popular majority. Here is the most influential one of the "cluster of social usages" constituting the institution of the presidency. Arthur W. Macmahon epitomizes the matter in his statement that "considered nationally political parties in the United States may be described as loose alliances to win the stakes of power embodied in the presidency."[11] The powers of the presidency are what our major

[10] Chas. C. Tansill (ed.), *Documents Illustrative of the Formation of the American Union*, 69th Cong., 1st Sess., House Document, No. 398, p. 663.

[11] *Encyc. Soc. Sci.*, XI, 596.

parties exist to capture and control. It is the competition for that very power that determines largely what the presidency as an institution has become and is today. No matter how bravely a president may proclaim his personal convictions, he is inevitably the organ of the most influential interest to whom he owes his election. And Franklin Roosevelt, President by the electoral votes of every state but two small ones in 1936, would possess and exercise power impossible to Rutherford B. Hayes, declared elected by the margin of a single furiously disputed electoral vote, and moreover only a minority of the official popular vote. It is a fair approximation to say that the presidency is today to no small extent what our political parties have made it. Here again is the handiwork of American folkways and mores with a minimum of stateways.

In our own generation the usages of the Electoral College have come to make the presidency peculiarly sensitive to minority groups concentrated largely in metropolitan centers. One of these usages that long ago became a stateway is the election of the presidential electors at large in each state, instead of by districts as they originally sometimes were. Thus in each state the election of presidential electors is, for the political parties, a game of all or none. For example, this makes it theoretically possible for the Negro vote in half a dozen big pivotal states to throw a presidential election to either party. This is true of other minorities sufficiently determined to act in concert on election day. The recent striking gains in civil rights are largely due to the balance of voting power wielded by such minority groups in the great cities of pivotal states. One need only read President Truman's veto of the Taft-Hartley Act to see that it was consciously designed to hold the party loyalty of a minority group, labor. The presidential elections of 1952 and 1956 only suspended the decisive functioning of these interest groups as balances of power. It was the stars in their courses that fought for General Eisenhower—the stars on his uniform—quite as they had done for General Grant. Judging by his elaborate legislative programs he learned promptly the art of wooing the support of these minority groups. The program of the welfare state stands secure. The ballots of minorities, with their balances of power functioning through the usages of the Electoral College, compel presidents and presidential candidates to play the game of outpromising each other in legislative programs. Thus they hope to capture the ballots of the minorities that collectively constitute the majorities required to elect presidents.

The letters of Washington just before he assumed the duties of the presidency reveal a deep concern as to what the public expected of him and what it would tolerate in his conduct of the new office. He was acutely aware of an utter lack of precedents for an American national chief executive.[12] He knew he would be establishing precedents, and he desired that they "may be fixed on true principles." The elaborate inaugural ceremony accompanying his taking the oath of office did not pass unchallenged. Today we generally recognize that, while the inauguration itself has no legal force, it nevertheless symbolizes the fact that the president is chief of state as well as chief executive. But to the post-Revolution purists the inauguration was a conspicuous violation of Republican simplicity and an inexcusable aping of monarchy.

The elective branch of the colonial legislature had clung to the control of finance with the tenacity of a bulldog. In this tradition Congress established the Treasury Department and required that it report directly to Congress, so that half a century later it was still being debated whether the Treasury was an executive department. Washington appointed Hamilton Secretary of the Treasury, and in accordance with the law and the requests of the House of Representatives, Hamilton made his famous reports to Congress on manufacturers and on finance and pushed through the houses his famous measures—the Hamiltonian program. What of Washington's legislative program? There was none. Hamilton, an inveterate Anglophile, immediately upon appointment had assumed that he was prime minister, even asking his friends to call him by

[12] James Hart, *The American Presidency in Action, 1789* (1948), pp. 7, 8.

that title, in the tradition of the British Chancellor of the Excheq-
uer. The conduct of the government was rapidly falling into the
pattern of a parliamentary system. Washington, without any conscious shirking of responsibility, was dropping into the background with a separateness suggestive of the British monarch.[13]
Here is a striking illustration of the extent to which the presidency
is at any time a "cluster of social usages." How often has the presidency come to a parting of the ways and taken one instead of
another fork of the road? As strong as the trend toward parliamentary usages then was, it promptly encountered adverse social
forces so strong and deep-seated in the emerging American political culture that the trend was soon reversed.

When Washington in person first delivered to Congress what we
today call the State of the Union Message, critics promptly dubbed
it the Speech from the Throne. When the reply to this message
was prepared by the two houses and then sent to Washington's
residence to be delivered by the Vice-President, it was pronounced
downright mimicking of British practice, which unquestionably it
was. A year earlier Patrick Henry, speaking in the Virginia Convention that ratified the Constitution, had declared that the Constitution "squinted toward monarchy." Before Washington had
been President half a dozen weeks he received a letter from a
friend in Virginia who wrote that Henry's phrase, "squints toward
monarchy," was in every mouth.[14] It was a dozen years later that
President Jefferson, a son of the Piedmont frontier and thoroughly
habituated to the American folkways, promptly ended the reign of
the "monocrats," as he had dubbed the Federalists, and "put the
Ship of State on its Republican tack," to use his own picturesque
phrasing. By then the trend had already set in that, in the milieu of
our own political mores, would transform the presidency into what
Grover Cleveland was long afterward to characterize as "peculiarly

---

[13] See W. E. Binkley, *President and Congress* (1947), p. 37.
[14] James Hart, *The American Presidency in Action, 1789* (1948), p. 14.

the people's office."

Washington soon needed advice—an advisory council. Every colony had been provided with a governor's council, and this organ had been evolving into the upper house of the legislature, but without losing all its executive functions. Elliott's *Debates* on the making and ratifying of the Constitution of the United States contains nearly a dozen scattered references to the United States Senate as a "council of appointment," or a body associated with the president "to manage all our concerns with foreign nations."[15] Indubitably the Senate is a legitimate child of the governor's council, and it carries to this day vestigial evidence of its ancestry. Among these vestiges are the confirmation of presidential appointees and the ratification of treaties.

Quite naturally, President Washington turned first to the Senate for his appropriate councilors. This was not strange at a time when the upper house had only twenty-two senators, two states not having yet ratified the Constitution. Washington made his first visit to the Senate chamber with a set of propositions concerning a proposed treaty with the Indians. What could be plainer than the Constitution's provision: "He shall have power, by and with the advice and consent of the Senate, to make treaties, provided two-thirds of the Senators present concur"? Now Washington took the chair of the Senate just as the governors customarily did when conferring with their councils. Vice-President Adams read the first proposition for the treaty and turning to the senators asked, "Do you advise and consent, etc.?" The question was greeted with stony silence. Here was a momentous instant in the laboriously emerging institution of the presidency. Senator Maclay of Pennsylvania finally broke the awkward silence by asking for some of the papers pertaining to the matter and a little later urged that the matter of

---

[15] Jonathan Elliot (ed.), *Debates, Resolutions and Other Proceedings in Convention on the Adoption of the Federal Constitution*, (1827–46), II, 47, 287, 306; III, 220, 221, 489, 493, 494, 496; V, 549.

the treaty be referred to a committee. Thereupon, according to Maclay, Washington "started up in a violent fret and said, 'This defeats my every purpose in coming here.' " When Washington left the Senate chamber that day, he is reported to have said that he would be damned if he would ever come back there.[16] Another fork in the road to be taken had been determined. Treaties would simply have to be negotiated by the president or his agent beforehand and the draft submitted to the Senate for its consideration in his absence as is done to this day.

In the first session of Congress the Senate confirmed all Washington's appointees but one. Here was another constitutional power suggesting the intention of the framers to make the Senate a council for the president that was to sit with him while considering the nomination of an appointee. Washington's one nominee who was not confirmed was to have been collector of customs at the port of Savannah, to which nominee the Georgia senators had objected. The astonished President sent the Senate a message suggesting that, in such cases, the Senate might ascertain the president's reason for the appointment. This was ignored, and the usage, euphemistically denominated "senatorial courtesy," had begun.[17] As a consequence it can be set down that usage has literally reversed the Constitutional provision, so that it is the Senate that virtually nominates and the president that gives consent. It was now clear that, no matter what the framers of the Constitution may have intended, the Senate simply would not serve as a council advising the president. Usage is a sovereign that can reduce a provision of the written Constitution with which it conflicts to sheer dead letters.

Washington finally got his executive council or advisory body scarcely by design but rather by accident. The Constitution, with

[16] James Hart, *The American Presidency in Action, 1789* (1948), pp. 86–96.
[17] *Ibid.*, p. 123.

apparently no suggestion of a council, authorized the president to require, in writing, the opinion of the principal officer in each of the executive departments upon any subject relating to the duties of their respective departments, and Washington was doing this as early as 1790. His first meeting with his department heads as a consultive group occurred in the third year of his presidency in order to consider what to do about the request of Congress for papers relating to St. Clair's disastrous defeat by the Indians in the Northwest Territory. The President here needed advice on a perplexing issue that had arisen, and he resorted to the expedient of calling his executive heads together. It is almost certain that he had no idea whatever of starting a new institution. It is but one more concrete illustration of the shrewd observations of the late James Bryce that "historical development is wiser than the wisest man" and "a succession of small improvements, each made conformably to existing conditions and habits, is more likely to succeed than a large scheme made all at once in what may be called the spirit of conscious experiment."[18] It is a significant fact, noted by the late George Burton Adams, that the British Cabinet system, every essential feature of which is pure usage, had matured so shortly before 1787 that the framers of our Constitution were not aware of its existence, and in fact the British Cabinet system was half a century old before its nature was sufficiently recognized that clear expositions of it as now understood were published.[19]

There was certainly no prompt recognition that a new usage had been contributed to the cluster constituting the presidency by Washington's informal conferring with his department heads collectively. Gradually, however, the term cabinet crept into the vocabulary of the newspapers and letters of the executive heads.[20] By the end of Washington's eight years the term was understood.

---

[18] *The American Commonwealth* (Commonwealth ed., 1908), II, 332.
[19] *An Outline Sketch of English Constitutional History* (1918), p. 167.
[20] H. B. Learned, *The President's Cabinet* (1912), p. 155.

It appeared in Congressional debates in 1798. Marshall used it in the Marbury decision in 1803.[21] By the end of Jefferson's presidency in 1809 it was a recognized institution. President Jackson was first to use the term *cabinet* in a presidential message. In 1907 it first appeared rather incidentally in a statute in the phrase, "the heads of the Executive Departments who are members of the President's cabinet."[22]

Jefferson's Secretary of the Treasury, Albert Gallatin, could not persuade his President to hold regular Cabinet meetings. When they were held, a vote was taken on issues discussed, with Jefferson having a single vote, but he had usually persuaded the Cabinet to the point of unanimity.[23] Jackson largely ignored his executive heads as counselors and turned instead to the coterie of cronies in his famous "Kitchen Cabinet." Some presidents have abided by the majority vote of their cabinets, notably Pierce and Buchanan. Lincoln was unquestionably the master of his Cabinet. To this day we can say that the Cabinet is not yet a stabilized institution but is still evolving. As recently as December 29th, 1953, Stewart Alsop was observing that President Eisenhower "has now made the National Security Council the chief instrument of decision on matters of vital importance, that he has been presiding over it in person, and that it has thus all but replaced the unwieldy cabinet reducing the out-dated cabinet to a shadow." During the first year of the Eisenhower administration the National Security Council is said to have won presidential approval of 305 major policy decisions.[24] Later Eisenhower did rather revive the Cabinet and convert it into a policy-shaping organ.

Why is the president the chief of administration? Practically all the reasons given by textbook or court opinion are not much

[21] Marbury *v*. Madison, 1 Cranch 137 (U.S. 1803).
[22] 34 *Statutes at Large*, Chap. 1639, p. 993.
[23] Francis A. Walker, *Making of the Nation* (1895), p. 91.
[24] The *Toledo Blade*, Dec. 29, 1953.

more than ex-post-facto rationalizations of the *fait accompli*. The Constitution is not specific on the matter, apparently because the framers failed to recognize the distinct character of administrative power—that is, the "management of men and materials in accomplishing the purposes of the state," as Leonard D. White so aptly put it.[25] At any rate the Constitution is not clear as to administration, and the legislative and executive branches of the Federal government throughout our history as a nation have competed for the control of that function. They are still competing for it today. The Eisenhower administration in the beginning even removed key administrators apparently as a consequence of senatorial pressure, and under the same kind of pressure made appointments to positions where the appointee could embarrass and harass the executive branch.

The question as to the presidential control of administration depends on whether the president has the constitutional power to remove executive officers of his own volition. That question was thoroughly debated in the first session of the First Congress. A bill investing the president with this very power of removal, without requiring senatorial consent, was considered then and dropped. This disposal of the issue has been called a "legislative decision,"[26] because it amounted to an interpretation that the Constitution implied the sole power of removal resided necessarily in the chief executive; he could not "take care that the laws be faithfully executed" if the Senate, by sharing the removal power, could compel him to retain subordinates he did not trust. A statute forbidding the Senate to share in removal power might have been repealed. An implication or a gentleman's understanding seemed safer.

It was Andrew Jackson who first put to test the president's power of removal as a means of control of administration. He even selected the most difficult office in the Cabinet on which to make the

[25] Leonard D. White, *An Introduction to the Study of Public Administration* (1926), p. 2.

[26] James Hart, *The American Presidency in Action, 1789* (1948), p. 155 ff

test. In 1833 he had appointed William J. Duane Secretary of the Treasury and advised him to remove the Federal deposits of money from the Bank of the United States, the renewal of whose charter he had just recently vetoed. Now Congress had by statute specifically vested in the secretary of the treasury exclusively the discretion to remove deposits from the Bank. Duane, relying upon the statute, refused to make the removal and stood firm despite Jackson's patient but persistent attempts at persuasion. Then Jackson removed Duane and appointed in his stead Roger B. Taney, who obediently removed the deposits. Jackson justified his removal of Duane by reasoning that "upon him [the President] has been devolved by the Constitution and the suffrages of the American people the duty of superintending the operation of the Executive Departments of the Government and seeing that the laws are faithfully executed."[27] Half a century later President Hayes, even in spite of a recently enacted Tenure of Office Act by which the Senate shared in removal power, defied the Senate by removing some New York customs officers, among whom was a future president of the United States.[28] And Grover Cleveland likewise removed a district attorney in the face of a furious senatorial protest.[29] It was only after President Wilson had removed a postmaster before the expiration of his term of appointment that the question was finally authoritatively decided in 1926 in the case of Myers v. United States.[30] The President has then the now unquestioned constitutional power to remove appointive executive officers and is consequently as much of a chief of administration as he has the competence and resolute will to be. Neither constitutional prescription nor statute has made him such, but rather over a century and a quarter of usage fortified finally by court opinion.

A quarter of a century ago Professor Howard Lee McBain

---

[27] James D. Richardson, *Messages and Papers of the Presidents* (1927), p. 19.
[28] W. E. Binkley, *Powers of the President* (1937), pp. 167–71.
[29] *Ibid.*, pp. 174–82.
[30] 272 U. S. 52, 42 Sup. Ct. 21 (1926).

denominated the president "Chief Legislator." "The prime function of the Executive," he wrote, "is not executive at all. It is legislative."[31] "Rightly or wrongly," he added, "the whole country looks to him, praises or blames him, for what Congress does or does not do, except of course, when both houses chance to be in control of the opposite party."[32] Here is a statement of plain fact that would have been incomprehensible in the early days under the Constitution and indeed at almost any time before 1900.[33]

It was President Theodore Roosevelt who established the first promising organic connection of the presidency and the Congress by means of White House conferences on pending legislation with the then master of the House of Representatives, Speaker Joseph G. Cannon.[34] The "dethronement" of the speaker in 1910 ended all possibility of institutionalizing that kind of liaison. In 1913 Woodrow Wilson initiated what he conceived to be the prime ministry of the presidency, which he believed the Constitution invited in the provision for the president to give Congress information of the state of the Union, and to recommend measures for their consideration.[35] Franklin Roosevelt would have already held conferences with leaders of his party in Congress in order to see, among other things, that the bill would be referred to hospitable committees. Moreover the message would probably have lying right under it the draft of an appropriate bill with the last *t* crossed and *i* dotted.[36] Congress became accustomed to presidents' submitting a bill along with a message.

[31] *The Living Constitution* (1927), p. 115.

[32] *Ibid.*, p. 131.

[33] John Sherman, *Recollections of Forty Years in House, Senate, and Cabinet* (1895), II, 1032.

[34] L. W. Busbey, *Uncle Joe Cannon* (1927), pp. 217, 218.

[35] Woodrow Wilson, *Constitutional Government in the United States* (1907), pp. 72, 73.

[36] "Congress's Reason for Delay in Passing the President's Bills," *United States News and World Report* (January, 1946).

So today "upon many of our most celebrated laws the presidential imprint is clearly stamped. Each of these was drafted in the President's office, introduced and supported by his friends, defended in committee by his aides, voted through by a party over which every form of discipline and persuasion was exerted and then made law by his signature."[37] Meanwhile the president may utilize the White House breakfast with his chief supporters and even obstructionists; the fireside chat to rally constituents; the press conference to express his dismay at Congress's "dragging its feet"; the ancient lure of patronage; the threat of veto to discourage shackling amendments.

Few usages have contributed more to making the presidency what it is today than the national nominating convention. Viewed from the galleries the convention looks as meaningless as a typical sitting of the national House of Representatives. In either case the significant action is invisible from the point of disadvantage in the gallery. Of course the convention looks utterly irrational. Successful institutions, however, are not products of reason and logic but of chance and circumstances. The key to an understanding of a national convention is that it is managed by professionals, politicians who are experts in social co-operation. These experts have one great objective, namely, manipulating the delegates so as to pick a potential winner and thereby capture control of the prestige, power, and patronage embodied in the presidency. In the strategy of picking a winner the managers exercise an acumen and shrewdness impossible for the rank and file of a party functioning individually in a national party primary. Inevitably the candidate nominated will be debtor to the powerful interests that swung the nomination to him, no matter how much he may protest his freedom from commitments and usually "methinks he doth protest too much." A President who has no powerful economic, social or party forces behind him rules with a palsied hand. Such are the

---

[37] Clinton Rossiter, *The American Presidency* (1956), p. 15.

realities of presidential power..For us the significant thing is that the nominating convention works, has worked for a century and a quarter, and is a faithful expression of the genius of the American people and of its folkways and mores. When we get a better nominating procedure, it will be one that emerges naturally just as the convention did; it will never be the brainchild of an inventive genius.

No interpretation of the presidency would be adequate that omitted the contributions of the great presidents to the making of the office. If we may borrow a term from the geologist, let us say that the administration of each of the great presidents has contributed its stratum of rich alluvial deposits. Washington's peculiar gift was in consequence of his superb character, which made its contribution even before he was chosen President. We have competent testimony to this fact in a letter written a year after the Philadelphia convention by Pierce Butler, one of the delegates. "Entre Nous," he wrote, "I do not believe they [the executive powers] would have been so great had not many of the members cast their eyes toward George Washington [President of the Convention], and shaped their ideas of the powers to be given the President by their opinions of his virtue."[38] To a degree the office is what it is because it was made for Washington. In office he gave it a good start.

It was Thomas Jefferson, the third President, despite all his acquired Eastern polish still a Piedmontese frontiersman at heart, whose role it was to reorient the developing office of the presidency away from foreign precedents toward its genuinely American character. Jefferson's keen eye had appraised Europe as accurately as any American of his day who had sojourned overseas, but he saw little there to be imitated. Here was our first astute American politician-statesman, a happy son of the American political mores, resolutely determined to make the presidency a republican and an American institution.

[38] Max Farrand, *The Records of the Federal Convention of 1787* (1911), III, 301.

A generation later an upsurge of the American masses, "the common man," put Andrew Jackson in the White House. Speaking in the then prevailing classical vogue, his partisans proclaimed him a "tribune of the people."[39] Just as the ancient Roman tribune had shouted his "veto" into the patrician Senate in defense of his plebeian constituents, so President Jackson converted the presidential veto into an instrument for the protection of the interest of the common man. When Old Hickory retired, it was impossible to turn the hands of the clock of history back and ever again make the presidency what it had been before. His impress persists today.

Even more than Jackson, Lincoln won the hearts of common folk—Lincoln, who casually touched his hat in return to an officer's salute but uncovered his head to the man in the ranks, as Noah Brooks observed.[40] Woodrow Wilson set the modern and apparently enduring pattern of legislative leadership. The 1920's constituted an interregnum, a decade of arrested development of the presidency. The Republicans as the spiritual heirs of the pre-Civil War Whigs who had entrenched themselves in Congress elected three typical Republican Presidents—Harding, Coolidge, and Hoover. But the spell broke suddenly on March 4, 1933, when Franklin Roosevelt seized the moment when the very disintegration of the nation seemed imminent to restore presidential leadership. When he announced, "I am prepared under my constitutional duty to recommend the measures that a stricken nation in the midst of a stricken world may require," it was apparent that another Woodrow Wilson was at the helm. At the ensuing mid-term election Republican congressmen appealed for re-election by insisting that they had supported Roosevelt's recovery legislation. In the opinion of Clinton Rossiter only Washington and Jackson did more than Franklin Roosevelt to raise the presidency "to its present condition of strength, dignity and independence."[41]

---

[39] See W. E. Binkley, *American Political Parties: Their Natural History* (1947), p. 135.

[40] Christian Gauss, *Democracy Today: An Interpretation* (1919), Appendix, p. 29.

[41] *The American Presidency* (1956), p. 119.

President Truman was determined that the Great Office would not be suffered to decline while he was President. It is the judgment of Rossiter that "Mr. Truman demonstrated a more clean-cut philosophy of presidential power than any predecessor except Woodrow Wilson."[42] No president did his "home work" more faithfully, and none has been shrewder or more proficient in delegating authority to subordinates. Consequently, despite having dealt with one earth-rocking crises after another, he left the White House fresh and chipper without the slightest suggestion of the "hair shirt" Herbert Hoover said he wore there. "The Office he handed over to Eisenhower was no less magnificent than the Office he inherited from Roosevelt and this may well be considered a remarkable achievement."[43]

The twenty years' contribution of Roosevelt and Truman to the institutionalizing of the presidency left Eisenhower no choice but to accept and continue it. Thus he inherited a strong presidency. By 1953 even Republicans expected him to seize the helm resolutely and propose and promote policies, and he was far oftener criticised for inaction than action. Building upon the already well-developed White House staff he had inherited, Eisenhower "has done himself and the presidency a great service by carrying the process of institutionalization at least a step and a half further."[44]

---

[42] *Ibid.*, p. 123.
[43] *Ibid.*, p. 125.
[44] *Ibid.*, p. 131.

II

Apprenticeship

for the Presidency

* I T   W A S   W H E N the New World was still young [writes Niles Blair]that a youthful giant rode into Williamsburg. He was only twenty-one and Governor Dinwiddie had sent for him. Although he had been to Williamsburg before he was not a familiar figure in the capital, for his home was on the Potomac. Yet because he was so immensely tall, and because, even in a country of fine horsemen, he stood out as a magnificent rider, people must have gazed admiring, curious perhaps to know who was this young centaur with the frank, cheerful face who rode down the Duke of Gloucester Street.[1]

The Governor of colonial Virginia was sending young Washington on the eve of what would turn out to be the French and Indian War upon a perilous mission far beyond the remotest settlements of the Virginia frontier in order to warn the intruding French away from territory well within the bounds of the Virginia Charter grant. In mid-November, 1753, with six frontiersmen Washington

[1] *The James* (1939), p. 109.

struck out into the wilderness and reached his destination (the present site of Pittsburgh) only to discover that the French had retired to winter quarters at Venango sixty miles deeper in the winter wilderness. Under the circumstances Washington might, with propriety have returned to Williamsburg, but instead he pressed on to Venango only to have the French commander there refuse to receive his message but insist that Washington deliver it to his superior, the commandant at Ft. Le Boeuf, a hundred miles still farther, to which Washington pushed on through water-clogged swampland. There Washington delivered Dinwiddie's ultimatum, which was courteously rejected. On his return trip the horses gave out, and he, with Christopher Gist, returned on foot, was shot at by a prowling Indian, and almost drowned amid ice floes of the Allegheny River. His report, *The Journal of George Washington,* when published by Governor Dinwiddie, created excitement on both sides of the Atlantic. The predestined first President of the United States had begun an incomparable apprenticeship for the great office a generation before it was created.

A year later Governor Dinwiddie sent Washington with a small force to anticipate the French in erecting a fort at the confluence of the Allegheny and Monongahela Rivers, but the French had already erected Ft. Duquesne there. A year still later the twenty-three-year-old colonel and commander-in-chief of the Virginia militia was assigned the defense of three hundred miles of frontier with three hundred men, and here, according to John C. Fitzpatrick, "Washington acquired the habit of thinking and acting for the welfare of a people. . . ."[2] At twenty-five he was urging Virginia, Maryland, and Pennsylvania legislatures to provide the troops to capture Ft. Duquesne. At twenty-seven he was a member of the Virginia House of Burgesses. Whoever is disposed to marvel at Washington's inexhaustible patience with and deference to the

---

[2] "George Washington," *Dictionary of American Biography* XIX, 512.

Continental Congress while serving as commander-in-chief of the Continental army should bear in mind that he had experienced personally the perplexing role of the legislator not only in the Virginia House of Burgesses but also in the very Congress to which he was responsible.

After Washington's twenty-seventh year there passed fifteen years during which he reveled in his heart's desire, the management of Mt. Vernon and his other plantations, all of which was done with an intelligence, enterprise, and efficiency rarely matched in the Old Dominion. Like the other great planters he developed a high sense of public responsibility, for, as Professor Max Farrand put it, there were things the Virginia planters as public servants would not do even in their own private interest. If, as Professor Thomas J. Wertenbaker concluded, the Virginia dynasty of presidents was a product of the tobacco plantation, here was but another stage of Washington's apprenticeship for the presidency. The supervision of these large-scale enterprises provided training in administration—the art of managing land, labor, and capital profitably—and at this Washington excelled. "As landed proprietor no less than as Commander-in-Chief he showed excellent ability, the power of planning for a distant end, and a capacity for taking infinite pains. Neither drought nor defeat could turn him from a course that he discerned to be proper and right."[3]

As commander-in-chief of the armed forces of the Revolution, Washington spent half a dozen distressing years patiently working under the authority of the Continental Congress (a Congress obsessed with a fear of the army) discretely avoiding every move that might augment the prevailing public phobia of military authority. Washington's extraordinary deference to the civil authority exercised by Congress revealed his shrewd comprehension of the political mores of the American people. Even when Congress, in desperate crises, twice granted him temporary powers of dictatorship,

[3] Samuel Eliot Morison, *By Land and By Sea* (1953), p. 173.

he used them sparingly. The deftness with which he exposed the Conway Cabal to supplant him and his magnanimity toward the exposed conspirators was veritably Lincolnesque. It was under the circumstances of these heartbreaking years dealing with cantankerous congressmen, conspiring generals, and an indifferent and fickle public that Washington perfected the high art of politics that made him the first statesman of the age. He completed the apprenticeship that was to make him the first President of the United States not so much by formal election as by the common consent of a greatful people.

A dozen years after Washington's first inauguration a veritable revolution in the climate of American political opinion and power brought to the presidency another great Virginia planter, Thomas Jefferson. By this time the pattern of federal administration had been firmly established thanks to Washington, the adept manager of men and materials in achieving the purposes of the new national state. Thus a firmly established and efficiently functioning federal government was the unintended bequest of the Federalists to the Jeffersonian Republicans. So Jefferson neither possessed nor required the genius of Washington in management. It was his role rather to provide the grand liaison between the national government and the frustrated frontiersmen and other neglected elements in American society and convince them that the national government was, after all, their very own—not their enemy. Instead of the adept administrator, this called for a kind of political evangelism capable of planting a political faith in the hearts of the people. How did Jefferson acquire this peculiar art? How did he serve the apprenticeship that was to prepare him too for a place among the front-rank presidents of the United States?

It was peculiarly appropriate that the first evangel of our emerging national democracy should have been a product of the Virginia Piedmont, the old colonial frontier.

[Jefferson] was the son of a western pioneer [wrote James A. Woodburn] living in a hot-bed of radical democracy, amid natives in their buckskin breeches and hunting shirts and coonskin caps. He was a man of education and eastern polish but he lived among small western farmers in crude cabins and he was in sympathy with their needs. ... What he did for democracy in Virginia was never forgiven by the landed aristocracy of his native state.[4]

No sooner had Jefferson attained his majority than he was appointed a justice of the peace. In Virginia the justices of the peace of each county collectively constituted the county governing board, thus giving the young Jefferson a taste of public administration of a sort. At twenty-six he was elected to the Virginia House of Burgesses, where he became the intimate associate of Patrick Henry the ardent leader of the irrepressible democracy of the back counties and the terror of the tidewater aristocracy, a leader of which he exposed as an embezzler of public funds. In 1774 Jefferson prepared for the consideration of the Virginia Convention "A Summary View of the Rights of British America," which proved too strong for the delegates. A year later he was a member of the Second Continental Congress into whose lap fell the management of the public affairs of the Union now at war. Within five days of his arrival he was put on a committee to draft a "Declaration of the Causes and Necessity of Taking up Arms." At thirty-three his masterly pen dashed off "at white heat" the burning phrases of the Declaration of Independence, his imperishable contribution to the American credo. Eighty-five years later President-elect Abraham Lincoln was to declare at Independence Hall, "I have never had a feeling politically that did not spring from the sentiments embodied in the Declaration of Independence."[5]

When Patrick Henry became Governor of Virginia in 1776, Jefferson inherited his leadership of the Virginia democracy in the legislature, where he proceeded systematically to break up the aristocratic system by promoting statutes abolishing land-holding

[4] "Radicalism in American Politics," *Mississippi Valley Historical Review*, XIII, No. 2 (1926), 149.

[5] Roy P. Basler (ed.), *Abraham Lincoln: His Speeches and Writings* (1946), p. 577.

in fee-tail and primogeniture and by disestablishing the Anglican Church. As War Governor, succeeding Henry, though he slighted no obligation, his term was a nightmare, for Jefferson was not of the executive type, and the British invaded the state, which was unprepared for successful defense. Back in Congress he drafted thirty-some state papers, the greatest of which was the report on government of the western territories that laid the groundwork of the Northwest Ordinance and the pattern of government for our territories ever since.

From 1785 to 1789 Jefferson was our minister to France, where he served his country as a diligent and skillful diplomat while he witnessed what turned out to be the prelude to the impending French Revolution. Returning home President Washington promptly appointed him our first Secretary of State, which office he conducted with the skill and understanding of the experienced diplomat. Soon he became the leading critic of Hamilton's financial measures and his loose construction of the Constitution as well as of the "monocrats," the term he coined to characterize the Federalists. By 1793 he had resigned and was back at Monticello convinced that he had finally retired from public life. But he had already become the "symbol of anti-Hamiltonianism" and as such the rallying point of what was to become the Jeffersonian Republican party, and by 1797 he was Vice-President. The four years he presided over the Senate were but another stage of his apprenticeship. From that post he witnessed the Federalists commit party suicide with their Alien and Sedition Acts savagely administered by partisan Federalist judges upon hapless Jeffersonians, and by 1801 he was President.

Jefferson's party constituted no disciplined phalanx such as the Federalist combination of interests but just a loosely associated aggregation of individualists extraordinarily touchy as to matters of personal liberty. Here were the ardent patriots who had read the new Constitution fresh from the Philadelphia Convention with burning indignation when they could find no bill of rights in it.

Not until they had been assured that very thing by amendments could they be calmed sufficiently to get the Constitution ratified by the necessary majority of the states. Jefferson's peculiar apprenticeship had prepared him precisely to be the only kind of president for those ardent devotees of personal liberty. With the flair of the adept political evangelist Jefferson struck a vibrant note for his disciples when he declared, "I have sworn on the altar of the living God eternal enmity against every form of tyranny over the mind of man."[6]

When Jefferson became President, he was prepared. "He was too astute a party leader to attempt to force his will upon the Republicans in Congress. He would suggest, he would advise; he would cautiously express an opinion but he would never dictate. Yet few Presidents have exercised a stronger directive influence upon Congress than Thomas Jefferson during the greater part of his administration."[7]

The lasting testimony to the political evangelism of Jefferson is the historical fact that he was to be the patron saint of every major party in our history, excepting only the Federalist. When, in the 1820's, his own party split into two branches, the Democratic Republican, which evolved into the Jacksonian Democrats, and the National Republicans, who were soon absorbed by the Whigs, each branch insisted they were the only true Jeffersonians. The patron saint of the new Republican party of the 1850's was Jefferson, frankly avowed as such in its first national party platform in 1856. And Lincoln, who became that party's first President, was to proclaim again and again, "The principles of Jefferson are the definitions and axioms of free society."[8]

Andrew Jackson, aged twenty, had been reading law with his companion John McNairy, and the two had been admitted to the

---

[6] Letter to Benjamin Rush, Monticello, Sept. 23, 1800.

[7] Allen Johnson, *Jefferson and his Colleagues* (1921), p. 32.

[8] Letter to H. L. Pierce and others, April 6, 1859, John Hay and John G. Nicolay (eds.), *Lincoln's Complete Works* (12 vols., New York, 1905), v, 126.

practice of law when, in 1788, the legislature of North Carolina elected McNairy Superior Judge of the extreme western district of the state now part of Tennessee. The two journeyed on the first wagon road to Nashville, then a remote stockaded village of log cabins. McNairy appointed Jackson attorney general, as the prosecuting attorney was then called in North Carolina, and Jackson, like Lincoln later, began riding the circuit with the judge and practicing law. In 1791 Congress organized Tennessee as a territory, and Jackson was appointed judge advocate of the Davison County militia regiment. In 1796, when the Territory of Tennessee held a constitutional convention preparatory to demanding admission to the Union, Jackson sat as a delegate. It was a recognition of professional standing that he was appointed a member of the committee that drafted the constitution that Thomas Jefferson was to pronounce the best of the state constitutions. Jackson was elected, without opposition, as the one Tennessee member of Congress in the national House of Representatives, where he took his seat December 5, 1796. Within a year the Tennessee legislature elected him to the United States Senate, but he soon resigned and returned home because of financial difficulties due to the severe depression of the mid-1790's. He aspired to and obtained the major-generalship of the militia of Tennessee, next to the governorship the most important office in the state. In March, 1814, having overcome a combination of obstacles, he thoroughly defeated the Indians at Horseshoe Bend. In recognition of this achievement he was commissioned a major general of the United States.

In 1815 with a motley and undisciplined aggregation of Tennessee and Kentucky militiamen, Creoles, Negroes, and pirates he confronted, before New Orleans, the hitherto invincible veterans of Wellington's Peninsular campaign. Passing down the tense lines in the pitch darkness of one o'clock in the morning before the battle and recognizing by voice and calling by name soldiers who gathered about and spoke to him, the future President was practicing the grand art of practical politics and all unconsciously serving well his apprenticeship for the presidency. The astounding victory at New Orleans "created a president, a party, and a tradition."[9] In 1821 President Monroe appointed Jackson Governor of the Territory of Florida.

We have the testimony of Vice-President Thomas Jefferson, while presiding over the Senate, that when Senator Jackson would rise to speak, his rage would almost prevent his expressing himself. But during the ensuing three decades he learned to control his emotions so that by the time he became President, his "tantrums" often consisted of sheer acting. Though he appeared to be self-willed and impetuous, he reflected carefully before making a decision. So well had he prepared himself for the great responsibility that in his cool, calculated judgment as to party strategy he persistently outwitted his proud and confident Whig opponents such as Clay and Webster. It would be difficult to point out a single victory of theirs over Jackson on a major matter. Accepting serenely the popular conception that he had been cast for the role of a tribune of the people, indecisiveness would have been an unpardonable defect in Jackson. It required a firm and resolute will on the part of the recognized champion of the common man to convince the old ruling elite that they were no longer in charge of public affairs. Jackson's whole adult life had been a preparation for just such a decisive presidency.

It was certainly no accident that James K. Polk turned out to be the ablest President in the twenty-four years between Jackson and Lincoln. By the age of twenty-eight "Young Hickory", as Polk has been called, was in the Tennessee legislature, where he won prompt recognition for his methodical ways and exceptional ability in debate. Two years later he was almost the youngest member of the national House of Representatives when his hero Andrew Jackson

---

[9] T. P. Abernathy, "Andrew Jackson," *Dictionary of American Biography*, IX, 529.

had become President of the United States. Congressman Polk was promptly recognized as an administration leader in the House. In the battle against the arrogant Bank of the United States Jackson turned to Polk, who was made chairman of the all important Ways and Means Committee. He became President Jackson's chief defender in his policy to remove the Federal deposits and thereby crush the Bank. By the age of thirty-four Polk was elevated to the eminence of Speaker of the House, an office already evolving into a position second only to the presidency of the United States in influence and power. No speaker of the House has ever been more savagely abused and sniped at by partisan opposition, but so thoroughly had Polk prepared himself that he was able to anticipate parliamentary difficulties before they arose, and he was consequently never caught unprepared. In his farewell address as Speaker he said: "It has been my duty to decide more questions of parliamentary law and order, many of them of a more complex and difficult character . . . than have been decided . . . by all my predecessors from the formation of the Government."[10]

It is significant that, although Polk desired to remain in Congress, his party drafted him to run for Governor of Tennessee. In this office he acquitted himself with his accustomed efficiency. Only a few weeks before Polk's election to the presidency Andrew Jackson wrote that "his capacity for business (is) great, and to the extraordinary powers of labor, both mental and physical, he united that tact and judgment which are requisite to the successful direction of such an office as that of Chief Magistrate of a free people."[11] No wonder the historian George Bancroft, who had been Polk's Secretary of the Navy, was to declare half a century later, "His administration, viewed from the standpoint of results, was perhaps the greatest in our history, certainly one of the greatest. He

---

[10] *Congressional Globe*, 25th Cong., 3rd Sess., p. 252.
[11] *Nashville Union*, Aug. 13, 1844.

succeeded because he insisted on being its center and in overruling and guiding all his secretaries to act so as to produce unity and harmony."[12]

Abraham Lincoln was given first place unanimously by the panel of fifty-five historians polled by Professor Arthur Schlesinger, Sr. to rank the presidents. What preparation had Lincoln for attaining that high eminence? He entered the presidency without a trace of administrative experience such as had prepared Washington to set the presidency going. Even Jefferson, whose disciple Lincoln repeatedly declared himself to be, had been Governor of Virginia. Like Jefferson however Lincoln was to be another exponent of the maturing American democratic culture. By Lincoln's time the railways and even more the telegraph had made possible the prompt dissemination of news and the consequent rapid formulation of public opinion on a continental scale, and Lincoln made the most of the opportunity these new media of communication afforded him.

If politics signifies primarily the determination of public policies, then Lincoln was our politician par excellence and this provides the clue to his pre-eminent rank among our presidents. From his mid-teens to his early fifties his life was one continuous preparation for the peculiar kind of president he was to be. Lincoln emerged into manhood in an Illinois community when "all Illinois then seethed in politics."[13] He was twenty-three when he announced his candidacy for the legislature in an "address to the people of Sangamon County" setting forth his stand on public policies. He lost the election, but the late Senator Beveridge, whose long political experience qualified him to judge the matter, wrote: "We see in the vagueness and dexterity of his first public utterance the

---

[12] Letter to J. G. Wilson, Mar. 8, 1888. Quoted by J. G. Wilson, *The Presidents of the United States* (1914), II, 230.

[13] A. J. Beveridge, *Abraham Lincoln* (1928), I, 114.

characteristics of the natural politician, a type of which he was to become, excepting only Jefferson, the supreme example. We observe too, that cleverness and caution which distinguished his every public maneuver and discomfitted the most skilful antagonists."[14] At the age of twenty-four he was appointed postmaster of the tiny settlement of New Salem. This is a neglected landmark in the political education of Lincoln, for he thus became the first to receive and read the newspapers that arrived—the *Sangamo Journal*, the *Louisville Journal*, *The St. Louis Republican,* and the *Cincinnati Gazette,*[15] and his tenacious memory seemed to retain almost everything he read.

At the age of twenty-five Lincoln was elected to the first of four terms in the lower house of the Illinois legislature and so apt was he as a parliamentarian that at the age of twenty-seven he was Whig floor leader and only the fact that the Whigs were in a minority prevented his being elected Speaker. It was customary, each night after adjournment, for the lobby to be thronged for speech-making and informal debate. The controversy over President Jackson's removal of Federal deposits from the Bank of the United States was then raging. Beveridge believed that

> the debate over it in the lobby more even than in the House, the discussion of it in taverns and wherever men met, afforded instruction in constitutional principles as thorough perhaps as Lincoln could have received at any college or university. The powers and duties of the President, the authority of Congress, the nature and disposition of patronage—well nigh nearly every subject with which he would have to deal one day was examined with sense and learning.[16]

Lincoln set out to persuade the legislature to move the capital from Vandalia to Springfield in his own county. The art of legislation

[14] A. J. Beveridge, *Abraham Lincoln* (1928), I, 118.
[15] Carl Sandburg, *Lincoln: The Prairie Years* (1926), p. 102.
[16] *Abraham Lincoln* (1928), p. 187.

then even as now involved the practice of logrolling. Lincoln and the "Long Nine," as the Sangamon county delegation was then called, traded votes and cast them with scarcely any other object- ive than the removal of the capital. Lincoln's triumph on this pro- ject at the age of twenty-eight was due to his extraordinary legis- lative craftsmanship and the fact that, as R. L. Wilson, one of his colleagues, put it, "his practical common sense, his thorough knowledge of human nature, then made him an over match for his compeers and for any man that I have ever known."[17]

At the age of forty Lincoln took his seat for his single term in the national House of Representatives and here experienced the invaluable discipline of adversity. As Congressman he made almost no impression on anybody in Washington, and what slight im- pression he did make was unfavorable. As a regular party man obedient to caucus decisions he joined in the concerted Whig crit- icism of President Polk for provoking the Mexican War while his constituents were ardently supporting the war. Back home he was denounced as a "second Benedict Arnold" for having pled the cause of the enemy. He had defied the "Sovereign"—the people— the people in Illinois, of all places, where it was an extraordinarily jealous potentate. Lincoln thus learned his greatest lesson in poli- tics. Henceforth this inveterate reader of newspapers would clair- voyantly perceive dominant opinion, catch step with popular move- ments, and march neither behind nor ahead of them. He would express only emerging popular opinion and feeling, which he dis- ciplined himself to register accurately.[18] "Never the apostle of a cause," wrote Beveridge, "he was to become the perfect interpre- ter of public opinion, thought and feeling and so the instrument of events."[19]

---

[17] Paul M. Angle (ed.), *The Lincoln Reader* (1947), p. 84.
[18] See Jesse Macy, *Political Parties in the United States, 1846–1861* (1900), pp. 248, 252, 253; A. J. Beveridge, *Abraham Lincoln* (1928), III, 143.
[19] *Abraham Lincoln* (1928), I, p. 107.

In 1856 occurred Lincoln's spectacular demonstration of maturity in the art of politics. At Bloomington, Illinois, he addressed the heterogeneous, even discordant aggregation of groups constituting the delegates to a convention of bitter opponents of the Kansas-Nebraska Act that had repealed the Missouri Compromise and thus opened the trans-Mississippi public domain to slavery. In the convention were represented the elements destined soon to constitute the then even unnamed Republican party. Resolved to stir their passions, Lincoln knew he must yet hold them in restraint. Hesitating Whigs needed to be convinced without alienating radical abolitionists. Germans must be conciliated without losing the anti-alien Know-Nothings. "With the politician's eye for vote getting and for uniting incongruous elements of his party, he avoided the language of the anti-slavery crusade and narrowed the issue to the clear-cut doctrine of slavery in the territories."[20]

Once when President Lincoln, in the midst of his term, was warned by one of his secretaries to be on his guard against a delegation of wily politicians waiting to see him, he promptly said, "Let them in. They won't fool me." The President who could write the magisterial, chiding letter to General Hooker, commander of the Army of the Potomac, had acquired the easy mastery of men, in the rough and tumble competition of the turbulent Illinois frontier. Who else could have remained unquestionably master of a Cabinet of cantankerous individualists at the very time that he was outwitting cliques of intriguing senators and representatives of his own party. So well had he served his apprenticeship that he alone was ready to steer resolutely the ship of state on the most tempestuous voyage of its history.

William McKinley's experience in responsibility began at the age of seventeen when he enlisted as a private in the Union army. There he promptly attracted the attention of his colonel, the future

[20] J. G. Randall, "Abraham Lincoln," *Dictionary of American Biography,* XI, 248.

President Rutherford B. Hayes, whose disciple McKinley promptly became. He rose by merit to the rank of captain and was mustered out as a major. After studying at Meadville College and in a law office and, for less than a year, at Albany Law School, he began the practice of law at Canton, Ohio. At the age of twenty-six he was elected county prosecutor, the local office that, above all others, has provided the springboard for many a notable political career. In 1876 when the coal mining firm of Rhodes and Company (Mark Hanna's firm) in the Massillon district imported some laborers from Cleveland to break a strike, rioting broke out, a mine was set on fire, and thirty-three strikers were jailed and indicted. In the hysteria that followed no lawyer would take the miner's case, none until former prosecuting attorney William McKinley volunteered to defend them and would not be dissuaded by the protestations of his friends. As Thomas Beer put it, "Major McKinley had the unbelievable stubbornness of the mild pliant man."[21] The competent young attorney obtained the acquittal of all the miners indicted except one, who served a short sentence—an astonishing achievement with juries from a community wrought up over the violence of the strikers.[22] This episode is significant indeed in McKinley's preparation for the presidency, since he then captured the lasting gratitude of a large segment of American labor. McKinley was the first President during whose incumbency labor, particularly organized labor, was cordially received at the president's office.[23]

At thirty-three McKinley began a career of fourteen years in the national House of Representatives. He entered Congress the day his old colonel, Rutherford B. Hayes, was inaugurated President of the United States. A protégé of Hayes, McKinley haunted the White House as no other congressman and so became familiar

[21] *Hanna* (1929), p. 79.

[22] F. P. Weisenberger, "The Time of Mark Hanna's First Acquaintance with McKinley," *Mississippi Valley Historical Review,* xxi (1935), 78.

[23] Samuel Gompers, *Seventy Years of Life and Labor* (1929), I, 552–53.

with the presidency long before his term as President. In four years McKinley earned by sheer merit the chairmanship of the most important committee of the House, the Ways and Means Committee, and this was long before seniority was almost the sole determinant of promotion. No other president had undertaken the responsibilities of the great office so expert in congressional legislation, and the consequence was that one has to go back almost a century to President Jefferson to find the prototype of President McKinley as the gentle but undoubted leader of Congress.[24] Erudite Senator George F. Hoar expressed the opinion that no other president, with the possible exception of Jackson, had exercised such influence over the Senate as McKinley.[25] Such were the consequences of a fruitful apprenticeship.

McKinley had rapidly become expert in the art of politics in county, congressional district, state, and national nominating conventions, presiding over them from time to time. He was permanent chairman of the Republican National Convention of 1892 when President Benjamin Harrison was nominated for a second term and would very probably have been nominated himself had he not insisted on Harrison's renomination. His declination increased his stature in the eyes of those who witnessed his resolute renunciation of the proffered crown.

In 1891 McKinley was elected to the first of two terms as Governor. The governor of Ohio did not then have the veto power, and uninformed publicists have blamed McKinley for not preventing certain legislation favorable to utilities. He did persuade the legislature to levy the first Ohio tax on corporations in the face of their determined opposition, and in a few years Ohio left the general property tax entirely to local government. As a champion of labor he urged the introduction of safety devices on railroads and trolley cars and arbitration in labor disputes. From the day of his inauguration McKinley had what it takes to be prepared for the office of president.

Just graduated from Harvard, Theodore Roosevelt was told that politics was so disreputable that it would "soil the linen of a gentleman." Unperturbed he promptly replied that he "intended to be one of the governing class" no matter how crude the politicians were. In the fullness of time he was to teach new techniques in the art of politics. Because a New York city boss needed a respectable candidate Theodore was nominated and elected to the state assembly at the age of twenty-four. He was a raw amateur with almost everything to learn about politics. Long afterwards he confessed to his intimate friend Jacob Riis his sudden disenchantment in the legislature.

> I stood for my own opinion alone. . . . I would listen to no argument, no advice. I took the isolated peak on every issue, and my associates left me. When I looked around before the session was well under way, I found myself alone. I was absolutely deserted. The people didn't understand. The men from Erie, from Suffolk, from anywhere would not work with me. 'He won't listen to anybody,' they said and I would not. . . . The things I wanted to do I was powerless to accomplish. I looked the ground over, made up my mind that there were several other excellent people there with honest opinions of the right, even though they differed from me, I turned in to help them, and they turned to and gave me a hand. And so we were able to get things done. We did not agree in all things but we did in some, and on those we pulled all together. That was my first lesson in real politics.[26]

So very rapidly did the amateur politician become expert that by his second year in the assembly, at the age of twenty-five, he was floor leader of the Republicans, and only the fact that his party was then in the minority prevented his being elected Speaker. At

[26] Quoted by Lawrence F. Abbott, *Impressions of Theodore Roosevelt* (1919), p. 45.

twenty-eight he led a forlorn hope as Republican candidate for mayor of New York. Appointed by President Harrison a member of the Civil Service Commission, the young reformer found the spoils system too deeply rooted in the prevailing political mores to be summarily eradicated, but this disillusionment too contributed to his political education. Appointed police commissioner of New York City, he took his duties so seriously that he became the terror of indifferent patrolmen. Coming in contact with the lowest levels of slum life he learned first hand of the vicious alliance of graft, politics, and crime. At last he became aware of poignant social problems on an extended scale, and his discoveries started his education in social reform, of which he had hitherto been so contemptuous.

When President McKinley, with understandable misgiving, appointed Roosevelt Assistant Secretary of the Navy, he proved to be a problem to his superior, Secretary John D. Long. Whatever the merits of Roosevelt's services he did acquire experience as a Federal administrator. Returning from Cuba from the San Juan Hill charge of the Rough Riders a thoroughly publicized hero, he was promptly nominated for and elected Governor of New York. Now thoroughly familiar with practical politics in this superpolitical state he pushed reform as far as he could without breaking with the state boss, United States Senator Thomas C. Platt. It was a game of wits between two semipros, and historians have not yet decided whether Governor or Senator was winner. At any rate Senator Platt was glad to manipulate delegations in the Republican National Convention of 1900 and manage to get Roosevelt nominated for and, as he assumed, relegated to the innocuous obscurity of the vice-president of the United States.

In dealing with the New York giants of business, finance, and politics Governor Theodore Roosevelt developed the practice of flexibility—of not insisting on the impossible—a preparation indeed for the larger office of the presidency. As he expressed it in an article published during his governorship, "Sometimes it is a sign of the highest statesmanship to temporize."[27] It is indicative of his progress that he would have spurned such a practice twenty years earlier. As Governor, instead of committing political suicide, he did enough tight-rope walking to learn not to lose his balance. As much could have been said of President Lincoln in the 1860's.

Although Theodore Roosevelt ranks high as an administrator in the presidency, he belongs rather with the evangelists in that office—that is with Jefferson and Lincoln. He had a pronounced flair for the dramatic, and he certainly succeeded in arousing the public on very significant issues. As his biographer expressed it "he possessed to an unusual degree the political asset of self hypnosis."[28] Let him who chooses disdain that peculiar trait, but it was an element of profound effectiveness in arousing the nation from its lethargy to the necessity of long overdue reform. "His flaws," declared his biographer, "were on the surface; his values were timeless."[29]

Young Woodrow Wilson's choice of a vocation was political leadership, and so certain was he of it that he considered himself a predestined and foreordained agent who was being "guided by an intelligent power outside of himself."[30] "He had been carefully, almost fearfully tutored by a perfectionist father in the mastery of the symbols of human communication. The deliberately poised phrase—the precisely pointed anecdote—the perfectly balanced paragraph were arrows in his quiver of political weapons."[31] In preparation for a public career young Woodrow painfully disciplined himself for oratory, and to the end of his public career he could influence crowds better than individuals or small groups.

---

[27] *Century*, June, 1900.

[28] H. F. Pringle, *Theodore Roosevelt a Biography* (1931), p. 80.

[29] H. F. Pringle, *Dictionary of American Biography*, XVII, 143.

[30] Walter Lippmann, "Woodrow Wilson's Approach to Politics," *New Republic*, Dec. 5, 1955, p. 15.

[31] Jasper Shannon, "Woodrow Wilson as a Domestic Political Leader," unpublished paper read at a round table of the Midwestern Conference of Political Scientists at Marquette University, May 4, 1956.

In his early twenties Wilson was captivated by Walter Bagehot's brilliant interpretation of the British Constitution, which was, in due time, to provide the budding scholar with a pattern for an interpretation of the American presidency. At the age of twenty-three he published his first article, "Cabinet Government in the United States."[32] He then held the American presidency in so little esteem that, not until many years later, did he aspire to it. Wilson's doctoral disseration, *Congressional Government*, published in 1885, was such a success that it struck the spark of ambition in him for a big public career. "I do feel a very real regret," he wrote his fiancee, "that I have been shut out from my heart's *first*—primary—ambition and purpose which is to take an active, if possible a leading, part in public life, and strike out for myself, if I had the ability, on a statesman's career."[33] After graduation from Princeton he studied law, was admitted to the bar, and started practice on the then prevailing assumption that law provided the high road to a political career.

By 1908 Wilson, now President of Princeton, was publishing his matured conception of the president as "the unifying force in our complex system, the leader both of his party and the nation."[34] Here he found in the president's State of the Union and other messages the constitutional authority for his functioning as a quasi prime minister.[35] Although he had written in 1902, "I was born a politician," there is no evidence in his writings and speeches that he had then any conception whatever of political machines, the work of the ward heeler or of everyday practical politics.[36] These were things to be learned later and outside of books.

Curiously enough Wilson owed his call to a political career to an overtly avowed conservative social and economic philosophy

[32] *International Review*, VI (Aug., 1879), 46–163.
[33] R. S. Baker, *Woodrow Wilson, Life and Letters* (1927), I, 229.
[34] *Constitutional Government in the United States* (1907), p. 54.
[35] *Ibid.*, pp. 72, 73.
[36] Arthur Link, *Wilson: the Road to the White House* (1947), p. 34.

bordering on that of a reactionary. The very year of his publication of *Constitutional Government in the United States*, he was publicly denouncing the whole program of government regulation of business as "socialistic."[37] The following year he was declaring, "I am a fierce partisan of the open shop and of everything that makes for individual liberty."[38] It was such views along with his eloquence in publicizing them that induced a coterie of conservative Wall Street Democrats to start grooming him for the presidency.

The plan of the president-makers was to get Wilson first elected Governor of New Jersey. He was pliable enough to assure the New Jersey Democratic leader, James Smith, that, as Governor, he would not "set about fighting or breaking down the Democratic organization and replacing it with one of (my) own," but he insisted on absolute freedom "in the matter of measures and men," and Smith accepted the terms, flattered with the role of president-maker. Wilson's acceptance of the nomination fully aware that it was being managed by the Smith-Davis political machines marked the transition from the academic to the practical politician. However, this alienated, for the time being, the Progressive Democrats, who assumed that Wilson had become the captive of the machine politicians.

The state convention nominated Wilson by a safe majority, whereupon the nomination was made unanimous. The delegates were preparing to disperse when it was announced that Wilson had left Princeton and was on his way to address the convention. In the midst of the address he declared, "I did not seek this nomination; it has come to me absolutely unsolicited with the consequence that I shall enter the duties of the office of Governor, if elected, with absolutely no pledge of any kind to prevent me

[37] "Government and Business," address before the Commercial Club of Chicago, March 14, 1908. Quoted by Link, *op. cit.*, p. 119.
[38] Quoted by James Kerney, *The Political Education of Woodrow Wilson* (1926), p. 34.

serving the people of the State with singleness of purpose."[39] The address closed with a burst of purple eloquence—an apostrophe to the flag. The convention was electrified, delegates stood on the chairs and shouted themselves hoarse, and the Progressives were reassured. No veteran in politics could have done it better. Woodrow Wilson was on his way.

It is evidence of his political dexterity that Woodrow Wilson went through the gubernatorial campaign holding the support of Progressives without alienating the party organization and the machine politicians.[40] But before the end of the campaign he had professed and proclaimed a completely Progressive program: utility regulations, direct party primaries, a corrupt practices act, and workman's compensation. "He seemed to catch public opinion as by wireless."[41]

After election and inauguration Governor Wilson pursued his purpose of having the legislature enact the measures he had advocated in his campaign speeches. When Democratic Boss James R. Nugent, lobbying against an administration measure, was summoned to the Governor's office, a heated altercation ensued during which Nugent hurled an insulting insinuation—and was promptly ordered out, to the glee of the Progressive Democrats.

Then the Governor broke precedent by meeting with and addressing the Democratic legislature caucus. He took advantage of the opportunity to practice his cherished pattern of executive leadership in legislation. Facing the caucus he alluded to the challenge of the opposition to his right to interfere in legislative matters. In a dramatic gesture he took from his pocket a copy of the Constitution of New Jersey and read: "He [the Governor] shall communicate by message to the Legislature at the opening of each

[39] Link, *Wilson: the Road to the White House* (1947), p. 167.
[40] *Ibid.*, p. 173.
[41] C. E. Merriam, *Four Political Leaders* (1926), p. 48.

session, and at such other times as he may deem necessary, the condition of the State, and *recommend such measures as he may deem* expedient." He added, "I stand upon the provision of the Constitution."

The pending measures proposed by the Governor were then discussed in the caucus with the Governor taking an active part. Thereafter he held daily conferences with members of his party and called in opposition members of the legislature. "He's a great man," declared one dumbfounded assemblyman. "He talked to us as a father would." When opposition to these practices arose, he threatened to appeal directly to public opinion.[42] He was accused of being stiff and exclusive whereupon at a planned social meeting he unbent, told stories and even danced the Virginia reel with one of the Senators.[43]

Wilson's theory of the executive as a prime minister was now emerging as a technique of practical politics eventually to culminate in the peculiar pattern of his presidential leadership in legislation. The session of the New Jersey legislature closed with the Governor's program of measures all enacted. "The newspaper men seemed dazed," Wilson wrote to a friend. "I wrote the platform, I had the measures formulated to my mind, I kept the pressure of public opinion constantly on the Legislature, and the program was carried out to the last detail."[44] As one reporter put it, the Governor had "licked the gang to a frazzle."[45] It all seemed just like a dress rehearsal for the first two years of Wilson's presidency.

In the autumn of 1911 Wilson met Colonel E. M. House, who, with George Harvey and others, was interested in promoting Wilson's candidacy for President. The association with House turned out to be what Sir Horace Plunkett pronounced "the

---

[42] H. J. Ford, *Woodrow Wilson, The Man and his Work* (1916), pp. 144-45.
[43] David Lawrence, *The True Story of Woodrow Wilson* (1924), p. 48.
[44] Quoted by Link, *Wilson: the Road to the White House* (1947), p. 274.
[45] R. S. Baker, *Woodrow Wilson, Life and Letters* (1927), III, 127.

strangest and most fruitful personal alliance in human history."[46]
House was a liberal with a belief in government responsive to the
needs of all classes, and he and Wilson came to see eye to eye.
House helped resolve the mutual antipathy of Wilson and Bryan,
which reconciliation led to the breath-taking coup in the Baltimore convention by which Bryan almost singlehanded threw the
nomination to Wilson after his candidacy had literally collapsed.
Wilson was learning the facts of life as to national politics and was
to enter the presidency better prepared than many a president with
ten times as many years of experience in practical politics.

Franklin Roosevelt was born amid books and may have rolled
about among them as a babe, which Doctor Oliver Wendell
Holmes considered so important. As a youth his intellectual pab-
ulum included Madison's *Notes on the Constitutional Convention*
and the *Federalist Papers*, both of which he absorbed by repeated
reading. He was twenty-eight when a group of Dutchess County
politicians persuaded him to run for the New York State Senate.
He is said to have toured the three counties of the senatorial district day by day canvassing every village, town and crossroad. It
was his ambition to call personally on every farmer. It is indicative
of his flair for politics that his most effective talking point was his
advocacy of a 96-quart standard barrel for apples—something the
farmers wanted. He became, with a single exception, the first
Democratic Senator elected in his district since the birth of the
Republican party fifty-six years earlier.

In the state Senate Roosevelt won promptly a statewide reputation by mobilizing reform Democratic senators and preventing the
election of Tammany's choice for United States senator. Herein
he revealed "leadership, heterodoxy, a courage bordering on audacity, adhesiveness and dramatic sense of timing."[47] Made chairman of the Forest, Fish and Game Committee, he had the opportunity to give full play to his enthusiasm for conservation as he

[46] E. M. House, *Intimate Papers* (1926–28), I, 44.
[47] John Gunther, *Roosevelt in Retrospect: a Profile in History* (1950), p. 204.

characteristically refused an appropriation for his own county because it did not need it. That he took a firm stand against the utility lobby and just as firm a stand for farm relief were prophetic. Setting up a temporary home in Albany, "the Roosevelt house burst with politicians day and night."[48]

A delegate to the Baltimore Convention of 1912, Franklin worked hard for the nomination of Wilson. Here he became acquainted with Josephus Daniels, soon to be Wilson's Secretary of the Navy with Franklin his Assistant Secretary. When war was declared in 1917, Roosevelt's work became mainly procurement contracts and labor relations. Invaluable for the future President was the art of high politics Roosevelt learned from Josephus Daniels, "a genius in handling recalcitrant Senators, and Congressmen and wheedling appropriations through committees."[49]

In 1920 Franklin Roosevelt, while still Assistant Secretary of the Navy, was nominated for Vice-President and made 800 speeches during the campaign. One year later he was stricken with the ailment that crippled him for the remainder of his life. It appears that even this misfortune that befell him in his early forties was a factor in his preparation for the presidency. While bedfast he read widely, aided by a system of card-indexing, keeping alive and expanding his already wide acquaintance with key men in his party throughout the nation by means of systematic and large-scale correspondence.

By 1929 Roosevelt was Governor of New York. An executive budget had just been voted into the state Constitution, and Governor Roosevelt promptly locked horns with the legislature, which was bent upon watering down the Governor's use of the budget power. The Governor was sustained in this controversy by the courts, whose decision helped ensure executive authority over state administration—one of the main purposes of the executive budget.

[48] John Gunther, *Roosevelt in Retrospect: a Profile in History* (1950), p. 205.
[49] *Ibid.*, p. 212.

Before the end of his first term as Governor, Franklin Roosevelt realized that farm aid was of extreme urgency. In his first annual message to the legislature he declared that his ultimate goal was that the farmer and his family be put on the same level of earning as his fellow citizens in the city. Three years later, campaigning for the presidency at Topeka, Kansas, he was telling distressed farmers, "I seek to give that portion of the crop consumed in the United States a benefit equivalent to a tariff sufficient to give you farmers an adequate price."[50]

Two years before he became President, Governor Roosevelt was directing his State Conservation Commissioner, Henry Morgenthau, to purchase and retire from cultivation tens of thousands of acres of marginal land to be reforested.[51] When he had persuaded the people of New York to vote an amendment to the state Constitution authorizing a bond issue to finance this, he received a telegram from Governor Dern of Utah reading, "Hurrah for trees."[52] As Governor Roosevelt acquired a reputation for leadership in farm legislation his prestige as a potential presidential candidate grew apace. His failure to persuade the legislature to pass legislation to protect bank depositors convinced him that Congress must provide that protection.[53]

Throughout his four years as Governor, Roosevelt showed an increasing flair for leadership. Never had a prospective president a better opportunity for practice games in the policies he was to establish as president. Campaigning for Governor in 1928 he was telling audiences that old-age pensions were no more socialistic than workman's compensation and this at a time when they were almost universally considered vicious. So he was to reap the benefits later of a reputation for persistent promotion of social legislation in the face of a hostile Republican legislature.[54] Likewise

[50] Bernard Bellush, *Franklin Roosevelt, Governor of New York* (1955), p. 94.
[51] *Ibid*, p. 94.
[52] *Ibid*, p. 98.
[53] *Ibid*, p. 125.
[54] *Ibid*, p. 190.

the legislature frustrated his efforts at labor legislation, but he helped educate the public by his lucid presentation of the matter. When inaugurated, President Roosevelt had already had three years experience wrestling with the economic problems presented by the Great Depression. Indeed, as the depression deepened, Governor Roosevelt in August, 1931, signed the bill for an eight-hour day and prevailing wages on all state highway contracts.[55]

In his first inaugural address as Governor, Franklin Roosevelt maintained that the state's water power belonged to all the people, and it was the duty of the legislature to see that the power was transformed into usable electrical energy and distributed at the lowest cost.[56] Yet his public power policy was so moderate as to be persistently denounced by the Socialists under the leadership of Norman Thomas. It was a culmination of Roosevelt's policy as Governor to sign, as President, the Norris Bill creating the Tennessee Valley Authority.[57] He had struggled throughout his four years as Governor to free the New York State Utility Commission from the domination of utility corporations. It was a sequel to this crusade when he signed the Wheeler-Rayburn Act of 1935 with its broad powers over the gigantic electrical power holding companies.

So thorough was Franklin Roosevelt's apprenticeship that the transition from the executive routine at Albany to that of the White House was made with scarcely a break. As Governor he had already

evolved most of the working techniques that were to be so useful to him as President, and the executive routine of his day had become fixed: how he arranged his appointments and so on in the White House exactly duplicated the system he set up at Albany. The later Fireside Chats grew naturally out of his

[55] *Ibid.*, p. 205.
[56] *Ibid.*, p. 209.
[57] *Ibid.*, p. 239.

innovation of direct radio talks to the New York electorate. In Albany he customarily held a press conference twice a day; so it was no great burden, in Washington, to do the same thing twice a week. Also he learned something of the incisive role he could play as a teacher, an educator, both to the public at large and to his immediate political associates.[58]

Scarcely any other occupant of the White House has executed the office of President with a more confident touch than Harry S. Truman. And this was in spite of the fact that he was compelled to undertake the great responsibility on a moment's notice, without a trace of briefing by his predecessor, and with a more meager apprenticeship than any predecessor who made a comparable mark in the presidency. In 1956 Clinton Rossiter, than whom there is no more competent authority on the American presidency, after summarizing the record of the Truman administration observed, "On the basis of this evidence I am ready to hazard an opinion, to which I also did not come easily or lightly that Harry S. Truman will eventually win a place as president, if not as a hero, alongside Jefferson and Theodore Roosevelt."[59]

Fortunately from youth Harry Truman had read widely and understandingly the history of his country so that he knew more than most of his predecessors of the nature of the presidential office. He served as a captain of artillery in World War I. At 38 he was elected as one of the three Jackson County, Missouri, judges, a nonjudicial board that administered county government and was twice re-elected, each time with enormously increasing majorities. Irving Brandt, then editor of the St. Louis *Star Times*, found Judge Truman to be the only Missouri official at a better-government conference who could discuss administration problems with the visiting experts. Eventually Truman was to say: "I had charge of spending $60,000,000 for highways and public buildings

[58] John Gunther, *Roosevelt in Retrospect: a Profile in History* (1950), pp. 260–61.
[59] *The American Presidency* (1956), p. 126.

in Jackson County. Nobody ever found anything wrong with that, and it wasn't because they did not look hard enough."

In 1934 he was one of three candidates for the Democratic nomination for Senator from Missouri in the primary election. He went stump speaking into 60 of Missouri's 114 counties making 6 to 16 speeches a day and won the nomination by a margin of 44,000.[60] Here was virtually a dress rehearsal for the whistle-stop campaign of 1948 when he upset the confident expectations of the pollsters, the gamblers, and the nation. If practical grass-roots politics is an essential equipment of a president, Harry Truman was prepared.

It was in the Senate that Harry Truman got the feel of national affairs. In the midst of World War II he conceived the idea of a special Senate committee to investigate war contracts. The Truman Committee, as it was popularly denominated, became the most famous committee of its time, veritably a household term on virtually everybody's tongue. Moreover it was literally a product of the man's personality. Its reports were clear-cut and unequivocal: the use of dollar-a-year men was not good for the defense program; denying raw material for producing automobiles was the way to persuade the motor industry to manufacture war planes; exorbitant war contracts ought to be renegotiated. And so the reports went on.[61] Some think the committee saved the nation billions, and competent contemporary authority expressed the opinion that, excepting only the president, Harry S. Truman through his committee contributed more to the winning of the war than any other civilian. Without the slightest preconceived design, the committee chairmanship turned out to be what led to the vice-presidency and the White House.

General Dwight D. Eisenhower had had a less relevant experience for the presidency than any president since General Grant.

[60] Harry S. Truman, *Memoirs* (1955), I, 141.
[61] Irving Brandt, "Harry S. Truman II," *New Republic*, May 7, 1945.

Most of his career had been outside the United States, and his unfamiliarity with significant issues of American life was apparent from the first weeks of his campaigning in 1952. "His only knowledge of government," observed Richard Rovers, "was what he had picked up as an Army lobbyist when Douglas MacArthur was Army Chief of Staff and, later, when he himself was Chief of Staff. . . ." In the light of such a meager apprenticeship the wonder is Rovere concluded, that President Eisenhower "has in general appeared before the world as a not unworthy successor of those few American Presidents whom the world has known and respected."[62] Clinton Rossiter, writing in the same year as Rovere, concluded, "Eisenhower already stands above Polk and Cleveland and he has a reasonable chance to move up to Jefferson and Theodore Roosevelt."[63] That would have put Eisenhower then among the first ten of the Schlesinger poll.[64]

[62] Richard H. Rovere, *The Eisenhower Years* (1956), pp. 368, 371.
[63] *The American Presidency* (1956), p. 435.
[64] Concerning the Schlesinger poll, see pp. 81, 83, 85, 93.

* **III**

Pressures on

the President

* **A PRESIDENT** who had been inaugurated with no adequate conception of what the office involved is reported to have protested, after a few months, that he was "getting damned tired of the pressures on him." He should have known that the very *raison d'etre* of the American presidency had become the reception and management of the public pressures through which the people conveyed their opinions and desires to their representative-in-chief. The most capable presidents have managed to manipulate the play of pressures and turn them to the promotion of the general welfare while others have been frustrated by their overwhelming force.

> Only through this office [wrote Herring] is there any hope for checking the minority forces that turn Congress to their will and make a mockery of representative democracy. Conditions being what they are in this country, the Chief Executive provides the only focal point about which policy can be developed and resistance offered to the pressure groups demanding consideration.[1]

No competent president today would think of evading this obligation.

[1] E. P. Herring, "Prescription for Democracy," *Annals of the Academy of Pol. and Soc. Sci.,* July, 1935, p. 142.

The perceptive realist in the presidential office knows that executive achievement will always be circumscribed by the means available to the purpose. To be effective the president's leadership in legislation and administration will be influenced by the pressures that impinge upon his office. He may become their slave as did some pre-Civil War presidents, which evidently induced Emerson to dip his pen in vitriol and write: "But the President has paid dearly for his White House. It has commonly cost him all his peace and the best of his manly attributes. To preserve, for so short a time, so conspicuous an appearance before the world, he is compelled to eat dirt before the real masters behind the throne."

The capable president may mobilize pressures, or play one against another, or at times by emitting a clarion call awaken dormant social forces and thereby mobilize public opinion behind him as did Franklin Roosevelt in the "hundred days" of 1933. That he will not accomplish the impossible is illustrated by the failure of three successive presidents to get the Eighteenth Amendment's provisions enforced upon a public containing a dissident minority apparently growing into an intransigent majority. Sooner or later every president reaches Lincoln's conclusion: "I claim not to have controlled events but confess that events have controlled me."[2]

It is axiomatic in the American system of separated powers that the dominant combination of interests—what the late Associate Judge Oliver Wendell Holmes denominated "the de facto supreme power"—will, in any given period, stake its fortunes on that branch of government on which it believes its security and the fulfillment of its desires depend. Thus the creditor, financial, mercantile, and planting interests that so largely framed the Constitution and came in time to constitute the Federalist party relied very largely on the presidency. The opposition to the Federalists, the Jeffersonian

[2] E. Hertz, *The Hidden Lincoln* (1940), p. 265.

Republicans, turned to Congress for the fulfillment of their purposes and in the quarter of a century when they were in power literally reduced the presidency to not much more than an agency of Congress.

In the second quarter of the nineteenth century a new preponderance of political power came with the vitalizing of the recently enfranchised American masses, who elected Jackson and practically remade the presidency into the people's office. Thereupon essentially the same combination of interests that had constituted the Federalist party now functioning as the Whig party entrenched itself in Congress, from which position it bombarded the executive. Today the Republican party with a similar group combination seeks to strengthen Congress by reducing the presidential power as by the Twenty-second Amendment and other proposed amendments such as the projected Bricker Amendment. With the exception of Lincoln and Theodore Roosevelt, both of whom lost favor with their party's leaders, the Republican presidents have generally accepted the party's theory of presidential subordination to Congress. Every Democratic president elected in the last hundred years has been a vigorous practitioner of presidential authority, which the Democratic group combination apparently expects.

Let no one assume that President Washington because of his monolithic prestige escaped pressures on the office. The fall of the Bastille in 1789 was hailed by Americans, one and all, as signifying the emancipation of the French people from autocracy. But when, three years later, they imprisoned their King and Queen, that was another matter so far as the conservative Federalists were concerned. The mercurial American masses however gave way to a hysterical French craze that swept the country. Mr. Jones and Mr. Smith became Citizen Jones and Citizen Smith. The French Tricolor and red liberty cap decorated taverns and coffee houses where met the American Jacobin clubs that sprang up across the nation.

For the first months of 1793 no ship, no news arrived from

France. April 3 a British packet beat into New York harbor bearing the news that the French Republic had guillotined the King and Queen and declared war on England and Spain. Swift couriers bore the news to the national Capitol at Philadelphia and then on to Mt. Vernon from whence Washington returned to Philadelphia to counsel with his Cabinet on the issue of war or peace. The problem was complicated by our Revolutionary treaty of alliance with France by which we were pledged to defend France's New World possessions and even still more by the fanaticism of hysterical pro-French Americans. These enthusiasts demanded a declaration of war despite the Spanish and restless Indian foes on our western border, the English on the North, and the lack of a navy with which to defend French possessions in the Caribbean against the overwhelming might of the British navy.

Under the circumstances President Washington did the inevitable and decided on peace proclaimed by the first presidential proclamation of neutrality. In our day a proclamation of neutrality is taken for granted as an incontestable exercise of presidential prerogative. Not so in 1793, when the opposition denounced it as a clear case of executive usurpation. Did not Congress have the constitutional power to declare war and by inference then to determine peace? In Jefferson's opinion, expressed in a letter to Madison, Washington's proclamation that the nation was at peace was equivalent to declaring it would not go to war, which took on the character of executive encroachment on the legislature. Moreover had not the President wantonly set at naught our treaty of alliance with France and thereby broken our plighted faith?

Washington stood firm on neutrality and may have been saved from the mad rage of the Francophiles by one of those strokes of fortune that from time to time tip the scales of history in a crisis. Vice-President John Adams wrote that "ten thousand people in the streets of Philadelphia, day after day, threatened to drag Washington out of his house and effect a revolution in the government, or compel it to declare war in favor of the French Revolution and against England."[3] In the midst of the tumult yellow fever broke out in Philadelphia spreading death and panic until over half the 43,000 inhabitants had fled the city or died. It was Adams' opinion that the yellow fever, more than Washington's prestige or any strength of the government, prevented a revolution. Thus the pressure of the Francophiles on President Washington was countered by an event. No president consults Congress before issuing a neutrality proclamation.

Persisting in his policy of peace, Washington sent John Jay to England to negotiate what turned out to be the ill-starred Jay's Treaty. Scarcely anyone was happy over it, but whatever advantages to the United States it provided operated to the benefit of northern interests, and the chambers of commerce of Philadelphia, New York, and Boston supported the treaty. Not a single item in it benefited southern planters and inland mixed farmers—in short, the Francophiles who attacked the treaty with savage fury. Jay was burned in effigy and Hamilton stoned in the street. Though Washington reluctantly sent the treaty to the Senate, he wrote to Alexander Hamilton, "At present the cry against the treaty is like that against a mad dog, and everyone in a manner is running it down.... The string which is most played on because it strikes with more force on the popular ear is the violation, as they term it, of our engagements with France."[4] He was misrepresented "in such exaggerated and indecent terms as could scarcely be applied to a Nero, a notorious defaulter—or even to a common pickpocket."[5]

Clearly the war between France and England growing out of the French Revolution had become the chief factor polarizing the party division between Federalists and Republicans. Jay's Treaty

[3] *Works* (1950–56), x, 47, 48.
[4] Worthington Chauncey Ford (ed.), *Writings of George Washington* (1889), XIII, 34. See also C. A. Beard, *Economic Interpretation of the Constitution* (1913), Chap. X.
[5] A. J. Beveridge, *John Marshall* (1928), II, 116.

had seemed so pro-British to France that the Directory broke off diplomatic relations with the United States, refused to receive C. C. Pinckney, whom Washington had sent there on a diplomatic mission, and compelled him, by a threat of the French police, to flee to Amsterdam. John Adams succeeded Washington as President and, indignant at the insult to Pinckney, called Congress into session to take such action as, he said, "shall convince France and the whole world that we are not a degraded people humiliated under a colonial spirit of fear and sense of inferiority."[6] But the pro-French Republicans insisted that, if only Adams would send a mission to France, all would be well. So Adams yielded and sent to Paris John Marshall and Elbridge Gerry to join Pinckney as envoys extraordinary to negotiate with the Directory. At Paris, three secret agents of the Directory, henceforth diplomatically designated as X, Y, and Z, met our envoys and declared that before they could be received there must be an apology for Adams' denunciation of France, each director must be paid fifty thousand dollars and tribute must be paid to France.

When Adams published the facts of this XYZ Affair, the Republicans were stunned into silence. Every French flag was pulled down from the coffee houses, the black cockade of our Revolutionary days replaced the red cockade, and an undeclared naval war with France began. A Navy Department was created, and Washington was appointed to command the army to be raised. Hamilton had been the power behind the Adams administration up to the spring of 1799. He was infatuated with dreams of conquest in which he would emulate the then rising Corsican corporal by leading an army that would capture New Orleans in co-operation with the British Navy, march into Mexico City and, with the co-operation of the South American patriot, Miranda, liberate Spanish provinces.

[6] J. D. Richardson (ed.), *Messages and Papers of the Presidents* (1927), I, 235.

The pressures of the Hamiltonian Federalists upon Adams for war with France appeared irresistible, and a declaration of war, when Congress would convene in December, seemed inevitable. But Talleyrand, the French Foreign Minister, realizing that war with the United States would give England another ally, let the information leak to Adams that a new mission would be courteously received. President Adams, confiding in no one but his wife, made one of the most momentous decisions in the history of the presidency. To the consternation of the now infuriated Hamiltonians he submitted to the Senate the nomination of a minister plenipotentiary to France. This wrecked the plans of the war party, set the Hamiltonians to sabotaging the Adams administration, and forecast the election of Thomas Jefferson and the demise of the Federalist party. To the end of his long life John Adams cherished the memory of how he had resisted and thwarted the pressures of the warmongers.

Jefferson, the third President, brought upon himself, by the Embargo Act, pressures that ultimately overwhelmed him though not until the last few days of his presidency. His plan was to bring Britain to her knees and thereby compel respect for our neutral rights by withholding our agricultural products from her. The Embargo Act, whose name his Federalist enemies spelled backward and thus denominated the O Grab Me Act, forbade American ships to sail to a foreign country unless the President suspended the act. "The enforcement act passed to sustain the embargo was a greater interference with the ordinary privileges of citizens than would have been necessary in the exercise of war powers,"[7] wrote Henry James Ford. Britain was not even greatly inconvenienced by the embargo, while American ships rotted in harbors, seamen were umemployed, agriculture languished, warehouses were empty, and economic distress gripped the nation. Jefferson confessed that

---

[7] *The Rise and Growth of American Politics* (1898), p. 132.

the Federal government rocked under the resolutions of the New England town meetings. On March 1, 1809, Congress, despite Jefferson's protest, repealed the Embargo Act.

Jefferson's successor, Madison, inherited from him the unsettled question of neutral rights. Like Jefferson he too was so dedicated to a policy of peace that an exasperated congressman once declared in the House that "he could not be kicked into a fight." However grievances grew during his first term—especially the exasperation of frontiersmen with the belligerency of the Indians incited by British agents—all of which built up irresistible pressures upon Madison for a declaration of war. By 1812 the time had arrived for another presidential election. National nominating conventions were as yet in the distant future, and presidential candidates were nominated by the congressional caucuses of each party. Madison was kept in uncertainty as to renomination for a second term, and action of the Republican caucus was delayed until the pressure upon Madison made certain that he would recommend a declaration of war. There is no evidence of a bargain on the matter, but Madison knew well enough that "No recommendation of war, no chance for a second term." How much this pressure motivated him no one can say.

The first President to meet head-on a gigantic economic pressure and not only overcome it but literally annihilate it was Andrew Jackson. The pressure was that of the Bank of the United States, and the secret of Jackson's overwhelming victory over it was that he was the first President to be elected by virtually direct, universal, white-manhood suffrage of the American people plus his ability to symbolize the Bank as a "monster" about to devour the American people. The Bank had been chartered by the United States government, which owned one-fifth of its stock, appointed one-fifth of its directors, and used the Bank as a depository and dispenser of Federal funds. The Bank had unquestionably performed valuable services both to business and the government, but its president,

Nicholas Biddle, was persuaded by Henry Clay, candidate for President against Jackson in 1832, to ask Congress to recharter the Bank four years before the expiration of its charter. Clay's purpose was to challenge if not fret Jackson into vetoing the rechartering, which is exactly what Jackson did as soon as Congress acted. Jackson's veto message was a masterpiece of propaganda mobilizing every popular prejudice against the Bank. After his reelection Jackson had the Secretary of the Treasury gradually remove Federal deposits from the Bank, without which it was soon unable to carry on. Jackson's ability to counter a hitherto irresistible pressure was a landmark in the history of the presidency. "The severance of official connections between the national government and the capitalist was one of the most important steps in American history. Thenceforth, the industrial interests were obliged to act underground and by lobby."[8]

One of the finest examples of a resolute presidential stand against tremendous pressure is that of Zachary Taylor's resistance to Clay's Compromise of 1850. The Mexican War had left a multitude of perplexing issues in its wake. Clay proposed to admit California as a free state while Taylor would have admitted it without raising the extremely provocative issue of slavery knowing it would be a free state in any case. Clay would have organized the other territory obtained from Mexico without mentioning slavery knowing it was not adapted to slavery anyhow. Texas, which had been an independent nation before its recent admission to the Union, now claimed a preposterous western boundary far beyond its present one. The expectation that the national debt of Texas would be assumed by the United States following its admission was not fulfilled, and holders of its depreciated securities thronged the lobbies and galleries of Congress clamoring for assumption of this debt. Here was probably the most immediate economic pressure upon President Taylor. Clay's Compromise would have satisfied these

[8] Frederick Jackson Turner, *The United States: 1830–1850* (1935), pp. 407–408.

holders of the Texas Republic's depreciated bonds by a payment of $10,000,000 to Texas out of the national treasury on the pretext of indemnifying the state for accepting what eventually became its present western boundary. Clay would placate northern antislavery opinion by abolishing the slave trade but not slavery itself in the District of Columbia and would have given the slavery interests a drastic fugitive slave law.

President Taylor had a thoroughly consistent plan of his own, one designed to avoid if possible the slavery debate that Clay's Compromises provoked. Even before Congress had met, Taylor had sent special messengers west to propose that the inhabitants of New Mexico and California adopt Constitutions and apply to Congress for admission, which California did. In his message to Congress when it convened, President Taylor recommended that California and New Mexico be admitted to the Union if they had prepared constitutions providing governments republican in form. Southerners filibustered against admitting two free states and in July Alexander H. Stephens and Robert Tombs, in a stormy conference with the President, wound up with a threat of secession. To this pressure President Taylor is alleged to have told Stephens and Tombs that he would hang those taken in rebellion "with as little mercy as he had hanged deserters and spies in Mexico."[9] Taylor was dead set against the introduction of two other controversial issues in the Compromise Bill, the slave trade in the District of Columbia and the fugitive slave bill because of the acrimonious debates they would certainly provoke. Time was to prove him correct as to the latter item, for the Fugitive Slave Law by its utter unreasonableness never for a single day after passage permitted the slavery question to become quiescent. Taylor was set to veto every part of the Compromise Bill when his sudden death ended his counterpressure against the compromise and elevated to the presidency Vice-President Fillmore, an avowed procompromise Whig.

[9] H. A. Weed, *Life of Thurlow Weed* (1884), p. 117.

There is just one instance in American history of a President practically asking Congress for a declaration of war and not getting it. Franklin Pierce had been elected President in 1852, with what many Southerners considered an implicit pledge to acquire Cuba. Then in February, 1854, the American Steamer *Black Warrior,* on its regular New York-Mobile run, was seized by Spanish authorities at Havana on a technicality. This seemed to President Pierce the heaven-sent opportunity, and within fifteen days he sent to Congress a message indicating he would use any authority or means Congress might grant in order to vindicate national honor. The thinly veiled objective of the annexation of Cuba with a consequent expansion of slavery was not missed by millions of Northerners already aroused by the pending Kansas-Nebraska Bill permitting slavery extension into free territories, and the ensuing surge of public indignation stopped the plan dead in its tracks.[10]

No president was more adept at dealing with pressures than Lincoln, and they confronted him months before his inauguration. As far as the popular vote was concerned he was a minority President having received slightly less than 40 per cent of it. The Republican party, upon which his power and prestige depended, was an extraordinarily heterogeneous aggregation of interest groups held together by a single issue—that slavery must be absolutely excluded from the territories. As the southern states were one by one passing ordinances of secession in the months before Lincoln's inauguration, there bore upon the President-elect a persistent pressure to agree to the Crittenden Compromise with its vital proposal to revive the Missouri Compromise line repealed seven years earlier at the insistence of slavery interests. This would have required a repudiation of the only issue that held the Republican party together and would have compelled Lincoln to be inaugurated virtually minus a party. Lincoln countered the pressure for the Crittenden Compromise with an inflexible determination to

[10] See Allan Nevins, *Ordeal of the Union* II, 349.

prevent the fatal dispersion of his party following. "Prevent as far as possible," he wrote a Republican congressman, "any of our friends from demoralizing themselves and our cause by entertaining propositions for compromise on slavery extension. There is no possible compromise upon it but puts us under again and leaves all our work to do over . . . on that point hold firm, as with a chain of steel."[11]

Lincoln demonstrated consummate political skill in countering the pressures to take the construction of his cabinet out of his hands even before his inauguration. His purpose was, as his secretaries John Hay and John Nicolay expressed it, to "combine the experience of Seward, the integrity of Chase, the popularity of Cameron; to hold the West with Bates, attract New England with Wells, please the Whigs through Smith and convince the Democrats through Blair."[12] But before he had settled the matter, Lincoln had to deal with the conservative or Seward wing that would have none of Chase and his kind. On the other hand the radical, Chase-and-Sumner, abolitionist wing of the party would rule out conservative Seward and his kind. "But Lincoln intended, come what would, to be master in his own house. He meant to rule by a balance of forces, in which he would hold pivotal authority. From the outset he had been determined, if possible, to have both Seward and Chase in his Cabinet and give the direction to neither."[13] Two days before the inauguration a crisis had come. Seward had presented an ultimatum: If Blair, Wells, and Chase went in—and he especially objected to Chase—he would go out. "There are differences between myself and Chase which make it impossible for us to act in harmony." That night a deputation of Seward men called on Lincoln to protest against Chase in the Cabinet. Lincoln listened patiently, but at the end drew a paper from a drawer and

[11] G. H. Putnam and A. B. Lapsby (eds.), *Complete Works of Abraham Lincoln* (1888–96), v, 196.

[12] Quoted by Carl Sandburg, *Lincoln: the War Years* (1939), I, 153.

[13] Allan Nevins, *The Emergence of Lincoln* (1951), II, 452–53.

explained that it contained both his careful choice of Cabinet members and an alternative list.

> Then he exploded his stick of dynamite. Mere mortals cannot have everything they like, he moralized. 'This being the case, gentlemen, how would it do for us to agree on a change like this? How would it do for Mr. Chase to take the Treasury, and to offer the State Department to Mr. William L. Dayton?' He added that he would make Seward minister to Great Britain. And he bowed the stupefied delegation from the room.[14]

This simply meant—no Chase, no Seward. It broke the deadlock, and he had both in his Cabinet.

No one should be puzzled as to why Lincoln appeared to be letting things drift for two months after his inaugural address declaring his purpose to "take care, as the Constitution itself expressly enjoins me, that the laws of the Union be faithfully executed in all the states." Let it never be forgotten that Lincoln had been elected by a minority party, that had given him only 39.91 per cent of the total popular vote, that a radical element of his party was even rejoicing that secession was at long last bearing the "curse of slavery" out of the Union, and even the Republican party oracle, Horace Greeley, editor of the *Tribune*, the very organ of the Republican party, was but publicizing a widespread public sentiment in his admonition to the seceding states, "Erring Sisters depart in peace." In the prevailing confusion of opinion Lincoln could perceive no consensus for decisive action for the simple reason that none existed.

It was the Confederate government itself that gave Lincoln the public pressure required for decisive action by its gigantic miscalculation as to the reaction of public opinion that it would provoke throughout the loyal states by the firing on Ft. Sumter. It was the latent though deep-seated reverence for the Union, symbolized by the nation's flag that had been shot at, that created an

[14] *Ibid.*, p. 454.

instantaneous and almost universal demand, outside the Confederacy, for presidential action. Equipped with an overwhelming popular mandate, or pressure, Lincoln acted promptly to mobilize the armed strength of the nation to overcome resistance to national authority. No longer was Lincoln sustained merely by his Republican party, but, for the time being, party lines practically disappeared and northern opposition to the forcible assertion of Federal authority was insignificant in the summer and autumn of 1861. With his unexcelled capacity for utilizing social forces Lincoln employed the now imperative pressures for maintaining nationwide Federal authority. Any earlier attempt to that end would have been made with a palsied executive hand.

Never was Lincoln's capacity for manipulating pressures and maintaining his mastery by playing one pressure against another demonstrated better than in the Cabinet crisis of December, 1862. It was a few days after Fredericksburg, the bloodiest of all the disasters of the Union army, when a caucus of Republican congressmen summoned by the radical (abolitionist) Senator Sumner appointed a committee of seven radicals to call on the President and demand a change of policies and Cabinet, particularly the dismissal of Seward. It looked for the moment as if Lincoln might have to surrender to Congress the constitutional privilege of determining his own counselors as the price of congressional cooperation in winning the war, for they were demanding that his Cabinet be reorganized to their satisfaction. Lincoln courteously asked the committee to return at an appointed time for another conference. When Seward heard of the demand of the committee, he sent the President his resignation. Now Lincoln knew that it was his Secretary of the Treasury, Salmon P. Chase, who was the marplot, a persistent informer of alleged dissension in the Cabinet.[15] When, at the appointed time, the committee returned, they unexpectedly found themselves compelled to resume their complaints

[15] See Lincoln's summary of Chase's conduct in John G. Nicolay and John Hay, *Abraham Lincoln: a History* (1890), VIII, 317.

in the presence of the Cabinet. Under the circumstances the distressed Chase felt compelled to eat his own words of talebearing and admit there was no Cabinet dissension. Furthermore, now completely discredited before President, Cabinet, and the caucus committee, the humiliated Secretary of the Treasury reluctantly decided to offer his own resignation.

This was precisely what Lincoln was maneuvering for. With the resignations of both Seward and Chase in his pocket he chose to accept neither, since each had a valuable personal following representing two wings of the Republican party, neither of which Lincoln could spare. "This," said he, "cuts the Gordian knot." Lincoln had rescued the very presidency from an extremely dangerous encroachment of congressmen. By a single shrewd stroke, scheduling the caucus committee to meet in the presence of his Cabinet, he had preserved his mastery of his own Cabinet, avoided the loss of the support of the followers of his two principal Cabinet members, and counteracted the design of congressional encroachment upon the presidency. The escape was nevertheless a narrow one. Lincoln's then intimate friend Senator Orville Browning had informed him that the radical strategy had been to surround him with a Cabinet of radicals with Chase as the premier. To this information Lincoln replied with emphasis that he was master, and that they would not be permitted to do it.[16] It is Samuel Elliott Morison's opinion that "in the Cabinet crisis of December, 1862, only Lincoln's astuteness saved him from becoming a mere Premier instead of a President."[17]

It was when confronted with a complex of clashing pressures that Lincoln utilized his incomparable artistry in resolving the problem by inventing a policy formula. The Emancipation Proclamation was just such a formula. His sense of timing was uncanny. He resolutely refused to be premature in meeting the issue. Thus

[16] H. Browning, *Diary of Orville Hicks Browning* (1925–1933), I, 64.
[17] *Oxford History of the United States* (1927), II, 254.

he told his friend Swett, "I can see emancipation coming; whoever can wait for it will see it; whoever stands in its way will be run over."[18] When a delegation of church leaders brought him a memorial for emancipation adopted by a great meeting in Chicago, he parried with the question whether it might not be as ineffective as the Pope's bull against the comet. How could he free slaves in regions where he couldn't even enforce the Constitution? They never knew that he had the draft of what they wanted lying on his desk and was waiting for the right moment to issue it.

Devising the peculiar formula of the Emancipation Proclamation called for a careful calculation of profits and losses among the potential supporters of the Lincoln administration by basing every item of the formula on the paramount purpose of the preservation of the Union. Horace Greeley in his famous "Prayer of Twenty Million" presented a demand that the President positively commit himself at once to universal emancipation. It disregarded the effect on the row of border states all holding slaves but still loyal to the Union and supporting Federal authority with its militia and volunteer regiments. These military forces from the border states must not be provoked into throwing down their arms in protest against fighting to free their own slaves.

When General Lee's attempt to invade northern states was prevented by his repulse at Antietam Lincoln decided that the opportune moment had arrived, and he issued his preliminary proclamation (September 22, 1862) warning "That on the 1st day of January A. D. 1863, all persons held as slaves within any state or designated part of a state the people whereof shall then be in rebellion against the United States shall be then, thenceforth, and forever free."[19] This warning passed unheeded and on the following January 1 the Proclamation of Emancipation was issued with the areas in rebellion to which it applied specifically designated. Close

[18] E. Hertz, *The Hidden Lincoln* (1940), p. 298.
[19] *U. S. Statutes at Large*, XII, 1268.

inspection of the Proclamation is required to get the formula by which Lincoln placated the pressures playing upon him without penalizing any of his slaveholding supporters. At last he made a grand gesture in response to the pressures of the abolitionists and while they were not satisfied with his cautious methods they were for the moment silenced. The slaveholding border states suffered no loss of a slave, and since the Proclamation applied only to areas beyond the Union armies it may not have then freed a single slave. But evidently President Lincoln had in mind especially the effect of the Proclamation on Europe, particularly England. The latter appeared to be teetering on the verge of recognizing the independence of the Confederacy, which would have been a severe blow to Lincoln's administration. But after the Proclamation was issued, the intense antislavery sentiment of British labor prevented any recognition of the independence of the Confederacy the British ministry may have contemplated. Lincoln had dealt a major stroke of international politics. The Proclamation had "lifted the Civil War to the dignity of a crusade."[20]

What Lincoln might have been able to do with the post-Civil War revolt against executive power no one can say. His successor, Andrew Johnson, had little if any of Lincoln's skill in countering pressures on the presidency, and consequently, despite his resolute courage, Johnson was overwhelmed by the pressures. It is customary to consider President Johnson as, by and large, the victim of rather aimless postwar prejudices. But the ideologies mobilized against policies he promoted in the public interest were little more than propaganda devices utilized by resolute economic interest groups in order to achieve their objectives. Johnson never was a Republican but had been selected by Lincoln as the vice-presidential candidate in order to have a southern state represented on the Union party ticket. As a Jacksonian Democrat, Johnson throughout his career was an uncompromising champion of the underdog,

[20] S. E. Morison and H. S. Commager, *The Growth of the American Republic* (1937), II, 590.

a perilous role even for the ablest president. As an East Tennessee Congressman he had introduced the first Homestead Bill as early as 1845. It was designed to give every homeless citizen a farm from the public lands.

The first Homestead Act to become law was signed by Lincoln in 1862. Three years later President Johnson saw with growing indignation that this law was being perverted by the greed of the railroads, mining companies, and the land speculators, all determined to grab the national domain. He voted two acts of Congress in order to prevent this and thereby alienated powerful economic interests. Johnson's first message to Congress (December, 1865) indicated his aversion to protective tariffs. This alienated interests that had assumed that the Civil War had been waged to overthrow the chief enemy of protectionism—cotton capitalism—and now Johnson seemed to be championing free trade.

More alarming still to powerful interests was Johnson's statement in 1867 that an aristocracy of the South based on $3,000,000,000 invested in Negroes, who were a productive class, had disappeared and in their place the political control of the country was being assumed by an aristocracy based on nearly $3,000,000,000 in the national debt. The bonds had been purchased at such a discount with a high rate of interest being paid in gold, which was at a premium over the circulating currency, that Johnson seemed to suggest a kind of repudiation, which created a wave of hysteria. He infuriated the promoters of western railroads by his adamant resistance to any more grants of government land that he would reserve for actual homestead settlers. Twenty-five years before the Sherman Antitrust Act Johnson recommended that Congress utilize its interstate commerce power to check the emerging rapacious monopolies of the post-Civil War epoch.

It was Johnson's misfortune to have entered the presidency without the backing of any powerful interests, and unlike Lincoln he provoked the wrath of the most powerful interests in the nation.

These interests were able to obscure the economic issues and turn against Johnson the torrent of passions aroused by the Civil War. Included in the combination of pressures that induced the Senate to come within a single vote of removing Johnson from the presidency were the bondholders, the banks, the protectionists, the monopolistic corporations, and the railroad promoters, all imperiled by the president's veto power, which in this case was wielded by an avowed Jacksonian Democrat.

Pressures piled up against President Hayes from the day of his inauguration so that he never experienced the customary presidential honeymoon. Fortunately he was expert in the art of politics, resolutely stood his ground, and won a signal victory. Only once since the Civil War has the Senate refused to confirm a president's nomination of a Cabinet officer. But the overconfident senatorial oligarchy that had come within a single vote of removing President Johnson and had held President Grant in the hollow of its hand started out to hold up Hayes' entire Cabinet list despite the fact that, as the late Professor John W. Burgess was to declare in 1916, "Taken all together, it was the strongest body of men, each best fitted for the place assigned to him that ever sat around the council table of a President of the United States."[21]

Hayes was the first President since the spoils system had been established to be wholeheartedly committed to civil service reform, and this was enough to make him *persona non grata* to the ruling clique of the Senate—Conkling, Platt, Cameron, Blaine, *et al.* Promptly upon receiving Hayes' Cabinet nominees, the Senate went into executive session and, departing from its time-honored usage of not challenging the president's choice of his official family referred the list to committees for investigation.[22] They made no exception to John Sherman, himself a Senator, and senators were usually confirmed promptly with the idea that a colleague required

[21] *The Administration of President Hayes* (1916), p. 65.
[22] C. S. Williams, *Hayes* (1914), II, 25.

no investigation. Each of the senators mentioned above had been urging his own choice of a Cabinet member upon Hayes, who was now to be disciplined for ignoring their recommendations. But the unprecedented conduct of the Senate fairly took the breath of the public, who assumed that some or even all of the list were to be rejected. The President was promptly deluged with mail urging him to stand firm, which Hayes would have done in any case.

With the rising tide of criticism the Senate leaders sought in vain to combine with southern senators against Hayes.[23] Soon the insurgent senators were being bombarded with telegrams from party men, political clubs, and chambers of commerce demanding confirmation. Newspaper opinion almost unanimously supported the President. Within seventy hours of receiving the nominations the Senate had been overwhelmed by the tide of public opinion and was impelled to confirm Hayes' Cabinet appointees with almost unanimity. Hayes was shrewd enough to stand his ground and wait until the pressure of the spoilsmen upon him had been countered by enlightened public opinion in support of him.[24]

Few presidents have ignored pressures to the extent that Cleveland did or paid as heavy a penalty for it. A striking example was his annual message to Congress of December, 1887, all of which was devoted to an emphatic demand upon Congress for the revision of the tariff. He had been shrewdly advised not to stir up a hornet's nest, but he was obstinate in his determination to do what was "right," a dangerous enough guide for a president in a world where even good men cannot agree on what is "right." Raising the tariff issue just then provided a golden opportunity for the protected interests to utilize the emotion-evoking issue to stir the prejudices of voters, and the consequence was the defeat of Cleveland for re-election and the election of a Republican Congress that passed the McKinley Tariff of 1890—the most extreme protectionist measure in our history to this date.

[23] R. B. Hayes, *Diary and Letters of Rutherford B. Hayes* (1922), III, 427, Mar. 14, 1877.
[24] *Ibid.*, II, 28.

In the maneuvering of the various interests in constructing the McKinley Tariff the duty of two cents a pound on raw sugar was removed, and it was given instead to the producers of raw sugar at nome. This incidentally produced a disastrous effect on American owners of Hawaiian sugar plantations and mills occasioning a loss estimated by the Minister of the United States to the primitive Hawaiian kingdom of $12,000,000 a year. In the midst of the crisis of the American sugar interest the Hawaiian Queen Liliuokalani gave vent to her intense hatred of missionaries and foreigners generally by initiating a policy of exclusion of them and revoking the constitution of 1887, which had given generous concessions to foreigners, wrung from her predecessor. The upshot was a revolt against her, managed mostly by Americans aided by American marines from a warship conveniently near at hand. The American flag was raised, and a mission sent to Washington, which was cordially received by President Harrison, who promptly sent a treaty of annexation to the Senate, which however took no action on it.

Soon after Cleveland became President again he withdrew the treaty. When the emissary sent by Cleveland to investigate the Hawaiian revolution reported to him, the President asked the provisional government to step down and restore the Queen, which was refused on the ground that President Cleveland had no authority to interfere in the internal affairs of Hawaii. What completely staggered Cleveland in the project was Queen Liliuokalani's avowed determination promptly after her expected restoration to behead as traitors the leaders of the revolution that had dethroned her—Sanford B. Dole among them. This was too much even for Cleveland, and when the provisional government with Dole as President declared its independence, Cleveland made an about-face, to the consternation of the idealists who had been applauding his courage, and he cordially greeted the new nation.[25]

[25] See Harry Thourston Peck, *Twenty Years of the Republic* (1906), pp. 333, 334.

There were tremendous emotion-packed social forces or pressures that handicapped Cleveland in the Hawaiian episode as well as in many other issues, such, for example, as his determination to eliminate frauds in the granting of pensions to Union army veterans. Wavers of the "bloody shirt" kept branding the Democratic party with the charge of treason and Copperheadism. Veterans of the Union army, numbering then far more than a million, were reminded in every party campaign that Cleveland had "hired a substitute" to escape military service. President Cleveland's determination to eliminate fraudulent pension claims by vetoing unwarranted special pension bills was used against him. It was his misfortune to order the return to southern states of Confederate flags captured by Union army regiments and in the custody of the Federal government only to discover that he lacked authority for such an executive order. But the crowning charge solemnly iterated and reiterated throughout the land was that Cleveland had gone fishing on Decoration Day. These things were taken seriously by a majority of the veterans and of their families, distributed widely enough among many congressional districts to hold balances of voting power. When Cleveland's determination to reinstate Queen Liliuokalani would have brought down the American flag that the revolutionists had raised in Hawaii with the later approval of President Harrison, who had been one of William T. Sherman's generals in the March through Georgia, there was heard again and again the ringing order of Secretary of the Treasury John A. Dix given on the eve of the Civil War, "If any man attempts to haul down the American flag shoot him on the spot." Of such stuff are made the pressures that sometimes determine momentous issues.

President McKinley seemed to perceive intuitively the equilibrium of social forces, and like Eisenhower he was adept at allaying the strife of conflicting interests. Henry Adams, certainly no devotee of McKinley, observed:

> Mr. McKinley brought to the problem of American Government a solution. . . .which seemed to be at least practical and

American. He undertook to pool interests in a general trust into which every interest should be taken more or less at its own valuation, and whose mass should, under his management, create efficiency. He achieved very remarkable results.[26]

Contrary to a persistent popular impression President McKinley could resist a pressure with adamantine resolution. Promptly following inauguration he appointed H. C. Evans Commissioner of Pensions. Evans promptly incurred the wrath of the pension attorneys by reforming abuses, exposing frauds and administering the office with the strictest integrity. The office had seldom if ever known so clean and upright an administration. The Union veterans' organization, one of the most notable pressure groups in American history, joined in attacking Evans and demanded his removal. "Enormous political pressure was brought to bear to secure this end but President McKinley resisted it like a man. He could not be moved and he gave unflinching support to Evans despite the clamor of venal claimants and maligners. The same pressure was applied to President Theodore Roosevelt. He withstood it for a while and then yielded,"[27] by appointing a Commissioner of Pensions more acceptable to the Grand Army of the Republic and the pension agents.

In the spring of 1898 President McKinley was subject to the most formidable aggregation of pressures for war that ever forced the hand of a peace-loving president. When he was inaugurated in 1897 an insurrection of the rural peons and urban working class was raging in Cuba. Driven to distraction by low wages and unemployment, they had revolted against the Spanish ruling class. Romantic-minded citizens of the United States translated the rebellion in terms of our own Revolutionary War with the insurgent leader Maximo Gomez cast in the role of George Washington. Two New York journalists, William Randolph Hearst and Joseph

---

[26] *The Education of Henry Adams* (1931), pp. 373–74.
[27] Harry Thurston Peck, *Twenty Years of the Republic* (1906), p. 674.

Pulitzer, plunged into a titanic competition for circulation of their respective newspapers. They took advantage of the Cuban civil war to fan the accelerating war frenzy of our citizens with fantastic tales of Spanish atrocities alleged to have been perpetrated upon hapless Cubans. An emotional explosion followed the publication, by Hearst's New York *Journal* (February 8), of a lurid translation of a letter stolen from the Havana Post Office by an insurgent spy. It had been written by the Spanish Minister to the United States, Enrique Dupuy de Lome, and contained disparaging comments about President McKinley pronouncing him, among other things, a "common politician." One week later the U. S. battleship *Maine,* which had been sent to Havana on a friendly visit, was sunk by an external explosion with the loss of 260 officers and men. Who was responsible for the explosion was never discovered, but it inflamed still more the public feelings against Spain.

Next the Pope, with the best of intentions, committed an error in dealing with the United States. He made an appeal to both Spain and the United States not to defile Easter time by an outbreak of war between two Christian nations. When the Catholic Archbishop Ireland went to Washington to plead for peace, many Protestant pastors were aroused. The American Protective Association, an anti-Catholic organization numbering millions, became agitated more than ever. "You have no idea," wrote the President's brother Abner, "of the pressure on William from religious peoples...."[28]—pressures for war, of course.

President McKinley meanwhile was pursuing a policy of diplomatic restraint that had the Spanish government, early in April, at the point of granting Cuba autonomy, independence, or even cession to the United States if only given a little time to prepare the Spanish people for the new policy. "War came in spite of the complete success of American diplomacy, and primarily because the American people wanted to have a war."[29] A new generation of

[28] Thomas Beer, *Hanna* (1929), p. 194.
[29] John D. Hicks, *The American Nation* (1941), II, 312.

Americans had been brought up on a romantic interpretation of the Civil War, nurtured on elementary history textbooks illustrated with stirring battle scenes. The consequence was an irresistible demand for a crusade to rescue an oppressed people. Let it be remembered that the Constitution vests in Congress the power to declare war, and that it is merely a custom to wait for the president's recommendation of a declaration of war. If McKinley had not placed the matter at the discretion of Congress, it would almost certainly have acted anyhow. McKinley might well have repeated Lincoln's words, "I claim not to have controlled events but confess plainly that events have controlled me."

President Woodrow Wilson demonstrated expert manipulation of social forces during his first administration when he was managing the translation of the "New Freedom" into one of the most consistent programs of legislation in our history. There is no more striking example of his technique than the way he countered the lobbyists, busy sabotaging the pending Underwood tariff bill. The measure had passed the House and gone to the Senate, where customarily tariff bills were rewritten to the heart's content of protected interests by the sinister pressures of well-heeled lobbyists. Wilson knew of the lobby activities, but he could not have known what was later revealed by an investigating committee. For example, the chief page of the House was employed by a lobbyist of the National Association of Manufacturers to haunt the cloak rooms and report conversations heard there and on the floor of the House. There was revealed evidence that the N. A. M. controlled the appointment of certain congressional committees, and a friendly congressman had permitted the N. A. M. the use of a room in the Capitol.[30]

President Wilson countered the pressures of the tariff lobbyists with a statement to the press. "It is of serious interest to the country," he said, "that the people at large should have no lobby and

[30] John F. Kennedy, "To Keep the Lobbyist Within Bounds," *New York Times Magazine* Feb. 19, 1956, pp. 40, 42.

be voiceless in these matters, while great bodies of astute men seek to create an artificial opinion and to overcome the interests of the public for their private profit.... The government ought to be relieved from this intolerable burden." Wilson's blast broke the back of the lobby, and consideration of the bill proceeded with the result that for the first time since the administration of James K. Polk the tariff was given a systematic revision by a Democratic Congress.

In the intuitive calculation of pressures and the manipulation of them to establish policies that he deemed to be in the public interest, Franklin Roosevelt stands high among the presidents. Thus he mobilized the pressures of the farmers in the mid-1930's to get Congress to establish for the rehabilitation of agriculture the Agricultural Adjustment Administration, the Farm Credit Administration, and the Farm Mortgage Corporation. Thus labor got the Wagner Labor Relations Act, Wages and Hours Act, Unemployment Insurance, Low Cost Housing, and Social Security. Those on relief got the distribution of surplus food through stamps, Old Age Insurance, and Old Age Assistance. Youth for the first time in history got special attention with employment provided by the National Youth Administration and the Civilian Conservation Corps. The adeptness of President Roosevelt in managing social pressures to these ends led one American scholar to declare that the President had "practically written a handbook on what every young President should know."[31]

The play of pressures upon a president who has not learned the game in the rough and tumble of party politics from the precinct up is downright baffling. For example, there was the tug of war for and against a bill H. R. 8002 recommended by the Hoover Commission that would have limited the validity of appropriations to a year at a time instead of setting no time limit. It was assumed that Congress would thereby be able to scrutinize expenditures more

[31] A Comment of T. V. Smith in a University of Chicago Round Table, Sunday noon, Jan. 5, 1936.

effectively and thus recover some of its lost control of finance. The Commission claimed the reform would save three billion dollars a year. This impressed President Eisenhower. He came out strongly for the bill, and it passed the Senate unanimously.

But when the bill reached the House Committee on Appropriations, it encountered the furious opposition of two veteran committee watchdogs of finance, Representatives Clarence Cannon of Missouri and John Taber of New York. Under questioning at a closed hearing of the committee, Secretary of Defense Charles Wilson was led to admit that the bill "might endanger the national security." Here was a Cabinet member in secret criticizing an administration bill. At this point ex-President Hoover dropped in at the White House determined to rescue the measure and so impressed President Eisenhower that he ordered prepared for his signature a letter to the House supporting the bill.

Even before the letter was signed John Taber got an appointment with the President and argued vigorously against the bill, maintaining that it would waste money instead of saving it and besides the procedure was unworkable. Thereupon the President admitted that this was "an entirely new point of view." At this turn of events Representative Clarence Brown, a sponsor of the bill and a member of the Hoover Commission that had proposed it, became indignant and called up ex-President Hoover in New York, who promptly telephoned the White House, following which Press Secretary James Hagerty issued a statement that the President was all-out for the bill. It was now Cannon and Taber's turn, and they promptly released the closed-session committee criticism of the bill by Defense Secretary Wilson who then felt impelled to deny what seemed to be the plain meaning of his words before the Committee.[32] The bill never became law.

Then there was the bill to provide Federal aid for school construction and designed to carry out President Eisenhower's recommendation. In a Cabinet meeting the bill was opposed by

[32] Stewart Alsop, *Toledo Blade*, August 7, 1957.

Secretaries Humphrey and Benson, who argued that it would mean Federal control of education, but Vice-President Nixon supported the bill. It was, of course, a special concern of Secretary Marion B. Folsom of the Department of Health, Education, and Welfare, who saw the President privately and urged him to come out with a strong statement before the House voted. But Senator Knowland, Senate minority leader, breakfasted with the President and berated the measure.[33] Supporters of the administration bill in the House waited for word from the White House, but none came and it lost by 3 votes. Veteran politician presidents such as the two Roosevelts or President Truman take such pressures in stride and with a smile, but it is otherwise with the less expert.

[33] "The Presidency: Can any one man do the job?" *United States News and World Report*, Nov. 22, 1957, pp. 50–72.

IV

The Influence

of Nominating Methods

* THE ADMINISTRATION of Andrew Jackson constitutes a well-known landmark in the evolution of the presidency. Verily a new Pharaoh reigned in the land, one that knew not Joseph. The "rich, the well born and the wise" had been in charge of the Federal government for a long generation, employing methods perfectly acceptable to them for choosing the chief magistrate. The very fact that the methods they used had invariably elevated to the presidency a particular type is indicative of the intimate relation between the method of nominating and electing the president and the kind of person put in the White House.

What kind of president would have been produced if the original method of electing the president by the exercise of the independent individual judgment of the presidential electors had persisted even for a season after Washington's retirement? The framers of the Constitution, of course, dreading as they did the possibility of national political parties, thought to avoid partisan conflict by creating for each presidential election an *ad hoc* assembly of notables, or rather assemblies, a separate one for each state, who would cast their ballots for the president. If their votes were so dispersed among many candidates as to prevent anyone receiving a majority, then the House of Representatives would be limited to voting for the highest five candidates (later changed to the highest three) in electing the president. Presumably the framers of the Constitution assumed that the electors would be selected from the landed and urban gentry and that their judgment would be acceptable to the complaisant lesser folk. One might speculate as to how many of our later presidents might have not been considered ineligible by such an elite functioning as the Electoral College.

The plans of the framers, of course, miscarried completely as to the Electoral College. The lesser folk and even some of the rural gentry promptly aligned themselves against the Hamiltonian financial program, and soon political parties emerged, very informal indeed at first, the Jeffersonian Republicans against the Hamiltonian Federalists. The biggest stake of national party politics promptly became the presidency with the prestige and power inherent in the office. With almost incredible clairvoyance Hamilton had once remarked to a friend that the time will "assuredly come when every vital question of state will be merged in the question, 'Who will be the next President?' "[1]

No sooner had political parties on a national scale emerged than there began a generation-long fumbling trial-and-error search for a way of getting presidential candidates nominated. For two or three decades no stabilized method developed, but concentration on a party candidate was characterized by a disconcerting informality. In 1796, with Washington now determined to retire, some sort of understanding appears to have been reached as to candidates probably by somewhat informal congressional caucuses—that is, two joint conferences of party members of both Houses, one a caucus of Federalists, the other of Republicans. At any rate Federalist presidential electors voted for Adams while Republicans voted for Jefferson, and Adams won by a margin of three electoral votes. For the quarter of a century following, the Jeffersonians employed the congressional caucus while the rapidly vanishing Federalists made abortive ventures with another method

---

[1] John C. Hamilton, *History of the Republic of the United States of America as Traced in the Writings of Alexander Hamilton* (1850–51), III, 346.

with secret national conclaves of party leaders not to be confused with the later national delegate nominating conventions.

The congressional caucus was a congenial organ to the old ruling class. The late Professor Edward M. Sait considered it "from almost every standpoint superior to the delegate convention that succeeded it,"[2] and John C. Calhoun more than a hundred years ago expressed a similar opinion.[3] Certainly the caucus confined its nominations to men of experience in public affairs so that its product, the first six presidents, has been called the statesman group of presidents. The jury of fifty-five historians polled by A. M. Schlesinger, Sr. did not rate one of the caucus-nominated presidents below average. Washington and Jefferson were rated "great" and John Adams "near great." No equal period of convention-nominated presidents reveals a comparable succession of well-qualified presidents.

Whatever may have been its merits, the congressional caucus as a presidential nominating institution had run its course by the 1820's. Though it had served satisfactorily the quasi aristocracy of the fathers, it was pounced upon and demolished by belligerent Jacksonian Democracy. William H. Crawford, the last caucus nominee, was discredited by the very method of his nomination. A chaotic interval of groping for a new method of nominating presidents followed during which presidential nominations were made by state legislatures, state legislative caucuses, state delegate conventions, and even large mass meetings in some states.[4]

The genesis and evolution of the national nominating convention is another example of the natural history of democratic institutions. Here is an institution absolutely indigenous to the American political soil—there is nothing whatever alien about it. Its persistence on a national scale, with only insignificant modifications, for more than a century and a quarter demonstrates its

[2] *American Political Parties* (1939), p. 313.
[3] *Works* (1851), VI, 249.
[4] M. Ostrogorski, *Democracy and the Party System* (1910), p. 16.

adaptation to the political folkways of our unique political society. The convention has influenced profoundly the nature of the American presidency and in a sense has reshaped it.

Somewhere in the heart of Pennsylvania a century and a half ago some Jeffersonian Republican, perplexed with the problem of getting the party ticket of county officers nominated, must have suggested to his fellow partisans, "Why not have the Republicans in each township select some delegates to a county meeting?" The suggestion was acted upon, and it proved to be just what was needed. Before long nomination by delegate conventions was an established institution in the counties of the middle Atlantic states. Soon congressional district conventions were nominating candidates for Congress, and state delegate conventions state party tickets. An established procedure based on practical experience had emerged for nominating state and local party tickets.

When the congressional caucus as a means of nominating presidential candidates folded up in the 1820's, something had to fill the vacuum created. This was no great problem for a people endowed with a gift for improvising social devices. What was more natural than for the local and state delegate conventions to make the transition into the national nominating convention? However this had to await the wide use of the steamboat for coastal and river travel. This came in time to make possible the Anti-Masonic party's national convention at Baltimore in 1831. Being a new party the Anti-Masons could not possibly have relied on a congressional caucus.

Three months after the Anti-Masonic convention at Baltimore, the National Republicans, soon to be incorporated in the emerging new Whig party, held a national convention in the same city and nominated Henry Clay. It should be noted that this convention, like our national conventions today, already had committees on credentials, on permanent organization, and on an address to the people, later to be designated the committee on resolutions. How could this national convention, the very first one of a major party, have these essential committees? The answer is that these earliest national conventions did not at all start from scratch but simply adopted the party folkways and usages already found in the county, congressional district, and state nominating conventions. The whole convention's system with its delegates selected in the precincts by caucuses satisfied the democratic aspirations of the recently enfranchised masses. The system represented a shift in political power from the old self-appointed elite to the people. Indeed it was the growing power of the West and of hitherto largely inarticulate urban lower-income groups that had doomed the congressional caucus. Henceforth these new elements had to be considered in nominating presidential candidates.

Consequent upon the national conventions and the national committees that soon appeared, the major parties got organized on a national scale, with a hierarchy of committees, national, state, county, and precinct. Even local as well as state and congressional elections became competitions related to the party effort to elect the president. The professional politician as a consequence of the Jacksonian revolution had snatched the party reins from the landed and urban gentry who had held the mastery during the first generation under the Constitution. The Convention signalized the conversion of the president from a quasi-congressional agent into a popular agent, a "tribune of the people," to use the favorite phrase of Jacksonian Democracy, based on the executive veto. Thus the intention of the framers to make the executive a check on Congress was restored after an epoch of near desuetude of the veto. But instead of the expectation that the veto would check the anticipated democracy of the legislature, the presidency itself had been converted into an organ of democracy.

The shift of political power from the old elite to the newly enfranchised masses profoundly changed the quality of the presidents for two or three decades. Of the eight presidents following Jackson, the first of the convention-nominated presidents, only James K. Polk was ranked "near great" and Van Buren as the only "average" by the panel of historians.[5] The remaining six were "below average," even considerably below. Franklin Pierce may have been the weakest willed of all the presidents. At any rate his loyal friend and campaign biographer, Nathaniel Hawthorne, expressed his deep concern over Pierce's election with the poignant exclamation, "Frank, I pity you—Indeed I do, from the bottom of my heart."[6] Pierce should probably be rated a failure as president.

A high physical vitality characterized the presidents of this pre-Civil War era so that when Lincoln was inaugurated there were five living ex-presidents, the greatest number at any one time in our history and this despite the fact that two of the eight had died in office. The last years of these five former presidents reflect the low prestige of the presidency in mid-nineteenth century. John Tyler died in January, 1862, after service in the provisional Confederate Congress and just before he would have taken his seat as an elected member of the Confederate House of Representatives. Martin Van Buren died six months later, despondent over the disasters of the Union army during the Peninsular campaign. Lincoln's high prestige was largely a posthumous phenomenon. "Never," wrote Claude Bowers, "has the Presidency meant less than during these years [the 1860's]."[7] The contempt for the presidency was revealed during the summer (1865) in outrageous insults to the three former Presidents then living in retirement. Buchanan, an old man in his beautiful country home of Wheatland at Lancaster, was the object of constant assaults in the press, and the publication of his "Vindication" overwhelmed him with abuse. Then, on Lincoln's death, Fillmore, hovering about the sickbed of his wife and ignorant of the request that private houses be draped, hung no crepe, and awoke one morning to find his house smeared with ink. At the same time the venerable Franklin Pierce, speaking at a memorial meeting, was interrupted with a yell, "Where is your flag?" and with scorn the old man flung back his answer, "It is not

---

[5] Polled by Arthur M. Schlesinger, Sr., in 1945.
[6] See Allan Nevins, *Ordeal of the Union* (1947), II, 41.
[7] *The Tragic Era* (1929), p. 12.

necessary for me to show my devotion to the stars and stripes by any special exhibition." Shortly the drive against the presidency was to culminate in the miserable fiasco of the impeachment of President Andrew Johnson. A Tocqueville or a Bryce who might have commented on politics in the United States in the 1860's could fairly have observed that the presidency had come to be held in very contempt.

The mid-century decline in the average quality of the presidents was doubtless due to the electoral revolt of the masses against the statesman type of chief executive drawn from the ruling gentry. The convention, far from being the cause of the decline, was merely the organ through whom the little people sought to nominate candidates drawn from their own ranks. Intellect had become somewhat suspect in this era of the rise of the common man. Even the Whigs, the heirs of the defunct Federalist party of "the rich, the well born, and the wise," won presidential elections only when they nominated military heroes—General William Henry Harrison and Zachary Taylor—figures fascinating to the masses.

The nomination of Lincoln at Chicago in 1860 marked a turning point in the general quality of presidents selected by means of the Convention. Of the thirteen presidents following that date as judged by the fifty-five historians only three were rated "below average"— Grant, Harding, and Coolidge. Woodrow Wilson and Franklin Roosevelt were adjudged "great," while Theodore Roosevelt and Grover Cleveland were considered "near great." Johnson, Hayes, Arthur, Harrison, McKinley, and Hoover were all rated "average."[8]

There has long been a tendency to accept uncritically James Bryce's contrast between the "natural selection" of prime ministers and the "artificial selection" of our presidents. The disparaging term "artificial" reflects, of course, on our nominating conventions. The two methods of "selection" are products of the political mores of two quite different peoples, and it cannot be

---

[8] Because of his brief incumbency Garfield was not judged nor was Truman, who had only recently succeeded to the presidency at the time of the judging.

demonstrated that either one is more natural than the other or in any way superior to the other. Each has from time to time brought forth conspicuous misfits. The late Harold J. Laski, in an article prepared for English readers, wrote that

if we make a numerical comparison between great American Presidents between Washington and Franklin Roosevelt and great Prime Ministers between the younger Pitt and Mr. Churchill the advantage is as much on the American as on the British side. . . .Most people would agree that, between 1789 and 1945, the great Prime Ministers were Pitt, Peel, possibly Palmerston, Disraeli, Gladstone, Lloyd George, and Churchill . . . .In the same period in the United States, it would be now generally agreed that Washington, Jefferson, Andrew Jackson, Lincoln, Theodore Roosevelt, Woodrow Wilson and Franklin Roosevelt were quite certainly Bryce's 'front rank' whatever the criterion by which he made the choice.[9]

According to Laski then the score would be even, "artificial selection" turning up seven "great" presidents in the century and a half while "natural selection" brought forth seven "great" prime ministers. Furthermore Laski dismissed the customary criticism of the American system for failing to elevate to the presidency such remarkable men as Clay, Webster, and Calhoun with the shrewd observation that

in each case their failure is explicable in terms of defects of character that, on the whole, is a tribute to the delegates who decided against them. . . . .Nor is it without significance that if 'artificial selection' in the United States excluded Clay, Calhoun and Webster, what Bryce calls 'natural selection' in Great Britain also excluded Lord Randolph Churchill and the great Irish leader Parnell from the influence that should have been theirs. And if men of such poor capacity as Franklin Pierce and Warren Harding became Presidents, Great Britain has little reason to be proud of Prime Ministers like Lord Goderich and Neville Chamberlain.[10]

[9] "The American Presidency," *Parliamentary Affairs*, III, No. 1 (Winter, 1949), 18.
[10] *Ibid.*, p. 19.

Unquestionably chance and circumstance play their parts in either system in determining who is to be the head of the national government.

Appropriating the matured usages of the state and local delegate conventions, the national nominating convention emerged full fledged over a century and a quarter ago without any state or national legislation, and so absolutely is the national nominating convention when in session a product of sheer custom and usage that its procedure and conduct cannot to this day be controlled by any state or national legislation. Only a constitutional amendment could give legislative power to regulate its sessions or even provide for national primaries for nominating presidential candidates.

The stability of the convention as an institution throughout its history is impressive. Disregarding such modern extraneous and unessential gadgets as radio, television, and newsreel cameras, it might be said that the more it changes the more it is the same thing. The maneuvering of factions and personal followings during the convention, the mass psychology, the deals and understandings between leaders, the play of patronage and pressure groups have persisted from the very beginning. It was at Baltimore in 1844 that the Democratic convention wrangled for two days over the seating of contested delegations from New York and wound up by seating both with half a vote for each delegate. It was in the same convention that ex-President Van Buren in eight ballots could not quite reach the then required two-thirds majority necessary for nomination, whereupon the convention nominated James K. Polk the first of all the "dark horses." So dark indeed was this "horse" that when the first telegraph line just constructed bore from Baltimore to Washington the first news telegram, conveying the news that Polk had been nominated, Democrats in the capital went about shouting "Hurrah for Polk," only pausing now and then to inquire, "Who the hell is Polk?" Dark-horse Polk turned out to be ablest President between Jackson and Lincoln. Bryce rated him as insignificant as Pierce, but that judgment was made before the publication of Polk's *Diaries* in 1910 revealed his quite superior ability.

Criticism of the convention, which breaks out quadrenially, concentrates upon its irrationality rather than on its product. The less he knows of the social drives, the seemingly blind forces that shape institutions, the more certain is the naïve novice that he can blueprint a better one. In practice he would inevitably experience what the philosopher John Locke did when he prepared as the constitution for the proprietary colony of the Carolinas an elaborate thirteenth-century feudal system, only to see the tough backwoods settlers serenely ignore it as a bit of constitutional romancing. Those who would suddenly supplant the deep-rooted convention system for nominating presidential candidates had better ponder Paul David's profound observation: "Almost any change in the nominating procedure is likely to have some effect upon the distribution of power in the social order."[11] In other words the forces of American political society functioning through the national convention sifts out a different kind of prospective president than a revamped convention or a national nominating primary would. Moreover the consequences of a shift to a different method of nominating candidates would be unpredictable and might turn out to be as striking as the consequence that resulted from the change from the congressional caucus to the convention method of nomination a century and a quarter ago.

Power politics provided the dynamics of every hotly contested nomination by a convention with patronage providing most of the leverage. Lincoln's nomination in 1860 would have been impossible without his managers' trading for state delegations by the offer of Cabinet posts despite Lincoln having forbidden such traffic. It was patronage, state patronage, that enabled the Eisenhower managers in the convention of 1952 to break the grip of the

[11] Paul David, Malcolm Moos, and Ralph Goodman, *Presidential Nominating Politics* (1954), I, 194.

"Old Guard" and ensure the general's nomination. Twenty years of Democratic presidents had left the Republican "Old Guard" absolutely bereft of federal patronage. It was the twenty some Republican governors who were equipped with state patronage, which they employed in managing their state delegations for Eisenhower, and, as Doris Fleeson put it, "They spared neither the carrot nor the goad."

The Pennsylvania delegation became the key to the nomination, and the managers of both Taft and Eisenhower sought to dazzle Governor Fine with prospects of a Cabinet appointment, an ambassadorship, or even the vice-presidency. They offered him the chance to be "Kingmaker" by making the nominating speech. Senator Duff, an ardent Eisenhower man but no friend of the Governor, was said to have been persuaded to promise to the Governor his own potential Federal patronage to get the Governor to deliver the Pennsylvania delegates for Eisenhower. But the most effective use of patronage for Eisenhower was made by Governor Dewey, who informed the New York delegates at their first caucus that he would be Governor for two and a half years more and that he had a long memory. Then he called their attention to the state jobs allocated to each delegate's district and to the fact that there could be new appointees two days after his return to Albany. No wonder one television close-up of the convention revealed Governor Dewey announcing the New York delegation's 95–1 vote for the Eisenhower "Fair Play" amendment to the rules. Let no one assume that a change to the national nominating primary would do anything to the play of power politics except to change the way it would be employed and very possibly for the worse. Power will be used when the stakes are as high as they always are in choosing a president.

There are certain important minorities interested in the protection of civil rights that would lose a powerful leverage they now possess in the convention system if a change were made to the national nominating primary. The same advantage would be lost if a change were made to a rigidly instructed delegate convention as has been proposed. These minorities are largely concentrated in the large cities of pivotal states where they can, when aroused, use the balance of power of their collective ballots to swing decisive majorities of electoral votes and thereby determine presidential elections. National conventions are therefore compelled to calculate the effect of the attitude of the Jewish, Negro, Catholic, and other religious and ethnic groups and select their candidates with respect to it. Thus it was the delegates from states where such minorities are potent and capable of shifting balances of electoral powers who compelled the Democratic conventions of 1948 and 1952 to recognize civil rights in their platforms. It was such delegates who sought to require a "loyalty pledge" of the delegates in the hope of thereby preventing another states' rights or Dixiecrat defection in 1952. In fact, the national nominating convention seems indispensable in choosing the type of candidate required as long as the Electoral College continues.

What would the substitution of a direct national nominating presidential primary do to the presidency? The convention has always had the obligation, seldom shirked, of finding a candidate with wide voter appeal—that is, a potential winner. It can and does, with rare exceptions, act with a collective intelligence by no kind of miracle possible for millions of party voters acting independently in the seclusion of the millions of polling booths of a national primary. Contrast the simplicity of the voter's function of deciding between the two major candidates for president in the general election with that of deciding among several possibilities whom to vote for as the party candidate in a primary election.

> A national primary [observed Paul David] would disregard the necessity for sectional, factional, and group compromises that are the price of union [but] the convention environment puts emphasis upon the process of compromise and adjustment through face-to-face negotiation. It brings representatives of every section and group together in one place where they are

required to think about the problems of the party from the national point of view.[12]

The primary, on the other hand, permits no opportunity for balancing of the interests and sections so necessary in selecting a potential chief executive of a multigroup society organized in a federal republic. The primary by making impossible the opportunity for elements of the party—the factions, sectional, economic, ethnic, and other kinds—to arrive at a negotiated consensus on platform and candidate would almost certainly, on occasion, prove disruptive of the party. In short the convention provides opportunity for the maximum of integration of which the loose federation of local parties constituting our national parties is capable.

If, under nation-wide presidential primaries, the indispensable collective party intelligence appears at all, it could be only by undersurface management. To be effective among millions of voters of a party this management would have to be well heeled indeed, and the good angels so necessary may be at hand in the oil multimillionaires fabulously enriched by the legal depletion deductions of 27 1/2 per cent before calculating Federal taxes. Here is an emerging new power group eager to play the role of twentieth-century American Warwicks. Instead of long since dethroned King Cotton or tottering King Corn the national nominating primaries might be the means of enthroning King Oil. But these same forces so easily concealed in the primary are, when operating in the convention, uncovered and tagged by shrewd news columnists, and their major moves are publicized almost as soon as they are made.

One thing is indisputable, a primary can never draft a candidate, which the convention sometimes does, and has thereby offered the electorate some superior candidates, for example Charles Evans Hughes in 1916 and Adlai Stevenson in 1952. If the national primary were established, "fate may then sometimes decree that only

[12] *Ibid.*, p. 203.

the most egregious self seekers and political charlatans shall be on the ballot as the choice to which the electorate must address itself."[13] By no means could the national primary frame the party platform, and a denatured national convention absolutely necessary for that sole purpose would be preposterous. Moreover the platform must precede the nomination of the candidate, who should be such a one as could consistently run on that platform. Nor would the primary be likely to nominate a suitable running mate for the presidential candidate. In short, as Sidney Hyman comments on the convention,"If it were abolished, the conversations it makes possible between trans-continental interests, the common language it gives to them, the common means of self protection, with which it arms them, the compromises it imposes upon them would come to an end. A Babel would rise on the debris."[14]

Edward S. Corwin and Louis W. Koenig express an even more vigorous condemnation, observing:

> Indeed the national primary instead of being a democratic device would be anti-democratic, because it would limit candidates to those few who could command the big money required for the campaign. Equally serious is the prospect that the national primary would have a devastating impact on party cohesion. The primary would serve to organize rivalry and strife between party personages on a national scale. The consequence might well be splits within parties that could not be healed within a single presidential term.[15]

In the convention the factions come face to face and have the opportunity to arrive at some understanding on differences, which they usually do. The primary would lack utterly such an institutional device for composing differences.

Nor should the quadrennial competition for presidential nominations between senators and state governors be overlooked. The

[13] Paul David, *Ibid.*, p. 200.
[14] *The American President* (1954), p. 165.
[15] *The Presidency Today* (1956), p. 109.

national nominating primary would almost certainly tip the scales heavily in favor of the senators, who have an advantage over governors in getting the attention of the nation. The evidence is overwhelming that the Senate provides no adequate apprenticeship for the presidency while a governorship has provided it repeatedly. Returning to the verdicts of the jury of historians, not one of the six "great" presidents had served a full term in the Senate.[16] Nor had one of the four "near great" ever sat in the Senate. The former senators cluster near the foot of the class. Three of the eleven "average" presidents, three of the six "below average" presidents, and one of the two "failures" had been senators. Half of the "great" presidents had been state governors, three-fourths of the "near great," and five of the eleven "average" presidents had been governors. There was only one governor among the eight presidents rated still lower. Meanwhile the American people might ponder well before changing the nominating process to a method that could give senators the edge in the competition.

What if we had selected our presidents through national nominating primaries instead of the convention during the last hundred years? Would it have given us better presidents? Of course we can never know, but some shrewd speculation based on historical data can be ventured. To begin with, we could not have had Lincoln, because a party primary in 1860 would have almost certainly nominated the less competent but nationally famous Senator William H. Seward instead of the then not-so-well-known frontier lawyer Lincoln, but a primary would have renominated Lincoln in 1864. Since General Grant's name was on every tongue a party primary would have done precisely what the convention did in 1868 and 1872. Indeed the chances appear rather strong that primaries would have done just what the conventions did in the nomination of Grant (twice), Cleveland (twice), McKinley (twice), Theodore

[16] Jackson had served a few months as an appointed Senator from Tennessee before resigning.

Roosevelt (1904), Taft (1908), Wilson (second term), Coolidge, Hoover (twice), Franklin Roosevelt (four times), Truman (1948), and Eisenhower (twice). This generalization is based on the assumption that the competition of the primary election did not, in any case, engender enough strife to upset the expected result.

A Republican party primary in 1876 would quite probably have nominated the magnetic but tarnished Senator James G. Blaine instead of the courageous and incorruptible Governor Rutherford B. Hayes, who could scarcely have competed successfully against Blaine in a primary. In 1880 either Blaine or the incompetent ex-president Grant would probably have been chosen by a primary instead of Garfield, who was certainly superior to either. In 1888 it might have been John Sherman with more than thirty years service as Congressman, Senator, and Cabinet member instead of Senator Benjamin Harrison. In 1912 it could easily have been the somewhat erratic Champ Clark instead of the much abler Woodrow Wilson. In 1920 it would have been General Leonard Wood or Governor Frank Lowden instead of Warren Harding. A peculiar set of circumstances that may never recur upset the normal functioning of the Republican convention in 1920. The three chief contenders, Wood, Lowden and Senator Johnson, were each strong enough to cancel out each other by creating a three-way deadlock, and since a Republican victory seemed certain in 1920, neither contender would give in. Since "any Republican could win" in 1920, a clique of Senators manipulated the nomination to one of their own number, Warren Harding, whom they considered pliable enough that the clique could dominate him as President.

The nomination of Harding seems to be the single instance out of twenty-four conventions that nominated candidates who became president in which the convention unquestionably did worse than primaries at corresponding dates might have done, which looks almost like the proverbial exception to a general rule. According to our estimate, in eighteen out of twenty-four conventions that nominated future presidents a primary would have done no better than a convention because it probably would have done exactly what the convention did. Discount all this as speculation as you please, the strong suspicion remains that the convention is as satisfactory in performing its function as any human institution can hope to be. No English scholar since James Bryce is more competent to judge our institutions objectively than Professor Denis W. Brogan, in whose opinion our national conventions provide "the maximum integration that the party system is capable of" and "they decide which candidates are available and then which of the available candidates is most available," a sifting process that a national primary could never even hope to do. Finally Brogan found that "the Convention system works, works as well, in its own sphere, as Congress does in its" and "no really effective substitute has ever been suggested."[17]

---

[17] *Politics in America* (1954), pp. 232, 234.

V

The Presidency as Molded

by the Campaign and Election

* **THE PRESIDENTIAL ELECTION** is
essentially a battle between the managers of the two major parties
to capture the presidency with all its prestige, patronage, and
power. Because the stakes are so enormous, the very nature of the
presidential office is inevitably profoundly affected by this quadrennial competition. No matter what the Constitution provides
with respect to the president, it is his virtually direct election by a
nationwide electorate, contrary to the intention of the framers of
the Constitution that has so largely converted the presidency into
what it has become. What if the first plan of the framers to have
the president elected by Congress and rejected just before adjournment had stuck? He might have become little more than the complaisant agent of Congress. What if the presidential electors had
continued to vote their individual judgment? He could never have
become the free choice of the national electorate. "How the President is elected does much to determine the ground rules under
which the social struggle proceeds in the political arena. The electoral vote system established by the founding fathers seen in this
perspective, shaped up as little less than an act of political
genius."[1]

[1] E. S. Corwin and L. W. Koenig, *The Presidency Today* (1956), pp. 129–30.

As Lincoln expressed it when responding to a serenade following his re-election in 1864, "The struggle of the election is but human nature practically applied to the facts of the case."[2] By and large the presidential election is an emotional rather more than a rational experience of the electorate but withal an exhilarating and wholesome one at that. One wonders how else the electorate as a whole could be made so acutely aware of the very existence of our national state, which most of the time is ignored when it is not casually just taken for granted. "I know of nothing grander," declared Walt Whitman, "better exercise, better digestion, more positive proof of the past, the triumphant result of faith in human kind, than a well-contested national election."[3]

But what does a presidential election do to the winning candidate? That depends on candidate and circumstances. There have been presidents elected who entered the office on inauguration day almost utterly innocent of what the election signified and what was expected of them—Ulysses S. Grant, for example. At the opposite extreme was Lincoln, the consummate politician, the inveterate reader of newspapers, clairvoyant discerner of public sentiment, and gauger of social forces. Lincoln was acutely aware of every component element of the group combination that had elected him. Unless he could hold intact that unstable combination, he could become as impotent as President John Tyler had been fifteen years earlier, when the Whig party that had elected him Vice-President turned against him as President and, in caucus, literally read him out of the party. What can be more futile than a president without a party? Perhaps it is the president oblivious to the elements that elected him or unaware of how to utilize them in order to govern with vigor.

The Republican party that elected Lincoln in 1860 was as incongruous an aggregation of economic and social groups as a

[2] Roy P. Basler (ed.), *Abraham Lincoln: His Speeches and Writings* (1946), p. 764.

[3] *Complete Prose Works* (1914), p. 218.

political issue—opposition to slavery in the territories in this case —had ever brought together. Laborers and farmers, mainly of the older native stock along with the Free-Soil Democrats, constituted the core of the new Republican party. It had swallowed almost *in toto* the northern Know-Nothing movement when the party had collapsed, but because of this antialien element the Republicans held only tenuously a contingent of recent German immigrants, whom it dared not alienate. Included also in the combination were radical Abolitionists, whom Lincoln abhorred, fanatical Prohibitionists, and some novel cults of that strange era of social ferment, even vegetarians among others. Lincoln's paramount purpose as President-elect was to keep this combination from disintegrating before his inauguration no less than afterward and all in the midst of a harassing spread of southern secession and defiance of Federal authority. These were the circumstances resulting from the election of 1860 and determining what President Lincoln might and might not do in March, 1861.

Before his election Lincoln had expressed to Leonard Swett, one of his campaign managers, his theory "that the pressure of the campaign was an external force coercing the party into unity."[4] On election day that particular integrating force completely vanished. Now there remained but a single proposition on which every last Republican agreed, "Keep slavery out of the territories." As secession spread, Republican leaders came under the most intense pressure to consent to the restoration of the Missouri Compromise, which had been repealed by the Kansas-Nebraska Act of 1854. This would have obliterated the one proposition that held intact the Republican party combination. Lincoln was adamant on this issue and wrote to a Republican congressman before his inauguration: "Prevent as far as possible any of our friends from demoralizing themselves and our cause by entertaining propositions for compromise on slavery extension. There is no possible compromise on it but which puts us under again and leaves all our

[4] Leonard Swett to W. H. Herndon, in E. Hertz, *The Hidden Lincoln* (1940), p. 297.

work to do over again . . . on the point hold firm, as with a chain of steel."[5]

It was the campaign of 1860 that created the crisis of 1861 and the set of circumstances that affected the presidency more profoundly than any provision of statute or Constitution. By inflexible adhesion to the one great cohesive issue of exclusion of slavery from the territories Lincoln held his party intact. Had he not done so, his oath "to preserve, protect and defend the Constitution" and "to take care that the laws be faithfully executed" throughout the entire nation would have been not much more than a symbolic gesture. The collapse of his following would have created a confusion bordering on anarchy, and he knew it. With no mandate to move at once against the Southern defiers of Federal authority Lincoln immediately after inauguration merely accepted and maintained the *status quo* bequeathed by Buchanan, who had himself resolved to defend Sumter if it were attacked. When the attack on Sumter came, the mandate given Lincoln by his party to keep slavery out of the territories was succeeded by the broader mandate of an electrified bipartisan northern public opinion to preserve the Union and enforce the supreme law of the land throughout its length and breadth.

Two generations before Lincoln's election Jefferson, the third President, had manifested the profound influence of a presidential election in shaping the presidency. During the campaign of 1800 this ardent agrarian prudently took in sail and toned down his strictures of 1782 against "the mobs of great cities who add just so much to the support of pure government, as sores to the strength of the human body."[6] "I had in mind," he explained during the campaign, "the manufacturers [manual workers] of the old country, at the present time, with whom the want of food and clothing necessary to sustain life, had begotten a depravity of morals."[7]

[5] G. H. Putnam and A. B. Lapsby (eds.), *Complete Works of Abraham Lincoln* (1888–96), v, 196.

[6] *Notes on the State of Virginia* (1782), p. 302.

[7] *The Writings of Thomas Jefferson* (Ford edition), (1892–99), III, 269.

The laborers of Boston, New York, Philadelphia, and Baltimore were worth luring away from their Federalist employers into the Jeffersonian party. Thus as early as 1800 a presidential candidate was taking cognizance of the fact that an urban minority had better be placated.

In this election of 1800 the Republicans had aimed to elect Jefferson President and Burr Vice-President, but under the original system provided by the framers of the Constitution for casting the ballots of the presidential electors a tie between them had resulted. This tie required election of the president by the House of Representatives with each state delegation casting one vote. Moreover this election was by a "lame duck" Federalist House of Representatives elected in the midst of the hysterical anti-French reaction of 1798 following the revelation of the XYZ Affair. Federalist leaders promptly set about planning to elect Burr President but were frustrated by his firm refusal to support Federalist plans if elected. He would serve only as a Republican President and, as a Tammany partisan, presumably would replace every last Federalist appointee with a deserving Republican.

Finding Burr to be an inflexible partisan Republican, Federalist leaders turned to sound out Jefferson through an intermediary. They hoped for assurances that Jefferson would maintain the Federalist fiscal system, adhere to the existing policy of neutrality, preserve and gradually increase the navy, and continue in office all Federalists except in the major departments. General Samuel Smith, acting as an intermediary for Senator Bayard, sounded out Jefferson on these matters apparently without his suspecting the purpose. Smith reported back to Bayard that Jefferson's views were in accord with Bayard's, whereupon the prolonged impasse in the balloting of the House of Representatives for president was broken by some Federalists absenting themselves or casting blank ballots. Ten states supported Jefferson to eight for Burr, and Jefferson was declared elected President.

Due to the peculiar nature of Jefferson's election he entered the presidency under circumstances requiring extraordinary caution on his part, and his conduct reveals that he knew it. The electoral college vote as between Republicans and Federalists had been close: Jefferson 73, Adams 65. Only twice has the electoral vote since then been closer. One can detect the consequent circumspection of the practiced and astute politician in Jefferson's administration. An irreconcilable minority could have rendered the government virtually impotent, and Jefferson had just such a minority in the potentially intransigent New England Federalists. Indubitably the election of 1800 had decisively circumscribed Jefferson's discretion. No wonder his first inaugural contained the ingratiating sentiment, incomprehensible to his partisan supporters, "We are all Federalists, we are all Republicans." He was to confide to a correspondent that the conciliatory tone of the inaugural was designed to lure back the Republicans who had been stampeded to the Federalists by the anti-French hysteria of 1798. In accordance with the tacit understanding that the Federalists assumed they had with Jefferson, he made no wholesale removals from office and filled vacancies as they occurred with his faithful followers, but erelong he was to inquire, "How are vacancies to be obtained? Those by death are few, by resignation none."[8] However let no one be too astonished to learn that this practical-politician President saw fit to make a federal supervisor out of James Linn, the former Congressman who had cast the deciding vote in 1801 shifting the New Jersey delegation of the House of Representatives from Burr to Jefferson and thereby ensuring Jefferson's election as President.[9]

President Jefferson was never averse to rewarding the elements in his constituency that gave vigor to the presidential arm. Believing that Hamilton had used the branches of the Bank of the United States as Federalist party patronage Jefferson expressed himself as "decidedly in favor of making all banks Republican by sharing

[8] Quoted by H. J. Ford, *The Rise and Growth of American Politics* (1898), p. 139.
[9] Henry Adams, *John Randolph* (1882), pp. 52, 53.

deposits among them *in proportion to the disposition they show.*[10]
The "midnight judges" authorized by the recent lame-duck Federalist Congress and appointed by President Adams had their offices jerked from under their feet by the new Congress' repeal of the legislation creating the judgeships. Imprisoned victims of the despised Sedition Law were pardoned, and Congress appropriated money to repay their fines. The erstwhile Whisky rebels rejoiced to see the hated excise tax repealed. Though retrenchment was Republican dogma, money was appropriated to build the Cumberland Road into the Ohio Valley, where Republicans thrived and Federalists were virtually nonexistent. Millions were gladly provided to pay for the purchase of Louisiana, to be inhabited in due time, it was assumed quite correctly, by almost none but Jeffersonians. For Jefferson "steered the ship of state by the headlands and not the stars."[11] Let the amateur politician longing for a handbook on "What Every Young President Should Know" give his days and nights to the study of the art of politics as practiced by our first master politician to occupy that office.

Andrew Jackson was extraordinarily sensitive to public opinion. It is no exaggeration to say that public opinion created what came to be known as the Jacksonian movement, and such an extraordinary opportunist was Jackson that, up to the time he became President, he had not contributed a single item to what came to be known as Jacksonian Democracy. Once a candidate for the presidency, however, Jackson, aided by professional politicians who knew how to exploit his prestige as a soldier, soon demonstrated dexterity in a vigilant search for issues that would attract and cement the elements of a Jacksonian following.

Jackson became the first President to participate vigorously in managing his own campaign for election to the presidency, as he did also in the one for his re-election in 1832. Thus, when Senator

[10] Beard and Beard, *The Rise of American Civilization* (1927), I, 384. Italics mine, W.E.B.

[11] *Ibid.*, p. 386.

Clay deliberately challenged Jackson with the passage of the bill to recharter the Bank of the United States, he vetoed it with a blistering message that practically ensured his re-election. Jackson's Veto Message is the best illustration to that date of how presidential campaigns were reshaping the presidency. Twenty-one years earlier Congressman Clay had torn to shreds the very idea of the Bank in his speech opposing rechartering the first Bank of the United States. Jackson chose to embarrass his opponent for the presidency, Clay, by incorporating in his Veto Message of 1832 the arguments of Clay's anti-Bank speeches of 1811. The Veto Message was expertly utilized to make a mass appeal against the Bank. Taking advantage of the universal pioneer phobia of monopolies Jackson's veto argued that the Bank was a monopoly unnecessary, inexpedient, unconstitutional, and injurious to the country. It was so phrased as to arouse the prejudice of state banks against the "monster" Bank as well as the poor against the rich. It did not miss the opportunity to stir the prevailing prejudice against the foreign stockholders of the Bank, mainly English, who received profits of the Bank in the dividends declared and thereby drained metallic money out of the country. In order to get a campaign document at public expense a Democratic congressman moved the printing of 16,000 copies of the Veto Message, and it carried. The incomprehensibly obtuse Whig leaders printed still more copies for distribution. The veto was a major factor in Jackson's re-election.

Theodore Roosevelt's campaign for a second and his only elective term in 1904 is abundantly illustrative of what the campaign can do to the presidency even when the incumbent is a "strong" president. Quite frankly Theodore Roosevelt's biographer H. F. Pringle entitles the chapter on the campaign, "Trimming Sail." No matter how deftly and unobtrusively it may be done, this indispensable trimming of sail is one of the factors that, through the virtually direct popular election of the president, effects a continuous reshaping of the presidency. Nor is this just a unique characteristic of our own office of chief executive. It is an essential feature of systems of self-government everywhere. In parliamentary governments the required trimming of sails is a function of the premier, whose office is thereby continuously reshaped.

As the campaign of 1904 drew near, President Roosevelt was confronted with the explosive issue of the tariff, which was then dividing the Republican party into revisionists and standpatters. Three years earlier President McKinley had virtually promised leadership in revising the tariff. "I do not want to promise the impossible," wrote President Roosevelt, "and I have to recognize a tendency in the majority to 'stand pat' while in a large and fervent minority there is a growing insistence upon a reduction of duties."[12] "I doubt whether it would be best to make a reduction in the year preceding election," he confided to J. B. Bishop.[13] A million veterans of the Union army were living then, and their chief organization, the Grand Army of the Republic, demanded more liberal pensions, and Roosevelt responded with an executive order granting pensions to all Union veterans between the ages of sixty-two and seventy whether disabled or not. This was done despite the fact that the Pension Act of 1890 limited payments to disability.[14] Such was the potential power of the veterans that the illegal order was not challenged in the courts.

> Even had Roosevelt been willing to shape all his policies in deference to expediency [wrote Pringle], it would have been suicidal to have done so. The President must serve two masters. He must convince the voters that their rights and desires are paramount. He must reassure potential campaign contributors that his program does not threaten business interests. Early in 1903, with Election Day still distant enough to make it feasible, Roosevelt continued to press his trust-control measures. He was tortured by pondering on their effects, but—to his credit—he did go on.[15]

[12] H. F. Pringle, *Theodore Roosevelt, a Biography* (1931), p. 353.
[13] *Ibid.*, p. 342.
[14] *Ibid.*, p. 345.
[15] *Ibid.*, p. 340.

However he was busy during the year before the 1904 election tempering his belligerent attitude toward greedy corporations. He offered to appoint Henry C. Frick of the United States Steel Corporation to the Isthmian Canal Commission. He sent a draft of his third annual message to James Stillman, president of the National City Bank, and promised to change passages pertaining to the currency question. He invited J. P. Morgan to the White House with the coy comment, "I should like very much to see you to talk over certain financial matters," he wrote. Even J. D. Archbold, vice-president of Standard Oil, who avowed he had "read every book he (Roosevelt) ever wrote" was invited to the White House. But once the election was over the Bureau of Corporations began investigating the petroleum industry. "Darkest Abyssinia," snorted Archbold, "never saw anything like the course of treatment we received at the hands of the administration following Mr. Roosevelt's election in 1904."[16] Full sail again, no more trimming. If this be cynicism, make the most of it, but here is what presidential elections can do to the presidency. They have done it. They still do it.

The reversal of the earlier economic and social philosophy of Woodrow Wilson that prepared him precisely for the presidency in 1913 amounted to an indubitable about-face. The statement of the late Charles A. Beard that he "turned his coat inside out to get into the White House" is even a plausible exaggeration. Bryan's program had been anathema to him. President Theodore Roosevelt was blamed for the panic of 1907. Wilson "expressed vigorously his opposition to the tendency of the times to regulate business by governmental commissions" and was condemning it as "socialistic." In short, he was asking the Democratic party to return to "the conservative principles which it once represented."[17] Wilson's conservatism is what induced George Harvey, the emissary of a group of New York financiers, to visit him at Princeton University, where he was President, and get what he thought

[16] *Ibid.,* p. 350–51.
[17] R. S. Baker, *Woodrow Wilson, Life and Letters* (1927), III, 185.

was a gentleman's understanding preliminary to the launching of a campaign to elect Wilson Governor of New Jersey as a stepping stone to the presidency of the United States.

The ideological transformation Wilson experienced in the following two short years may have been almost unconscious. No matter how naïve he had been during the ferment of progressive ideas, he rapidly developed a clairvoyance with respect to emerging popular opinion. He seemed to "catch public opinion by wireless."[18] Even before Wilson plunged into the campaign of 1912 Louis D. Brandeis had proposed to him that he make the restoration of economic competition his main issue. The idea was not new to the candidate, but he lacked the clear understanding of the problem and the pertinent information with which Brandeis was loaded.[19] As a consequence in his first major campaign speech in 1912 Wilson forecast what was to become his legislative program amounting to a war on monopoly. Brandeis provided him with live ammunition in the large quantity of social data accumulated by Brandeis' researches.[20] The candidate also blasted away at the protective tariff, thus portending the Underwood Tariff revision. By the end of September the erstwhile condemner of government commissions was ready to accept Brandeis' proposal of an industrial commission to ensure competition through regulation of business enterprise to be actually realized soon in the Federal Trade Commission.[21] Early in October the candidate who three years earlier had declared himself to be "a fierce partisan of the open shop"[22] was promising safeguards to labor to be realized eventually in the Clayton Act specifically exempting labor from the antitrust laws so far as statute could do it. For the first time in history the speeches of a presidential candidate came close to developing in the very midst of the campaign the blueprint of a specific legislative program.

[18] C. E. Merriam, *Four Political Leaders* (1926), p. 48.
[19] Arthur S. Link, *Wilson: the Road to the White House* (1947), pp. 488–89.
[20] *Ibid.*, p. 493.
[21] *Ibid.*, p. 509.
[22] *Ibid.*, p. 127.

Since the advent of practically universal white manhood suffrage coincident with the election of Andrew Jackson revolutionized the presidency by making it pre-eminently the people's office, every "great" president has had to be more or less an opportunist. The art of political opportunism consists largely in discovering emerging popular demands for public policies and converting them into plausible and persuasive rationalizations of the public interest. In this art it is not clear as to which of the two Presidents Roosevelt was the more apt. Certainly Franklin Roosevelt proved adept at playing the breaks at almost every opportunity, and fate gave him plenty of them. In 1932 he became the Democratic candidate for President against hapless President Hoover, in whose administration the market crash of 1929 had ushered in the worst depression in our history. Hoover was the first President to assume leadership in Federal action in dealing with a depression, but the efforts proved inadequate—too little and too late, at any rate, so it then seemed to most of the electorate in 1932.

The thumbnail platform Franklin Roosevelt dashed off for the 1932 Democratic convention was "synthesized overnight out of opportunism." It exploited the advantage of the "outs" and constituted a summation of reactions to red-hot current sore spots. Thus it promised unemployment relief, labor legislation, old-age insurance under state laws, farm relief, conservation of natural resources, public power, regulation of holding companies, security exchanges, and utility rates, reciprocal trade agreements, a balanced budget, sound currency, and repeal of the Eighteenth Amendment. Fortunately Franklin Roosevelt had grown up economically loose footed and in contrast with Herbert Hoover was unaffiliated with any major economic group. Neither agriculture, business, nor labor had tagged Roosevelt. His economic outlook, if he had any, was rather that of the Hyde Park country squire with its traditional contempt for millionaires, "money changers," and "economic royalists." This may even have provided a somewhat judicial objectiveness with which to deal with the temporarily paralyzed and thoroughly bewildered economic interests of the early 1930's.

Franklin Roosevelt's inveterate opportunism inspired his appropriation of the phrase the "forgotten man," who was now to be remembered. It was an infuriating stroke, a challenge to the Republican formula of nurturing business as a sovereign remedy for the disease of poverty. The "forgotten man" was a formula with which to capture the attention of the unemployed worker, the impoverished farmer and the harassed consumer. A deliberate and successful bid was made for the "Hoovercrats," who had deserted the Democratic party in 1928. Roosevelt's campaign addresses offered fairly specific benefits for each element in the new group combination he was building. Farmers demoralized by thirty-five-cent wheat learned of a "Domestic Allotment Plan" designed to strike a balance between demand and supply of farm produce. The unemployed were promised direct Federal relief when local relief resources ran out. Labor exchanges, that is Federal employment agencies, vetoed by Hoover, were to be established and public works expanded. Business was to be bolstered by more generous loans by the Reconstruction Finance Corporation. Reminiscent of the first Roosevelt were plans for reforestations and erosion- and flood-control. Consumers heard of the possibility of breaking rigid and excessive electric power rates in the proposed conversion of Muscle Shoals into a yardstick for determining the cost of producing power while "forgotten men" were cheered by the plan to convert the Tennessee Valley into a model of a happier way of life. Stock-market victims heard with satisfaction the promise of rigid regulations. Handicapped by infirmity though he was, Franklin Roosevelt toured the country with the most vigorous campaign ever carried out by a successful presidential candidate.

If the balanced budget and sound currency promises of the Democratic party and candidate are excepted, Franklin Roosevelt's first administration represented almost as neat a translation of a campaign program into public policies as that of the first campaign and term of Woodrow Wilson. With the exceptions just noted every item in the summary of platform planks and candidate's promises was enacted into law. With the banks of the country closed at the moment of Roosevelt's inauguration it is no exaggeration to say that the national economy touched the bottom of the trough of the depression on inauguration day. With his flair for the dramatic the President seized the opportunity through apt use of biblical phrases and the promise of "action and action now" to inspire a despairing people with his own infectious confidence. So captivating was it at the time that ere long one nationally known businessman, resenting some criticism of the President, asserted that he had voted for Herbert Hoover but hoped God would forgive him for it, and he believed that Franklin D. Roosevelt was the greatest leader since Jesus Christ.[23]

The flood of legislation of the "hundred days" that ushered in Roosevelt's presidency was, by and large, a fulfillment of the promises of the preceding campaign. Thus it fell to the lot of the new Congress to enact banking legislation authorizing retroactively the closing and reopening of the banks directed by the President and Secretary of the Treasury under color of uncertainly applicable earlier legislation.[24] By enacting the Economy Statute a dazed Congress acceded to the President's request for authority to reduce sharply department budgets and cut Federal salaries and veterans' pensions and benefit payments, thereby carrying out a plank in the Democratic platform persistently promised by Roosevelt during the campaign as essential to recovery. To carry out a project proposed by the President during the campaign Congress authorized the Civilian Conservation Corps, which soon had a quarter million unmarried young men at work, a number later doubled. Whether sound or not, the Roosevelt policies were largely consequences of campaign exigencies.

A president can miscalculate as to the mandate of an election as did Franklin Roosevelt following his overwhelming re-election in 1936. It induced a cockiness revealed in his inaugural address and his belligerent address on the State of the Union in January, 1937 —"I have only just begun to fight." Here he proposed a still more elaborate reform program and sweeping administrative reorganization. Most of all had he been frustrated by the fact that, in the

---

[23] John T. Flynn, "Other People's Money," *New Republic,* December 11, 1935.
[24] Carl Swisher, *American Constitutional Development* (1954), p. 299 n.

face of what he considered the popular mandates of his election in 1932 and 1936, the Supreme Court had struck down a dozen major New Deal statutes. Brooding over what to do with the Supreme Court following the election of 1936 when he carried every state but two, Roosevelt seized the bull by the horns only to be thrown. His proposal to appoint an extra member of the Supreme Court for every sitting member of the Court who would not voluntarily retire with full pay at the age of seventy provoked a prolonged debate and defeat of the proposal. An unfortunate aftermath of the so-called Court-Packing Bill was the reception of the administrative reorganization bill, which conservatives smeared with the epithet the Dictator Bill and which passed only in a watered-down form. Thus the election of 1936 left its lesson so that never again is a president likely to read as much into an overwhelming re-election majority.

The campaigns of 1952 and 1956 linked the presidency to business as almost never before. Early in the 1952 campaign it began to appear that unless General Eisenhower could break the solid South, his election might be quite in doubt. Long before his nomination he had expressed his belief that Federal authority over offshore oil deposits rightfully belonged to and should be transferred to the states, all unaware of Supreme Court decisions holding that the Federal government had a paramount interest in them. So, when speaking in Texas and Louisiana, the eager candidate went the limit on the issue. In his excitement the general was denouncing President Truman's veto of the bills quitclaiming Federal title to the offshore oil land as a "shoddy deal" and a "grab," terms impossible to reconcile with the pertinent Supreme Court decisions. The big-city press of Texas promptly came out for Eisenhower and oil men; ranchers and real estate interests began contributing heavily to Republican campaign funds. Governor Shivers of Texas obtained an opinion of his Attorney General that Texas voters might scratch out Democratic candidate Stevenson's name and write in Eisenhower's on the Democratic ticket. Candidate Eisenhower may not have known that the 27 1/2 per cent depletion allowance to oil companies before computing their Federal taxes was creating a fabulously wealthy group of oil magnates capable of financing campaigns of their favorite candidates. The expectations of the oil interests were promptly satisfied by the new administration's legislation transferring offshore jurisdiction to the states. Not in a long generation had business come out of a campaign so fortified to influence the presidency. One consequence was a Cabinet decidedly unbalanced as among the interests constituting American society by its preponderance of representatives of big business, a bias epitomized by a catch phrase, "Eight millionaires and a plumber."

In the midst of a speech delivered in the closing days of the 1952 campaign General Eisenhower, acting on the suggestion of a speech-writer, astonished the nation with a pledge to "forego the diversions of politics and ... concentrate on the job of ending the Korean War. That job requires a personal trip to Korea. I shall make that trip. I shall go to Korea."[25] The startling declaration was probably the most telling single stroke of any campaign in a long time. Its electoral effect was incalculable. Seldom had a candidate made a more specific commitment. It was, in due time, faithfully executed and in one way or another the shooting was stopped. Eisenhower was irrevocably pledged to a policy of peace.

General Eisenhower's accidental discovery of the unsuspected potency of the peace issue in the campaign of 1952 led eventually to an unfortunate new trend in the presidency, a reduction of the freedom of the commander-in-chief in the free exercise of the discretionary power vested in him by the Constitution. President Truman had taken pride in maintaining that power unimpaired. When the North Korean army made its surprise invasion of South Korea in the summer of 1950, President Truman had to act promptly if at all. His order to General MacArthur to use American armed forces in resistance to North Korean forces was given as Commander-in-Chief and in compliance with obligations agreed

[25] See James Reston, "Korea is Now Eisenhower's Most Telling Issue," *New York Times,* Nov. 2, 1952, Sect. 4, p. E3.

to by Article 43 of the Charter of the United Nations. This obligation was in consequence of our ratification of the Covenant by the
treaty power, and treaties are of course a part of the supreme law
of the land as the Constitution declares. In the heat of the campaign of 1952 it became a part of Republican strategy to disregard
the legal basis of Truman's action in Korea and to brand him as a
warmonger.

It was evident enough that the criticism, during the 1952 campaign, of Truman's prompt use of American armed forces in Korea
had done something to the presidency when President Eisenhower
in January; 1956, asked Congress for emergency authority to use
armed forces to protect Formosa. This amounted to a request for
Congress to authorize the President to exercise a power already
vested in the president by the Constitution and that had been exercised promptly by presidents ever since McKinley had suddenly
sent troops into China to protect American citizens against the
Boxer rebels in 1900. President Eisenhower's request for permission to exercise a constitutional power already vested in him was a
new departure creating a precedent that would make it difficult
for future presidents to act as freely as circumstances might make
absolutely necessary. Of course the Republican party campaign
strategy of critizing Truman as a warmonger in 1952 had made
President Eisenhower's request practically necessary in 1956. In
1957 he was seeking congressional sanction in advance of possible
armed intervention in the Middle East, but failed to obtain it.

The campaign of 1956 again revealed what a presidential election can do in determining a trend in the presidency. Since President-elect Eisenhower had gone to Korea and had brought about
an apparently stable armistice, the Republican party leaders assumed credit for the "peace" and made the most of the issue in
the 1956 campaign. It proved overwhelmingly effective. So impressed was a vast segment of the voters, especially mothers, that
pre-election interviewers of voters such as Samuel Lubell and the

Alsop brothers heard again and again the monotonously reiterated refrain "Eisenhower stopped the war in Korea" and "Democrats always get us into wars." So when, within a week of the
election of 1956, war broke out in the Near East with Israel's invasion of Egypt, President Eisenhower reassured a nervous nation
that he would not use our armed forces without calling Congress
into special session, thus more securely than ever fastening upon
the commander-in-chief the extraconstitutional limitation upon
his freedom of action deemed so essential by the framers of the
Constitution. Verily the presidential campaign does persistently
shape and reshape the presidency.

VI

The President

as Party Leader

* **THE PARTY LEADERSHIP** now expected of the president is an example of nothing else than pure and simple custom. The Founding Fathers anticipated nothing of the sort, and the very idea would have been abhorrent to them. In their minds political parties, especially on a national scale, represented pure poison to the body politic. The provision for the election of the president by presidential electors, each one exercising his personal judgment and without knowing which of his two ballots might help elect a president or which a vice-president, was deliberately designed to discourage the development of national parties. The term party brought vividly to the minds of the Founding Fathers the only example of such a thing they knew of on a national scale, the contemporary personal following of English politicians, the most notorious of which had been the servile, patronage-hungry partisans of George III, the "King's Friends" as they had been denominated, the party sustaining the English ministry whose arbitrary policies had driven the colonists to revolt.

President Washington could never have understood, in his day, the turn of events that were eventually to make every president the titular and often the actual chieftain of his party. It never even occurred to Washington that the Federalists were anything else

than loyal supporters of decent government—and not at all a political party. Otherwise he never would have included in his Farewell
Address:

> Let me . . . warn you in the most solemn manner against the
> baleful effects of the spirit of party generally . . . It serves always
> to distract the public councils and enfeeble the public adminis-
> tration. It agitates the community with ill founded jealousies
> and false alarms; kindles the animosity of one part against
> another; foments occasional riot and insurrection.[1]

Washington's immediate successor, John Adams, was just as
antipathetic to political parties as our first President. "There is
nothing I dread so much as the division of the Republic into two
great parties, each under its leader," he lamented. "This, in my
humble opinion, is to be feared as the greatest evil under our Constitution."[2] His son John Quincy Adams, who was elected President a quarter of a century later, would not even then recognize
the *fait accompli* of political parties. Thurlow Weed, a contemporary professional politician, was to declare, "Mr. Adams during
his administration failed to cherish, strengthen, or even recognize
the party to which he owed his election; nor, as far as I am informed, with the great power he possessed did he make a single
influential friend."[3] John Quincy Adams would not, even if he
could, create a majority coalition as President for "like George
Washington he did not believe in political parties, or in sections,
the essential realities of American politics—and they did not believe in him."[4] Adams removed no enemy from office, not even his
Postmaster General, who was busy distributing patronage against
him. He even prevented his supporters from copying the damaging
public record of a court-martial decision on six militiamen Andrew

[1] Jas. D. Richardson, *Messages and Papers of the Presidents* (1927), I, 218.
[2] Quoted by W. M. West, *History of the American People* (1918), p. 333 n.
[3] Quoted by E. M. Carroll, *Origins of the Whig Party* (1925), p. 13.
[4] Samuel Flagg Bemis, *John Quincy Adams and the Union* (1956), p. 55.

Jackson had executed for fear it would be construed as "a measure of hostility against General Jackson."[5] Since Jackson was the opposing presidential candidate, such abstinence represented the very antithesis of presidential leadership of his party.

Thomas Jefferson was the first President to assume and practice leadership of his party in that office. He was already the unquestioned symbol as well as manager of the group combination constituting his Republican party. Jefferson's distant and quite critical cousin, Chief Justice John Marshall, with clairvoyant prescience predicted accurately what was to be the pattern of Jefferson's party leadership while President.

> Mr. Jefferson appears to me to be a man who will embody himself with the House of Representatives. By weakening the office of President he will increase his personal power. He will diminish his [the President's] responsibility, sap the fundamental principles of government, and become the leader of the party which is about to constitute the majority of the legislature.[6]

It was precisely this party leadership of the President that constituted the innovation so obnoxious to Marshall and Federalists generally as what they conceived to be a perversion of sound government.

When the first Congress in Jefferson's administration was organized, not only the Speaker but the chairman of every committee was a personal lieutenant of President Jefferson. Ostensibly the House had freely chosen its officers and selected its chairmen of committees, but Jefferson's wishes confidentially conveyed had determined this official personnel as certainly as if the President had publicly nominated them. The time would come when such things would occasion no lifting of eyebrows, but in 1801 it was a consequence of what Federalists considered perfidious intrigue.

Jefferson busied himself writing letters to likely Republican

---

[5] J. Q. Adams, *Memoirs* (1874–79), VII, 275.
[6] Hamilton (H. C. Lodge, ed.), *Works* (1885), VI, 501–503, quoted by A. J. Beveridge, *Life of John Marshall* (1916), II, 537.

leaders encouraging them to run for Congress whenever a competent leader retired. When John Randolph, at the President's behest, was deposed from chairmanship of the Ways and Means Committee for refusing to move an appropriation of $2,000,000 desired by Jefferson for the purchase of Florida, Jefferson encouraged another Republican to run for Randolph's seat in the next congressional election, the earliest attempt at a presidential purge—an unsuccessful one at that. Young Senator John Quincy Adams observed, "His whole system of administration seems founded on the principle of carrying through the legislative measures by personal and official influences."[7] It is no mean tribute to the political genius of Thomas Jefferson that this system worked with almost infallible efficiency.

Precedent-smashing President Jefferson did not confine himself to private conferences and letters in exercising his mastery of the party. He worked also through the congressional party caucus, sometimes meeting with it, and was alleged to have presided over some of its sessions. On the floor of the House his personal representative was at hand to hold wavering partisans in line.[8] Nor was Jefferson as free from utilizing patronage for party purposes as has usually been assumed. Thus he was not averse to suggesting "a judicious distribution of favors" to the Bank of the United States in order "to engage the individuals who belonged to them in support of the administration."[9] Incredible as it may seem, Jefferson removed a larger percentage of civil servants for purposes of patronage than did Andrew Jackson, who is the reputed founder of the spoils system in the Federal government.

Freedom from any hard and fast social philosophy permitted Andrew Jackson a flexibility as to policies promoted that was to put him in the front rank of American political leaders. Instead of

[7] *Memoirs* (1874–79), I, 403.

[8] Washington, *Federalist,* Feb. 21, 1802, cited by R. V. Harlow, *The History of Legislative Methods in the Period before 1825* (1917), p. 188.

[9] Quoted by Henry Jones Ford, *The Rise and Growth of American Politics* (1898), p. 131.

initiating what came to be denominated Jacksonian Democracy, the already developing movement by and large appropriated the general as its symbol and leader. As W. E. Dodd put it, Jackson could, "by intuition, scent the course the public mind would take particularly in the West."[10] Thus he followed when he seemed to lead. No doubt Jackson convinced himself, as he did his followers, that he was guided always by eternal principles of justice. Instead he was, like the ablest political leaders, more or less unconsciously a pragmatic opportunist.

President Jackson gathered about him a coterie of devoted and expert politicians who persistently sought the centripetal issues to hold intact the Democratic group combination. When Jackson saw impending in Congress a gigantic log-rolling appropriation bill for local improvements at Federal expense, such as for rivers, harbors, canals, and turnpikes, he let out a blast against such internal improvements. This was his veto of the bill for the twenty-mile improvement of the Maysville road in Kentucky selected for veto by Secretary of State Van Buren at the President's request because it was in such a strong Democratic district that the Congressman could not be defeated by the veto. By and large the regions of Jackson's strength did not need improvements, but the veto did enrage the Whigs pretty generally. Jackson's veto of the act to recharter the Bank of the United States raised to ecstasy the underdog elements so evident in the Jacksonian following. Jackson was crushing the "Monster," the money power. Incidentally it won to Jackson the powerful state banks, which hated the Bank of the United States because of its power to check their bank-notes issues by presenting the notes for redemption in specie thus curbing inflation, so popular in the money-starved pioneer communities. Jackson's order of removal of all Federal deposits from the Bank of the United States, which ruined it, bound most of the elements of Jacksonian Democracy together more securely than ever. He planned it that way.

[10] *Expansion and Conflict* (1915), p. 37.

Senator Henry Clay persuaded the Senate to pass a resolution censuring the President for ordering the removal of Federal deposits from the Bank of the United States, and the Resolution of Censure was entered on the *Senate Journal*. Against this action Jackson formally protested and asked to have his protest entered on the *Senate Journal*, but the Senate refused. Thereupon Senator Thomas H. Benton declared he would not rest until the censure was "expunged" from the journal. At this point President Jackson, as party chieftain, set to work. Under his relentless pressure and that of his partisans one state legislature after another forced the resignation of senators who had voted for the censure resolution. As new senators were chosen in their stead, Jackson men gradually gained control of the Senate.[11] Four years after passage of the Resolution of Censure the Jackson senators were strong enough to pass a resolution providing for the formal and ostentatious expunging of the Resolution of Censure from the *Senate Journal*.[12]

The party chieftain had a narrow escape on his last great move of party leadership. He was confronted with a party revolt against his determination to impose on the Democratic Convention of 1836 the nomination of his personal favorite, Vice-President Van Buren, as the candidate to succeed himself. So far as service to their chieftain and the Democratic party was concerned Senators Thomas H. Benton and Henry Lawson White, Secretary of the Treasury Roger B. Taney, and House Speaker James K. Polk had claims superior to Van Buren. The seriousness of the revolt became evident enough when the legislature of Jackson's own Tennessee nominated White for President and eventually cast its electoral vote for him. The revolt spread to other states, but Jackson would not yield on his choice of Van Buren for President. He dictated not only the nomination of Van Buren by the convention but also of Richard M. Johnson as the candidate for Vice-President. The choice of Johnson was an almost incomprehensible act

---

[11] Henry A. Wise, *Seven Decades of the Union* (1871), p. 137.
[12] *Senate Journal,* Dec. 20, 1837.

of defiance to the insurgents, since Johnson openly acknowledged a Negro mistress and was alleged to have tried to have his two Paris-educated octoroon daughters introduced into society. That Jackson could get away with the dictation of nominees for both offices by the Democratic Convention in the face of a determined opposition was a demonstration of presidential party chieftainship scarcely matched anywhere else in the history of the presidency.[13]

James K. Polk was such a thoroughgoing party man as to become the first President to give official recognition of political parties, in this case in his inaugural address.[14] Young Hickory, as Polk came to be called, was as much a regular party politician as Old Hickory himself. He had been a faithful Jacksonian Democrat as Speaker of the national House of Representatives and as Governor of Tennessee. As President he took complete charge of his administration, and even Andrew Jackson was to discover that Polk as President made his own decisions. He prepared a form letter for prospective Cabinet members, which stated that "the principles and policies of the administration were to be found in the Democratic platform" and that each Cabinet member was expected to devote his time and energy to the administration and not be a candidate to succeed him. Polk had committed himself to serve but a single term. As the historian Schouler put it, "What Polk went for he fetched."[15]

Polk began his administration confronted with a serious party division. The annexation of Texas, just before his inauguration, had aroused the Van Buren Free-Soil Democrats, who assumed it was a plot of the proslavery Democrats for more slave states. Like a genuine party chieftain Polk was determined to end the intraparty rivalry, which explains his requirement that Cabinet

[13] See H. A. Wise, *Seven Decades of the Union* (1871), pp. 153–56; Marquis James, *The Life of Andrew Jackson* (1938), pp. 694–95.

[14] J. D. Richardson, *Messages and Papers of the Presidents* (1927), IV, 382.

[15] James Schouler, *History of the United States Under the Constitution* (1880–1913), IV, 498.

members retire if they became aspirants for the presidency. The Cabinet had been shrewdly constructed to represent sections and party factions.

Polk's election signified the triumph of exuberant pioneer expansionism, and, as it turned out, he became territorially the greatest expansionist of all the presidents. It was Polk's confident expectation that he could settle the boundary dispute with Mexico and acquire by peaceful negotiation the territory later practically conquered. But when he asked Congress for an appropriation to carry on the negotiations, an antislavery Democratic Congressman from Pennsylvania, David Wilmot, moved his famous rider to the appropriation bill that any territory acquired through the appropriation must be freesoil. Although the Wilmot Proviso was defeated, the friction it created ended only at Appomattox nineteen years later.

It is indicative of President Polk's role as a genuine party chieftain that he regarded antislavery David Wilmot's "Proviso" a "mischievous and foolish amendment" at the same time that he considered proslavery Calhoun the "most mischievous man in the Senate." He opposed the extremists on each wing of the party; they "would destroy the union." He would have extended the Missouri Compromise line to the Pacific. Siding with neither wing of his party, he was disliked by both and was charged alternately with autocracy and weakness.[16]

Consistent party man though Polk was, he utterly despised the spoils system. The pressure of Congressmen to get offices for constituents led him "to distrust the disinterestedness and honesty of all mankind."[17] However, this was an era of the triumphant spoils system, and Polk could not serenely brush it aside. As it turned out, somewhat more than three hundred removals were made. Even such an ardent Whig as Daniel Webster, recognizing Polk's

[16] See E. I. McCormac, "James K. Polk," *Dictionary of American Biography*, xv, 38.

[17] *Diary* (1910), ii, 278.

devotion to his party, was nevertheless to admit that he appeared "to make rather good selections from among his own friends."[18]

No president entered the great office more adept in the high art of party politics than Abraham Lincoln. To most contemporaries his nomination and election must have looked like a major accident of American history. Between election and inauguration he had effectively exercised party leadership by his inflexible determination not to give up the one issue that held the Republican group combination together—opposition to the spread of slavery into the territories. To this end he persuaded Republican senators and representatives in Congress not to agree to the Crittenden Compromise, which, among other things, would have revived the repealed Missouri Compromise thereby approving slavery extension in territory south of 36 degrees and 30 minutes north latitude. Thus he was enabled to begin his administration without the otherwise inevitable disintegration of the party that had elected him.

To most Republicans in 1861 it must have seemed a miscarriage of the logic of events that such a national statesman as Senator William H. Seward with a long generation of public service in state and national politics had not been nominated and elected President instead of the still relatively unknown and ungainly frontier politician Lincoln. When only a month after his election Lincoln offered Seward the headship of his Cabinet, the Senator may have jumped to the conclusion that the leadership of the Republican administration and party was within his grasp. A scant month after Lincoln's inauguration Seward, in his strange memorandum entitled "Thoughts for the President's Consideration," was to propose among other things that Lincoln virtually abdicate his presidential powers to his Secretary of State. We have already seen that just before the inauguration Seward had even assumed that he might dictate the composition of Lincoln's Cabinet. A deputation from Seward met the President-elect and declared that

[18] Frederick J. Turner, *The United States, 1830–1850* (1935), p. 539.

Seward would not serve with Chase, only to be floored with Lincoln's counterproposal to leave both Seward and Chase out of his Cabinet. Thus early did Lincoln demonstrate that he and he only was the Republican party chieftain. When the Lincoln administration was but three months old Seward was to write to his wife, "Lincoln is the best of us."[19]

The firing on Ft. Sumter required a sudden reorientation of party policy and never has a party chieftain made a more prompt and thorough transition to the leadership of a new party alignment. No longer was the paramount issue to be the exclusion of slavery from the territories by congressional legislation but instead the preservation of the Union and the enforced maintenance of Federal authority throughout its length and breadth. Slavery was now a secondary matter and on this point Lincoln was just as adamant as he had been on exclusion of slavery from the territories before Sumter. If he could save the Union by freeing none of the slaves, he would do it; if by freeing all the slaves, he would do that; if by freeing some and leaving some in slavery, he would do it that way, which is just what the Emancipation Proclamation eventually declared.

Indeed, after Sumter, the very composition of the Republican party began to change as some War Democrats came over to it, and it consequently adopted the name of the Union party. Lincoln readily accepted the prevailing party usages, and patronage was dispensed to Unionists, not just to Republicans. Appointments, especially the postmasterships, were dispensed with a view to cementing party organization in the states, cities, counties, and precincts. After distributing the post offices to persistent partisans, Lincoln turned to the creation of captaincies, colonelcies, and brigadier-generalships to cement the new Union party combination. His friend Whitney said Lincoln even made colonels and brigadier generals of politicians to keep them out of the Democratic party. Illinois Republican newspapers complained that forty

[19] Benjamin P. Thomas, *Abraham Lincoln* (1952), p. 254.

out of seventy Illinois regiments had Democratic colonels and other Republican papers protested there was only one Republican among six major generals appointed by President Lincoln and that he appointed eighty Democrats among a total of one hundred and ten brigadier generals.[20] Leonard Swett explained that "in the close calculation of attaching the factions to him he counted upon the abstract attraction of his friends as an element to be offset against some gift with which he might appease his enemies."[21] So supremely important to Lincoln was the preservation of the Union that this great end justified his utilizing patronage as the party chieftain saw fit.

Lincoln's Cabinet had itself been a masterpiece of the politician's art constructed to cement party factions and geographical regions of party strength marred only by two members appointed to pay off convention pledges for the support of state delegations contrary to Lincoln's instructions. The key members of the Cabinet were Seward, recognized leader of the Conservative Republicans, and Chase, darling of the antislavery wing. It has been related elsewhere how, in 1862, a delegation of Republican senators and representatives, incited by Secretary Chase's talebearing of Cabinet discord, confronted Lincoln with a demand that he get rid of Seward. It will be recalled that Lincoln serenely invited them to return for a later conference. When at the appointed time they returned, they were astonished to find they were to meet with the Cabinet. Under the circumstances Chase denied reports of dissension, and by the daring coup Lincoln saved his Cabinet intact and demonstrated again who was party chieftain.

President Lincoln maintained a continuous interest in state politics, particularly the election of what came to be called the "war governors," that is Republican or Union party state governors. The most notable of these contests was the Ohio gubernatorial

---

[20] Carl Sandburg, *Lincoln: the War Years* (1939), I, 334.
[21] Letter to Herndon in E. Hertz, *The Hidden Lincoln* (1940), p. 299.

campaign of 1863 between Unionist John Brough and the Democratic candidate, the notorious Copperhead Clement L. Vallandigham. Lincoln hung around the Washington telegraph office the night of the Ohio election waiting for returns, more anxious, he admitted than when he had been a candidate himself in 1860.

> About ten o'clock Lincoln telegraphed to Columbus: 'Where is John Brough?' He was in the telegraph office came the answer. 'Brough, what is your majority now?' wired Lincoln. 'Over 30,000.' At midnight Brough reported 'over 50,000'; at five o'clock in the morning 'over 100,000'. 'Glory to God in the highest,' wired Lincoln, 'Ohio has saved the nation'.[22]

Lincoln had no hesitation about asking generals in the field to furlough soldiers to go home to vote in close election of those states that had not authorized their soldiers to cast ballots in the field. Many states at that time had October elections for state officers and November balloting for the presidential and congressional elections. In 1864 the re-election of Lincoln was in such doubt that in August Lincoln himself was convinced he would not be re-elected, but the capture of Mobile Bay by Admiral Farragut and the fall of Atlanta to Sherman's army raised the hopes of the Union party. Lincoln, in a letter sent to General Sherman by special messenger, suggested "Anything you can safely do to let her [Indiana's] soldiers or any part of them, go home to vote at the state election will be greatly in point. They need not remain for the presidential election, but may return to you at once." Not only did Sherman grant wholesale furloughs to Indiana troups, but two of his generals, Blair and Logan, returned home and made campaign speeches. Union party victories in the October state elections indicated Lincoln's re-election in November.

After Lincoln it is necessary to by-pass seven presidents until one reaches in William McKinley the next indisputable presidential party chief. In the light of the evidence it seems absurd that it is necessary to show that McKinley always kept National Chairman

[22] Benjamin P. Thomas, *Abraham Lincoln* (1952), p. 399.

Mark Hanna aware—sometimes painfully aware—that he was subordinate to the party chieftain McKinley. McKinley's private secretary, George B. Cortelyou, who had a high opinion of Hanna's political competence, considered McKinley an abler politician than Hanna.[23] Herbert Croly in his laudatory biography of Hanna, published the year before he founded the *New Republic*, wrote, "McKinley was the master, Mr. Hanna was only the able and trusted Prime Minister."[24] There is also the testimony of Elihu Root, McKinley's Secretary of War, that "Hanna was a strong and vigorous man, but McKinley was the controlling spirit of the two."[25] But it took the urbane John Hay to express himself bluntly on the matter only two weeks before McKinley's first election as President: "There are idiots who think Mark Hanna will run him."[26]

In the spring of 1900, preceding the campaign for McKinley's re-election, McKinley seems to have acted deliberately so as to make Hanna's subordinate relationship emphatically evident. Hanna waited impatiently for the President's indication that he wanted him to conduct the 1900 campaign. So worried was Hanna that late in April he had a heart attack while writing in his office and fainted away, and his intimate friends attributed the attack to his distress because of the President's prolonged silence. His prestige was at stake.[27] A little later Hanna was elated when McKinley asked him to accept management of his campaign for re-election.

In the Republican National Convention of 1900 McKinley showed Hanna again that he was but the party chieftain's lieutenant. Senators Platt of New York and Quay of Pennsylvania with their respective state delegations in their vest pockets decided to embarrass Hanna by nominating Governor Theodore Roosevelt

[23] Herbert Croly, *Marcus Alonzo Hanna* (1913), p. 365.

[24] *Ibid.*, p. 365.

[25] Charles S. Olcutt, *The Life of William McKinley* (1916), II, 347.

[26] In a letter to Henry Adams, Oct. 20, 1896. Quoted by Tyler Dennett, *John Hay* (1933), p. 178.

[27] Croly, *Marcus Alonzo Hanna* (1913), p. 329.

of New York as McKinley's running mate. Hanna had his own
ideas as to a proper vice-presidential candidate and moreover had
a strong aversion to that "damned cowboy," as he once put it, and
wanted no likelihood of his getting into the White House. Thus
challenged, Hanna decided to fight and would almost certainly
have been overwhelmed by the prevailing pro-Roosevelt enthusi-
sam, had not Charles Dawes telephoned from the convention at
Philadelphia to the White House. He bore the President's reply
back to Hanna, "The President's close friend must not undertake
to commit the Administration to any candidate.... The Administration wants the choice of the Convention and the President's
friend must not dictate to the Convention."[28] The chief had spoken,
the lieutenant obeyed as usual.

Perhaps the most striking instance of McKinley's mastery of
party politics, particularly as related to National Chairman Hanna,
occurred in the midst of the campaign of 1900. On August 3,
Hanna wrote a letter to President McKinley conveying the information that the New York State Republican Chairman was
concerned over the transfer of work from the Brooklyn Navy Yard
to that in Boston, thereby creating labor unemployment and loss
to Brooklyn merchants. Also one Sergeant Dugan at Iowa Island
on the Hudson was employing Democrats, and he contemptuous-
ly threw aside a protesting letter from a Republican member of
Congress. Among other things McKinley's reply contained the
statement:

> It would not be right and I am sure you would not have the
> [Navy] Department employ men at the Navy Yard who are not
> needed, nor would you have work done there which could be
> done at some other Navy Yard in the country.... If elected I
> have to live with the administration for four years. I do not
> want to feel that any improper or questionable methods have
> been employed to reach the place, and you must continue, as

[28] Charles G. Dawes, *A Journal of the McKinley Years* (1950), pp. 232, 233.

you always have done, to stand against unreasonable exactions, which are so common at a time like this.

After reading the President's letter Hanna threw it on the floor in exasperation, but once again it had been demonstrated that President McKinley was as certainly the party chieftain as any president since Andrew Jackson.[29]

Mark Hanna was the Republican National Chairman when Theodore Roosevelt succeeded to the presidency upon the death of McKinley. Despite his misgivings about Roosevelt in 1900 Senator Hanna became as loyal a supporter of the Roosevelt administration as he had been of McKinley's. Nevertheless President Roosevelt was suspicious of his party chairman as revealed in a letter to young Theodore, "Senator Hanna has been intoxicated by the thought that he could be nominated himself or at least dictate the nomination."[30] All the available evidence indicates that Hanna never aspired to the presidency and was in fact failing in health at this time. He died only a year later.

The issue was brought to a crisis by Senator Hanna's Ohio colleague Senator Foraker, seeking to provoke a break between Hanna and the President. One month before the 1903 Ohio Republican Convention Foraker gave out a news statement intimating that Hanna's friends were planning to oppose a resolution in the state convention endorsing Roosevelt as the Republican candidate in 1904. Now Hanna as National Chairman thought it improper to be usurping the function of the national convention of the following year and accordingly sent the President a telegram saying that since the issue had been forced upon him, he would have to oppose such a resolution. This confronted the President with a dilemma. Theodore Roosevelt had a habit of resolving crises with lightning-like strokes perfectly timed, and he now dealt Hanna a brutal blow. His telegram in reply to Hanna after saying

[29] See the letters in Herbert Croly, *Marcus Alonzo Hanna* (1913), pp. 329, 330.
[30] H. F. Pringle, *Theodore Roosevelt, a Biography* (1931), p. 347.

that he had nothing whatever to do in raising the issue, continued, "Inasmuch as it had been raised, of course, those who favor my administration and my nomination will favor indorsing both and those who do not will oppose." A national chairman must always seek to promote party unit, and Hanna had no choice but to wire the President, "I shall not oppose the indorsement of your administration and candidacy by our State Convention."[31] Just as in McKinley's administration National Chairman Hanna had once more been subordinated by the party chieftain, but in this case by a battle ax instead of with the unfailing courtesy of President McKinley.

When the 1904 Republican National Convention met, President Roosevelt's handpicked choice for temporary chairman was his Secretary of War, Elihu Root, who according to custom made the keynote speech, directed by the President to emphasize a dozen specified issues. Senator Henry Cabot Lodge, the President's former Harvard history professor, was planted as Roosevelt's choice for the strategic chairmanship of the Committee on Resolutions and "drafted the platform under orders from the White House."[32] Roosevelt chose as National Chairman to manage his campaign George B. Cortelyou, his Secretary of Commerce and Labor in which department a Bureau of Corporations had been established to investigate the oil, packing, tobacco, steel, and other industries and furnish material for prosecution under the antitrust laws. The Democratic convention fell into the hands of conservative leaders who ignored the twice-defeated Bryan and nominated a colorless conservative candidate, Judge Alton B. Parker of New York.

Parker remained quiescent at his home until late in the campaign, when he went on a short speaking tour and began attacking "Cortelyouism," and on November 3 he committed the *faux pas*

[31] For the telegrams, see Croly, *Marcus Alonzo Hanna* (1913), pp. 425, 426.
[32] H. F. Pringle, *Theodore Roosevelt, a Biography* (1931), p. 353.

of describing the contributions of corporations to the Republican campaign as "blackmail" and intimated that they were made in return for silence concerning damaging information gathered by the Bureau of Corporations.[33] This gave President Roosevelt an opportunity for a characteristic lightning stroke. Denying that corporation contributions had been "extorted," not that they had been made, he declared, "Mr. Parker's accusation against Mr. Cortelyou and me are monstrous. If true they would brand both of us forever with infamy, and inasmuch as they are false, heavy must be the condemnation of the man making them." Challenged to furnish proof, Parker refused to divulge the source of the information given him in confidence. Not until eight years later did a congressional committee ferret out the fact that 72 1/2 per cent of the contributions to the 1904 Republican campaign had been made by corporations, but President Roosevelt could scarcely have known this. He had turned Parker's charges to his own advantage, and Parker, having shot his bolt, carried no state outside of the South.

Four years later President Roosevelt virtually handpicked William Howard Taft as his successor. He used the Federal machine with its patronage to pack the National Nominating Convention. Of 125 Federal officeholders who were delegates, 97 were for Taft. The Taft forces controlled nearly all the southern delegates. The President "dictated the Platform."[34] His intimate friend Senator Lodge made the principal address as permanent Chairman. The President deluged Taft with letters and suggestions throughout the campaign. Bryan was again the Democratic candidate. Early in the campaign it was discovered that Charles N. Haskell, the Treasurer of the Democratic National Committee, was connected with the Standard Oil Company, whereupon he resigned. In an epistolary controversy with Bryan over Haskell,

[33] New York *World*, Nov. 2, 4, 1904.
[34] H. F. Pringle, *Theodore Roosevelt, a Biography* (1931), p. 502.

the President caught Bryan at a disadvantage. So active did the President become in the campaign that candidate Taft became relatively inconspicuous. President Roosevelt had busied himself as if he were Taft's campaign manager.

Five years before his inauguration as President, Woodrow Wilson had pointed out the growing popular tendency to recognize the president "as the unifying force in our complex system, the leader both of his party and the nation."[35] Wilson was an avowed party man. It could hardly have been otherwise in such a devotee of parliamentary government—one who read into the Constitution's provisions for the State of the Union and other presidential messages the invitation to the president to assume a premiership. "He must be the leader of his party. He is the party's choice and is responsible for carrying out the party platform. He therefore should have a large influence in determining legislation."[36] The President "cannot escape being the leader of his party except by incapacity and lack of personal force because he is at once the choice of the party and the nation."[37] So the president carries a mandate from his party which consists of a majority of the nation. Within the party councils he can control its program through his position as leader and through his personal force.[38]

Soon after his election in 1912 Wilson received a letter from A. Mitchell Palmer, soon to be appointed Attorney General, suggesting that he promote an amendment to the Constitution carrying out the Democratic platform plank favoring a single term for the president. This brought a vigorous refusal from the President-elect, who was certain that the president ought not to be hampered by the denial of the strength derived from possible re-election. Here was one more opportunity to assert that the president "is expected by the nation to be the leader of his party as well as the

[35] *Constitutional Government in the United States* (1907), p. 54.
[36] *Ibid.*, pp. 60–61.
[37] *Ibid.*, p. 67.
[38] *Ibid.*, p. 69.

chief executive officer of the government and the country will take no excuses. . ." One must not overlook the refrain of "party, party, party" in Wilson's expositions of his conception of the president's proper role. His first fourteen months in the presidency were a demonstration of this role as he put on the statute books the Underwood Tariff, the Federal Reserve Act, the Clayton Act, and the Federal Trade Commission Act. Fortunately for his theory of party government this first Congress was young, political patronage only partly distributed, and the Democratic majority, after many years of Republican administrations, obedient to the kind of party discipline Wilson believed in.

The party leadership of President Wilson was nowhere better demonstrated than in the Underwood Tariff Act. The Ways and Means Committee, busy framing a bill weeks before inauguration, had put a complete draft in Wilson's hands when he had been in office only three weeks and found him ready to support it with all the influence of the presidency.[39] The caucus was consulted about nearly everything, and after thorough discussion there the membership went to the floor of the House prepared for united action.[40] Without closure or even a motion to limit debate the bill passed the House without material change and by a large majority. The President's astute leadership was evident also in the Senate. Promptly after his address to Congress he appeared in the President's Room just off the Senate Chamber to confer with the Finance Committee on the tariff bill. The bill was hotly argued in the Senate Democratic Caucus, and on July 7 it declared the bill to be a party measure and urged the duty of all Democrats to support it. In the opinion of Professor Frank W. Taussig, "President Wilson had quietly assumed leadership and secured a hold on his associates which astonished friend and enemy."[41]

---

[39] H. J. Ford, *Woodrow Wilson, the Man and His Work* (1916), p. 182.

[40] O. W. Underwood, *Drifting Sands of Party Politics* (1931), p. 171. G. R. Brown, *The Leadership of Congress* (1922), pp. 185–86.

[41] Quoted by H. J. Ford, *Woodrow Wilson, the Man and His Work* (1916), p. 185.

One of Wilson's former Princeton students, David Lawrence, believed that Wilson's ill-fated appeal of October, 1918, for the election of a Democratic Congress at the ensuing mid-term election was but a natural consequence of his cherished theory of party responsibility.[42] The would-be "prime minister" appealed to the country for a national vote of confidence. The "solemn referendum" on the Treaty of Versailles, especially the Covenant of the League of Nations asked for in the presidential election of 1920, reflected a similar pattern. Twice during his presidency Wilson considered resigning, in the fashion of a British prime minister, if Congress rejected major administration measures, the repeal of the exemption of American vessels from Panama Canal tolls and the McLemore Resolution warning American citizens against traveling on armed vessels of belligerents, but he was sustained on both of these issues.

Franklin Roosevelt entered the presidency the most adept politician of his time. He was a consummate artist in the game of party politics, confessedly in the role of a "quarterback" calling the plays and taking advantage of the breaks as they became apparent. During the "hundred days" when legislation to deal with the economic crisis was pending, congressmen who came to the President anxious as to the "loaves and fishes" were dismissed with the coyly whispered information, "We haven't got to patronage yet." That could wait till these same congressmen had earned the right to patronage by their votes for administration bills. Such was the Spartan discipline of the Roosevelt party organization that a congressman's sharing of patronage might depend on his answer to the question, "What was your preconvention position on the Roosevelt candidacy?"[43] Democratic National Chairman James A. Farley is said to have kept a list of "eligible" applicants for jobs, each bearing the cryptic initials F. R. B. C. (for

[42] *The True Story of Woodrow Wilson* (1924), p. 319.
[43] E. P. Herring, "The First Session of the 73rd Congress," *American Political Science Review*, XXVIII, No. 1 (1934), 82.

Roosevelt before Chicago). Roosevelt unhesitatingly accepted the fact that his name was magic among the city machines since his prestige enabled them to elect their local candidates. They did not care much about the New Deal "but needed Roosevelt who was to them 'the resurrection and the life.' "[44] Nor was Franklin Roosevelt a whit more critical than Lincoln had been as to such means to the ends sought.

Party chieftain Roosevelt was human enough to be misled by his overwhelming re-election of 1936, when his opponent Landon received only eight electoral votes. It stimulated the pride that preceded a fall, in this case the failure to get Congress to reconstitute the Supreme Court. In bitterness over this failure he planned the abortive purge of 1938, the plan to pressure the Democratic primaries to vote down the renomination of selected senators and representatives whose opposition to the Court Bill had incurred the President's wrath.

James Farley, Democratic National Chairman, relates that in January, 1938, the President's secretary, James Roosevelt, telephoned to him saying that candidates for the Senate would file for the Democratic primary in Illinois the following day and the President wanted a statement of the National Chairman on the attitude of the party organization on the nominees. Farley promptly prepared and telephoned to James a two-hundred-word statement, the essence of which was that the Democratic National Organization "has absolutely no concern with the primary or convention struggles for these nominations." The statement closed with the following two sentences: "These nominations are entirely the affair of the States or the Congressional districts, and however these early battles may result the National Committee will be behind the candidates the people themselves choose. This goes for every State and every Congressional district." Ten minutes later

[44] Edward J. Flynn, *You're the Boss* (1947), p. 146.

James telephoned back to Farley, "Father has struck out the last two sentences." Ten years later Farley stated in his autobiography concerning the episode, "An albatross not of my own shooting, was hung around my neck. From that time on I knew no political peace. I have the copy of the statement before me now, the one from which I struck the two sentences by order of the White House."[45] There was no doubt as to the party chieftainship of President Roosevelt no matter how imprudent the attempted purge turned out to be. With a single exception the incumbents Roosevelt attempted to purge were re-elected.

"In 1948 I was in a position to control the nomination," wrote Truman in his *Memoirs*.[46] "When I made up my mind to run those in the party who turned against me could do nothing to prevent it." It certainly did not look like that a week before the delegates assembled at Philadelphia for the Democratic Convention of 1948. An aggressive clique of Democrats, including sons of Franklin Roosevelt, Americans for Democratic Action, some senators and representatives, both northern and southern, big-city Democratic bosses, and even some Democratic governors and state chairmen combined to "dump Truman." This rebellion collapsed when both General Eisenhower and Associate Justice W. O. Douglas refused to be their candidate. The late Grove Patterson, then editor of the *Toledo Blade*, reported an interview he had with President Truman at the White House in the midst of the turmoil the day preceding his renomination. "I had never before seen such an example of faith, serenity, and atomic belligerency in any one human being," wrote Patterson. "I'll give these Republicans the toughest fight they were ever up against," he said. "I'll go into every town of over ten thousand people in America. I'll do so-and-so and so-and-so and so-and-so," which turned out to be precisely what he

---

[45] *Jim Farley's Story, the Roosevelt Years* (1948), pp. 120–21.
[46] 1955, II, 186.

did, as Patterson put it. "And the thing that made the situation fantastic," continued Patterson, "was that apparently not a man, woman or child in the United States believed he could do it." J. Howard McGrath was the Democratic Chairman, of course, but the party chieftain was President Truman himself.

In President Truman's acceptance speech delivered to the convention at 2 A. M. following his nomination, he seized the initiative and put the Republicans on the defensive by one of the boldest coups in party history. In the midst of his address he said: "My duty as President requires that I use every means within my power to get the laws enacted the people need in such important matters and I am therefore calling the Congress back into session on the 26th of July." He had pointed out that the Republican platform advocated the very laws he wanted. This was the famous Republican eightieth Congress—the "do-nothing Congress" as Truman denominated it—and it met in boiling wrath and did nothing some more. Clark Clifford, the President's legal counselor, who had helped him reach the decision to call the special session of Congress, said: "We've got our backs on our 1-yard line with a minute to play; it has to be razzle dazzle."

And razzle-dazzle it was throughout the campaign, which the chieftain kept always on the offensive. Such slam-bang speeches by a President of the United States shocked some Democrats almost as much as the Republicans. He blazed away at every Republican head that showed itself. Republican policies were worse than wrong, they were dishonest and vicious. If midwest farmers helped to elect a Republican Congress, they would have only themselves to blame for the consequences. The election of Dewey would mean a depression if not an atomic war, and all declared in one-syllable words that the have-nots could understand, and they outnumbered the haves. "Old Doc Truman was Roosevelt without kid gloves and the golden voice. It was barehanded Harry calling a spade a bulldozer.... The guy was just too busy to attend his own funeral."[47] His few feeble advisers were horrified, but the party chieftain was in charge and knew exactly what he was doing.

Not many presidents have begun their administration so very much an amateur in party politics as was Dwight D. Eisenhower in 1953. Packing his Cabinet with businessmen instead of making it representative of a balanced cross section of the outstanding interests of the nation revealed the romantic amateur in the art of politics. He could not have known of such an axiom as that expressed by V. O. Key, "Men with the minds of tradesmen do not become statesmen,"[48] or the even more pungent observation of the elder Senator Henry Cabot Lodge, "The business man dealing with a large political question is really a painful sight."[49] The unexpected consequence however was the fact that President Eisenhower was never obsequious to these business tycoons but from the very beginning of his administration was the master of his Cabinet. Even at the pre-inauguration meeting of his Cabinet, held January 12, 1952, when the President brought up the question of trade between the East and the West involving even some commodities of military value and Charles Wilson demurred with the comment, " I don't like to sell fire arms to the Indians," the President-elect retorted almost sharply, "Charlie, I am talking common sense."[50] Four years later President Eisenhower was reported to be very sharp and short-tempered with Charles Wilson over his delays in shaping a Defense Department budget and over leaks of information.[51]

Throughout the Eisenhower administration the Secretary of the Treasury, George M. Humphrey, was reputed to be the President's strong man of the Cabinet, the member in whom the President especially confided. Less than two months after his inauguration President Eisenhower decided to ask Congress for stand-

[47] Grove Patterson, *Toledo Blade*, November 3, 1948.
[48] *Southern Politics* (1949), p. 27.
[49] Quoted by Malcolm Moos, *The Republicans* (1956), p. 390.
[50] Robert J. Donovan, *Eisenhower: The Inside Story* (1956), pp. 10–11.
[51] "Washington Whispers," *United States News and World Report*, December 21, 1956.

by credit controls as a safeguard against inflation. Secretary of the Treasury Humphrey emphatically objected to the controls. But the President persisted in the demand, declaring that he wanted to show that the administration was interested in the "little fellow." He was irked by the persistent charge that his was a "business man's administration."[52] Here were early indications of the budding party chieftain. Four years later when the 4-H Club (Humphrey, H. Hoover, Jr., Hollister, and Rowland Hughes) wanted the Mutual Assistance program continued with no great increase of expenditures, the President, ignoring their advice, went ahead and asked Congress for an increase of more than 55 per cent over the previous year for that purpose—that is, countering Russia's drive for influence in Asia. In January, 1955, at a joint meeting of the Cabinet and congressional leaders, the President "ribbed" Humphrey for stating positively that a tax cut was possible and cautioned him that a heavy reduction of expenditures was not in sight.[53] Three months later Humphrey was urging a tax cut to stimulate business and produce a Treasury surplus, but the President insisted he would have to see a surplus in black and white before he would consent to tax reduction.[54] The President frequently rejected outright the tax proposals of Humphrey.[55]

Early in 1954 Eisenhower apparently woke up to his responsibility as party leader. He became eager to get Congress to enact a program on which a Republican Congress could be elected, a political "umbrella," as he called it, for Republican Congressmen who would support it. He told congressional leaders that the time had arrived when the Republican Administration must face up to its responsibilities. Again, mindful of the "little fellow," he was insistent upon housing legislation, maintaining that it would fulfill one of the basic needs of the people. In the face of conservative

[52] R. J. Donovan, *Eisenhower: The Inside Story* (1956), pp. 34, 35.
[53] *Ibid.*, p. 314.
[54] *Ibid.*, pp. 353–54.
[55] *Ibid.*, pp. 224–25.

opposition he refused to hold it back.[56] At conference after conference with congressional leaders the President urged passage of the pending program. A Republican leader at one of these conferences ventured a protest against the President

> pushing an independent Congress too far. This remark stung Eisenhower. He shot back that he had no pride of authorship in the program. In the drafting of it, he said, he had sought every possible bit of legislative advice. He was intent solely on doing what was good for the country. He said that so far he had been fighting quietly under cover. But if he had to, he asserted, he would carry it into the open.[57]

Disregarding controversies as to the validity or wisdom of his policies, it cannot be denied that, by the end of his first term, President Eisenhower was rapidly maturing as a practitioner of the art of party leadership. In the beginning he was weak, for example, when he cut out the tribute to General Marshall upon the advice of Governor Kohler in his campaign speech at Madison in 1952. Early in his administration, frustrations led to emotional outbursts of the President, but by 1956 perplexing problems were dealt with calmly. In the campaign for re-election National Chairman Leonard Hall and Presidential Assistant Sherman Adams were listened to, of course, but the decisions as to strategy and tactics were Eisenhower's, and no one took issue with him about them. By this time the President was better informed as a consequence of his habit of reading the newspapers. He was making the transition from the vague and undefinable theories with which he had been obsessed, such as "free enterprise" and "states rights," over to deep convictions growing out of four years of experience with stern realities. His economic adviser had even persuaded him to stop referring to the TVA as "creeping socialism." In the presidency Eisenhower had taken "the most difficult

[56] *Ibid.*, p. 224.
[57] *Ibid.*, p. 230.

cram course in the world" and was making the grade. As an Eisenhower intimate put it, "the fact is Ike has grown up."[58]

Indicative of an early grasp of the role of presidential party leadership was Eisenhower's New Republicanism with its moderate program, a deliberate attempt to transform the party into a genuine major party, even the majority party. He had been President only a few months when he expressed privately his exasperation over the opposition of the National Association of Manufacturers and the United States Chamber of Commerce to continuing the excess-profits tax. He protested that they did not realize that his middle-of-the-road course was the only way they could have a share of influence in the government. If a Republican administration was to succeed, he maintained, they would have to make concessions. Lodge and Benson reassured the President with the information that no stand taken by the National Association of Manufacturers or the United States Chamber of Commerce could do him much harm. Thus the amateur politician was learning the facts of political life.[59] The new President quite early concluded that the New Deal represented permanent reforms responsive to the dominant forces of American politics, and he decided even to extend it. Every item of its program was incorporated in that of the New Republicanism. Eisenhower was resolutely determined to utilize the Federal government to maintain a continuous expanding prosperity despite the persistent protests of Secretary Humphrey. The President took a stand on civil rights that, in 1956, was designed to induce a movement of Negro voters back to the party of their Great Emancipator. Though it failed in its purpose the intent exemplified the traditional role of the president as party chieftain.

[58] The two quotations are from Joseph and Stewart Alsop's column, "Eisenhower Today Different From Man Elected in 1952," *Toledo Blade*, Nov. 10, 1956. The second quotation however is not a statement of either of the Alsops.

[59] See R. J. Donovan, *Eisenhower: The Inside Story* (1956), p. 61.

By the campaign of 1956 the party chieftain had so maneuvered as to leave the Democrats scarcely one effective issue.[60] Even his veto of the Gas Bill, which would have transferred control of the price of gas at the well from the Federal Power Commission to the state utility agencies, was a master political stroke comparable to Jackson's veto of the rechartering of the Bank of the United States in 1832. Eisenhower's veto was due to the attempt at bribery of a senator by the agent of an oil company. The veto gratified, for the time being, the consumers of gas at the same time that it held out to the gas-producers the clear implication that the President would sign another such bill *if re-elected.* The consumers and producers were both to be comforted, the consumers at once, the producers eventually—quite a coup for an election year.

Eisenhower even excelled Franklin Roosevelt in utilizing personal charm, incidentally without arousing the intense animosity that developed toward Roosevelt. Even Roosevelt's fireside chat was appropriated by Eisenhower and rendered more effective by television. A majority of the voters were deeply impressed by President Eisenhower's apparent sincerity, his high ethical standards, his dignity, his ability to compose conflicting opinions by his search for areas of agreement, his organization of the executive branch, as well as the prestige he had brought to the White House from the very day of his first inauguration. President Eisenhower managed to restore the morale of the dispirited Republican party and make it once again a serious competitor in the battles of the two-party system, for the time being at any rate. That was no mean achievement for the party chieftain in the White House.[60]

---

[60] See Ernest K. Lindley, "Ike's Blue Print," *Newsweek,* June 18, 1956.

The President

and Congress

* **M U S T E R E D   O U T** after four years of service in the Union army Captain Oliver Wendell Holmes was back home in Boston. Presently he went out to call on his old philosopher friend at Concord. Emerson's conversation flowed on smoothly as he aired his transcendental abstractions of life and death, conscience and duty. The veteran of many a bitterly contested battle left convinced that Emerson was out of touch with reality. Battle experience had made Captain Holmes a stark realist who would henceforth translate life in terms of struggle. In 1872 Lord Justice Brett, under the Criminal Law Amendment of 1871, sentenced the London gas-stokers' leaders to prison for a year for merely preparing to strike.[1] Thereupon the act was condemned by some as class legislation, which criticism induced Holmes to expound his theory of legislation in a brief but illuminating article published in the *American Law Review*, of which he was now editor.

"The more powerful interests must be more or less reflected in legislation ... The objection to class legislation is not that it favors

[1] See G. D. H. Cole and Raymond Postgate, *The British Common People, 1746–1938* (1939), pp. 353–54.

a class, but either that it fails to benefit the legislators, or that it is dangerous to them because a competing class has gained in power, or that it transcends the limits of self-preference which are imposed by sympathy .... But it is no sufficient condemnation of legislation that it favors one class at the expense of another; for much or all legislation does that; and none the less when the bona fide object is the greatest good of the greatest number .... If the welfare of the living majority is paramount, it can only be on the ground that the majority have the power in their hands. *The fact is that legislation in this country, as well as elsewhere, is empirical. It is necessarily made a means by which a body, having the power, put burdens which are disagreeable to them on the shoulders of somebody else.*[2]

When Holmes in the same article wrote that "whatever body [legislature] may possess the supreme power for the moment is certain to have interests inconsistent with others which have competed unsuccessfully," it sounds like a comment on American labor's serious set-back in the congressional elections of 1946. His observation on British labor legislation of the 1870's that "the more powerful interests must be more or less reflected in legislation" would be just as applicable to the Taft-Hartley Act three-quarters of a century later. When the farm bloc induced Congress to establish a permanent policy of parity prices by which citizens, first as taxpayers, support the price of farm products by keeping them off the market even if the government must destroy valuable food supplies (potatoes for example) in order that these citizens, in the second place as consumers, may be compelled to pay higher prices—there can be no doubt that legislation is "necessarily made a means by which a body having the power puts burdens disagreeable to them on the shoulders of somebody else."

Such then is how the Congress functions in the stage to which civilization has thus far advanced. Of course, the social structure

---

[2] "The Gas-Stokers' Strike," *American Law Review*, VII (1873), 583–84.

of the United States is fundamental in the dynamics of congressional law-making, and the constantly shifting strength of the competing interests results in ever-changing points of equilibrium among them and consequently different kinds of legislation. One of our concerns here and now is the question as to how accurately the congress, through its structure and habits, registers these balances of the competing forces of American society. Herein we may find fundamental causes of the recurring clashes between president and Congress.

The persistent usage requiring a representative in Congress to be a resident of the district that elects him makes him extraordinarily obsequious to his constituents, except in the "safe" or practically one-party districts, where he will almost certainly reflect the prevailing social philosophy of the dominant interests. The reason is that the American member of Congress when defeated cannot, like the English member of Parliament, seek election in another district. When there is a near balance of parties in an American congressional district, the representative's function tends to become quasi-judicial as he weighs the claims of competing interests. Thus he must seek to discover points of equilibrium when confronted with controversial issues on pending legislation.[3] This signifies that the congressman's legislative function is the translation of dominant public opinion into public policy, but as John Dickinson observed, "The only opinion, the only will, which exists is the opinion, the will, of special groups.... The task of government and hence of democracy as a form of government, is not to express an imaginary popular will, but to effect adjustments among the various special wills and purposes which at any given time are pressing for realization."[4] The congressman's calculation as to the point of equilibrium or the balance of forces in his district constitutes his bid for re-election, which is an essential feature of the

---

[3] See Harvey Walker, "Who Makes the Laws," *State Government,* XII (1939).
[4] "Democratic Realities and Democratic Dogma," *American Political Science Review,* XXIV (1930), 291.

representative process as established by American usage. But there are 435 representatives and 96 senators, each one presumably engrossed with his own problem of satisfying the dominant interests of his constituency, while it remains for the president to seek for common denominators of national policy in the jigsaw puzzle of these 531 constituencies.

The problem of the president in dealing with Congress is complicated by the fact that the House of Representatives is so constituted that rural population not only has more than its proportionate share of representatives in Congress, but also because, as a consequence of the use of seniority in determining committee chairmen, the representatives from predominantly rural districts almost monopolize the chairmanships of the House committees. This is because rural constituencies are in the habit of re-electing their representatives repeatedly until they have attained high seniority. Thus urban constituencies not only fail to get their proper number of Congressmen, but those they do elect largely fail to attain the positions of power in the organization of the House that control important legislation because of an urban propensity to shift from one party to another. One exasperated critic has declared, with pardonable exaggeration, that we have a "rotten borough Congress."[5]

The House of Representatives was established originally on the plan that representation should be approximately proportionate to population. The failure to maintain that principle is due in the first place to the delay of state legislatures in remapping congressional districts after a decennial reapportionment of congressmen among the states. In many populous states the rural population, though a minority, can dominate the state legislature and thereby maintain an antiquated distribution of congressmen. For example, Ohio was redistricted in 1913 for representation in Congress on the basis of the census of 1910, after which date by 1950 the population had concentrated intensively in a few urban

[5] See J. A. Durham, "Congress, the Constitution and Crosskey," *Indiana Law Journal*, xxix (Spring, 1954).

counties. This left two-thirds of Ohio's congressional districts with less than the national average of population per representative, and sparsely populated districts were of course predominantly rural districts. But in the second place when a state legislature remaps its congressional districts, it is likely to crowd the urban population in a relatively few districts and distribute the rural population in more than its proportionate share of the districts. When the Ohio legislature at long last, following the 1950 census, redistricted, it gave the rural 15th district 226,341 inhabitants and the urban (Columbus) 12th district 503,410.[6]

If urban population suffers from the mapping of their vast population in fewer than their fair share of congressional districts, even far more is it penalized by the rule of seniority in determining the leadership in the House of Representatives. The sovereignty in the House of Representatives is concentrated emphatically in the speaker, the Rules Committee, the majority floor leader, and the chairmen of important standing committees. Long continuous service in Congress is an almost absolute prerequisite for occupancy of these places of power. Obviously this all signifies that these masters of the House represent the "safe" or practically one-party districts, which are by no means confined to the Democratic party and the solid South. An examination of the occupants of the top seventy-six positions of the Republican organization in the Eightieth Congress revealed an average previous tenure of 14 1/2 years. Such a tenure spanned the entire epoch of the New Deal despite its near total eclipse of Republican power. The control of legislation was thus transferred to those who generally represented the ideology of the 1920's and were in a sense an incarnation of a cultural lag. Moreover these seventy-six Republican congressmen, with rare exceptions, represented predominantly agrarian districts. Their constituencies were intensely property- and production-conscious and consequently provided ready allies of business,

---

[6] *Congressional Directory, 83rd Cong., 2nd Sess.*, pp. 113, 114.

industrial management, and finance. The election of 1946 brought some new Republicans to Congress from urban-industrial districts, but their lack of seniority relegated them to unimportant committees, despite the fact that these Republican congressmen were more in step with the cultural trend. Indeed urban districts manifest a less stable party tendency, change congressmen more frequently, and thus fail to attain commanding positions of power in Congress. As a consequence whenever the president urges upon Congress controversial measures in behalf of the distinctly consumer-conscious urban masses, such, for example, as rent or price control or housing legislation, he plays the game with Congress against heavily loaded dice.[7]

Though based on French experience the following observations of Emile Giraud are just as pertinent to the United States. He concluded that the legislature must be directed by the executive, the organ with "unity of thought," "capacity to acquire a view of the whole," and "possessing, by virtue of its participation in administrative and diplomatic activities, adequate information." "A feeble executive means a feeble state, one which fulfills badly its function of protecting the individual against political, economic, and social forces which, without the state, tend to swallow him up."[8] The principle is easily stated, but just how the executive is to "direct" the legislature or how the two great organs of government are to be integrated for the smooth and efficient functioning of government is a problem not yet solved by any nation—not even by Britain.

The evidence is conclusive that the fathers of the Constitution were far less fanatical devotees of the dogma of separated powers than their great grandchildren. The framers did not specifically prescribe the separation of powers in the Constitution but merely

---

[7] For the data on Republican congressmen in the Eightieth Congress and freshmen Republicans I am indebted to Mr. Dwaine Marvick, when a graduate student of Columbia University, who constructed several tables revealing, among other things, the generalizations above.

[8] Quoted by E. S. Corwin, *The President: Office and Powers* (1957), p. 486.

implied it and then specifically modified it by the contrary principle of checks and balances, which commingles instead of separating powers. The courts have been compelled to resort to none-too-certain principles of jurisprudence in giving their judgments as to whether one or another branch of the government may "constitutionally" exercise a disputed power. Certainly the framers did not forbid the heads of the executive departments appearing in or even having permanent seats in the houses, although the Constitution does forbid their being members. The records of the first several Congresses provide incontrovertible evidence of the framers' assumption that the department heads would provide the initiative in legislation. At any rate eighteen delegates of the Constitutional Convention later sat unprotesting in the First Congress as one outstanding legislative problem after another was referred for study and report to the heads of executive departments. Congress had Secretary of the Treasury Alexander Hamilton, in his assumed role of the "prime minister," prepare and send to the House of Representatives the famous *Reports* on which were based the monumental statutes of the Hamiltonian legislative program. Evidently these framers who sat in Congress thought it not improper that Hamilton use, as he did, his personal influence to persuade Congress to support these measures. So smoothly did this legislative-executive arrangement work that, to the Federalists, who were by and large the framers of the Constitution and who put it in operation, the relation of Congress to the executive must have seemed to have been properly, firmly, and permanently established.

For better or for worse the Federalist adjustment proved to be transient. It was indeed but the first of many different adjustments of Congress to the executive that had come about as a consequence of the play of the forces of American society upon the national government. It can be set down as a fundamental principle that whether Congress or the executive is dominant in the government depends upon which of the two, in a given period, is the more adequate medium of governmental control for the dominant interests of the nation. The Federalist group combination had been so harassed by the "omnipotent" agrarians who dominated state legislatures during the 1780's that they had vested strong executive powers in the presidency and then fortified those powers by the usage of executive initiative in legislation, that is, initiative of the heads of the executive departments, especially Secretary of the Treasury Hamilton. Their opponents, the Anti-Federalists who had at first opposed the ratification of the Constitution, were infuriated by the Hamiltonian practices and policies, rallied under Jefferson, captured the Federal government, and turned the Federalists out in 1801. These Jeffersonians had found the state legislatures satisfactory organs for their purposes, and they consequently made the national legislature their peculiar organ by terminating its dependence upon the heads of the executive departments. They established instead a system of congressional committees to take the place of the executive departments in proposing and considering legislation, thereby setting a pattern that persists to this day. Under the later Jeffersonian presidents, Madison and Monroe, the presidency gradually declined to an organ of relative insignificance in the Federal government.

It was the awakening of the American masses in the 1820's, their revolt against what they considered the failure of a government dominated by the rural and urban gentry entrenched in Congress to satisfy their needs, and their consequent turning with passionate devotion to a party messiah in Andrew Jackson that ended the hegemony of Congress. Jackson proclaimed himself a "tribune of the people" and, through the veto power and his leadership in legislation, made the presidency practically a third branch of the legislature. A new dominant interest, that of the "common man," had found the presidency to be the most convenient organ for achieving its desires, and it has ever since turned to the presidency for redress of grievances whenever stirred by a conviction of crisis. Thus Jackson, Lincoln, and the two Roosevelts have been pre-eminently "tribunes of the people" and have brought to bear upon Congress the pressures of public opinion crystallized by presidential leadership.

When "the people" captured the presidency under Jackson and made the office peculiarly their own, it brought an about-face in the old group combination that had once been the Federalist party but which now constituted the Whig party. The president as a popular leader—"demagogue" was the favorite Whig epithet—was now considered a potential dictator who ought consequently to be held rigorously subordinated to Congress. The present Republican party inherited the Whig attitude toward the presidency. For more than a century now Congress has been the chief reliance of the industrial-finance-transportation complex of interests. Their conception of the proper relation of president to Congress was only too frankly expressed when, in the midst of the presidential campaign of 1864, the majority leaders of the two houses of Congress of Lincoln's own party in the notorious Wade-Davis Manifesto declared that "the authority of Congress is paramount." It is significant that Theodore Roosevelt, the only other Republican President notable for vigorous executive leadership, had no happier time than Lincoln in dealing with the high command of his party and finally felt impelled to lead the Bull Moose secession from the party. The Republican party consists of a group combination historically intolerant of executive leadership. It is scarcely improper to designate the Republican party as virtually a congressional party. The late Senator John Sherman knew thoroughly the genius of his Republican party when he advised President-elect Benjamin Harrison to "have no policy distinct from that of his party and that is better represented in Congress than in the Executive."[9]

The Republican dogma of congressional supremacy over the executive is almost certain eventually to decline in practice, however much it may be proclaimed in theory. It was indeed a Republican president, Theodore Roosevelt, who gave the first marked impetus in this century to the practice of the legislative leadership of the

[9] *Recollections of Forty Years in the House, Senate, and Cabinet* (1895), II 1032.

president. "A good executive under present conditions of American life," he wrote in his *Autobiography*, "must take an active interest in getting the right kind of legislation in addition to performing his executive duties with an eye single to the public welfare." Reminiscent of the Federalist liaison between the executive and Congress is the contemporary comment of Senator Dolliver of Iowa in the fifth year of the presidency of Theodore Roosevelt: "There are at least five acts of legislation, all of them referring to this and similar questions, that were put through Congress in the last five years practically without change, as they came from the office of the Attorney General of the United States." Shortly afterward it was admitted on the floor of the House that the pending Food and Drug Act originated in a similar manner.[10]

It was President Wilson who gave the first great demonstration in this century of executive leadership in legislation. As a student of politics he had become fascinated with the parliamentary system, and he thought the Constitution provided both an opportunity and an invitation to introduce it in the national government in the clause that authorized the president to give Congress information on the state of the union and make recommendations for their consideration. So pronounced was Wilson's revolution that by 1917 a perceptive commentator could observe that "outside of Washington the old suspicion of executive power is dead, and popular sentiment has become so entirely uninterested in the process of politics as to ask only for substantial results.[11]

The mental pattern of the parliamentary system can be seen between the lines of Wilson's ill-fated appeal for the election of a Democratic Congress in 1918. Even the election of 1920 was a "solemn referendum" on the Covenant of the League of Nations.

---

[10] *Cong. Rec.*, 79th Cong., 2nd Sess., Vol. 92 (April 5 and June 5, 1906). See E. S. Corwin, *The President: Office and Powers* (1957), p. 268.

[11] *New Republic*, Sept. 29, 1917.

Wilson set the pattern of legislative leadership for his chief disciple, President Franklin Roosevelt, no matter how very different the ways of the latter may have been.

In the full tide of the reaction against Wilson's leadership, candidate Warren G. Harding mortgaged his presidential leadership by pledging himself to be a "constitutional" president, only to find himself shackled in office when he sought to carry out party pledges. When he appeared before the Senate to urge his erstwhile colleagues not to ignore the budget estimates but to keep appropriations within the income, the address was condemned as executive participation in debate and "veto by argument." No matter how reluctant Calvin Coolidge was to assume legislative leadership, such had been the effect of Theodore Roosevelt and Woodrow Wilson on the presidency that he admitted it to be "the business of the President as party leader to do the best he can to see that the party platform purposes are translated into legislative and administrative action."[12] Coolidge even went as far in recognizing the legislative role of the president as to draw up legislation to apply the unexpended balance of the Deficiency Appropriation Bill of July 3, 1926, to the prosecution of litigation to cancel the Fall-Sinclair-Doheny oil leases.[13] It was as an ex-President however that Coolidge expressed his most notable recognition of the president's appropriate function with respect to Congress when he declared, "It is because in their hours of timidity the Congress becomes subservient to the importunities of organized minorities that the President comes more and more to stand as the champion of the rights of the whole country.[14]

According to Robert Luce, President Hoover "sent drafts of several important proposals to the Capitol to be introduced by

[12] *Autobiography of Calvin Coolidge* (1929), pp. 231, 232.
[13] *House Journal*, 69th Cong. 2nd Series, p. 194.
[14] "The President Lives Under a Multitude of Eyes," *The American Magazine,* cviii (1929), 146.

leaders"[15] despite the fact that later as an ex-President he declared the "militant safeguard of liberty" to be "legislative independence" and that "the weakening of the legislative arm does lead to encroachment by the executive upon the legislative and judicial functions, and inevitably that encroachment is upon individual liberty."[16]

The twentieth-century trend toward presidential leadership in legislation was greatly accelerated in the 1930's by the concurrence of a poignant crisis with the accession to the presidency of a genius in the translation of current social forces into outstanding public policies. The studies of Lawrence H. Chamberlain indicate that almost half (eight out of nineteen) of the notable Federal statutes of nearly three-quarters of a century (1873–1940) that were mainly due to presidential leadership fall within the presidency of Franklin Roosevelt. As a further striking evidence of President Roosevelt's leadership in legislation Chamberlain found that of the thirty-five great statutes since the 1870's due predominantly to congressional initiative only two fell within the long presidency of Franklin Roosevelt, constituting one-sixth of the period.[17]

President Truman was far less systematic than his immediate predecessor in promoting legislation, failing even to keep his own majority party organization in the Seventh-ninth Congress informed as to his plans. However Congress had by this time become so accustomed to looking to the executive for legislative initiation that during the Republican Eightieth Congress even Senator Homer Ferguson of Michigan, an outstanding Republican leader, uttered a mildly critical comment concerning President Truman because he had let his dissatisfaction with certain pending legislation leak out of the White House instead of sending a message and a bill embodying just what he wanted.[18] Nothing can bring into bolder relief the

[15] *Legislative Problems* (1935), p. 260.
[16] *The Challenge to Liberty* (1934), pp. 125, 126.
[17] *The President, Congress, and Legislation* (1946), pp. 450–51.
[18] "What Is Your Congress Doing," *University of Chicago Round Table*, No. 483, p. 4 (1947).

present generation's trend toward executive initiative in legislation than a Republican Senator's complaint that a Democratic President had failed to send a prepared bill to a Republican Congress. When President Truman sent Congress a proposal for certain legislation in the summer of 1948, a critical commentator remarked, "If President Roosevelt had recommended that legislation a bill would have been found lying right under the message."

Inch by inch then we seem to be resuming somewhat the original pattern of executive initiative in legislation with which the Federalists under Hamilton's leadership started off the government in 1789. Evidently we are coming in full cycle. At any rate over half the bills dropped in the congressional hoppers are said to originate in the executive departments[19] so that "much legislation is tailor-made in the departments and sent to the Speaker or appropriate committee chairman for introduction in the House."[20] Many of these measures are prepared in compliance with requests of congressional committees, which is suggestive at least of the practice of the First Congress asking the departments for reports on projects. Before administration measures are transmitted from department to congressional committee, they are routed through the Legislative Reference Division of the Bureau of the Budget to determine whether they conform with the President's general program. Many congressional committees regularly refer bills to the department affected and report favorably only if the matter is approved by that department. Of course it is the routine and non-controversial measures by and large that can be handled by this procedure. This trend may be temporarily checked when Congress and president belong to opposing parties, a situation that might suspend but not reverse a trend so pronounced as to represent a wholesome developing usage.

[19] George B. Galloway, *Congress at the Crossroads* (1947), p. 150.
[20] *Ibid.*, p. 6.

It is in the enactment of such major matters of legislation as social security, civil rights, or labor laws affecting, as they do, powerful interest groups and sections of the nation, that the stresses and strains inherent in the American social structure become apparent. It is obviously erroneous to attribute the resulting clashes and deadlocks of president and Congress mainly to party differences, since Congressional votes on such measures often manifest a tendency to ignore party affiliation. The enactment of Roosevelt New Deal legislation was stopped dead in its tracks in 1938 by the "unholy alliance," as it was called, of southern Democrats with Republicans. President Truman's program for domestic legislation encountered the same obstinate combination, and it is significant that the Republican Congress that countered Truman's legislative program in 1947 served only to emphasize an executive-legislative deadlock already nine years old—nine years of Democratic presidents and Congresses. Twentieth-century Republican presidents, as a rule, have been rather less happy than Democratic presidents in getting Congress to enact their programs.

The clash of president and Congress is intensified by the striking differences between the ways in which pressures play upon the Congress on the one hand and upon the president on the other. For example, important elements such as labor, racial, and certain other groups are peculiarly weak in urging their desires upon Congress. Consequently they quite naturally and properly seek to exert a leverage on the government through their voting strength as balances of power in presidential elections. Indeed, here is a counterbalance against the immense advantage the interests of property and production hold in Congress due to the under-representation of urban voters and to the fact that the practice of seniority in determining control of the House of Representatives also reduces considerably the fair share of power of the urban voters. Such is the predominance of rural constituencies that the majority of congressmen can ignore the desires of the urban masses with impunity, while the president does so only at his peril.

When the city voters are aroused on issues that affect them, a presidential candidate who does not pledge himself to heed their demands can scarcely hope for election. More and more presidential campaigns are becoming competitions in bidding for the city vote, and election returns reveal the reason. In 1944 Governor Dewey appealed strongly, though in vain, for the metropolitan vote. His half-million majority in up-state New York was more than cancelled by President Roosevelt's majority of three quarters of a million in New York City. And it was simply because the metropolitan majorities of President Roosevelt in half a dozen other key states with big electoral votes wiped out Dewey's majorities in the rest of those states that Roosevelt was elected for a fourth term.

Thus a new president almost inevitably enters office pledged to issues and owing his election to elements that are inhospitable to the dominant groups in an overwhelming majority of the congressional districts. This explains why a leading Republican Congressman declared in 1945 that all the recent Republican candidates—Landon, Willkie, and Dewey—have been "too New Dealish." The presidency has become almost an "urban institution."[21] That Dwight D. Eisenhower became aware of this fact is indicated by his campaign speeches as well as by his addresses to Congress. Republicans who have not learned that social forces and not presidential fiat, by and large, determine administration policies can never understand the resemblance of the Truman and Eisenhower legislative programs. Each was bidding for the support of the same electorate.

In the nature of the case then the president, whether Democrat or Republican, normally comes face to face with a predominantly rural and hence potentially hostile Congress. The so-called presidential honeymoon turns out, in due time, to have been little better than an armistice. At any rate this has been the experience

---

[21] See J. A. Durham, "Congress, the Constitution and Crosskey," *Indiana Law Journal*, XXIX (Spring, 1954), 355–366.

of every president in this century. The persistent growth of cities underrepresented in Congress will certainly not reduce the tendency of Congress to clash with presidents. A potential factor in intensifying this conflict has been the almost unnoticed restoration of the near dictatorship of the speaker of the House. It is to be doubted whether Joe Martin in the Eightieth Congress was, in effect, any less a czar, that is, master of the House, than was "Czar" Joe Cannon in the heyday of his speakership. Joe Martin did not need to appoint and be Chairman of the omnipotent Rules Committee as Joseph G. Cannon had been when Martin could, through the power of recognition, block any move of that committee not to his liking. Martin was indeed, in effect, as one commentator put it, "ex-officio chairman of the Rules Committee." Statements of Speaker Rayburn carry the authority of a latter-day czar, although now it is the genial voice of Sam instead of the gruff bark of Joseph G.

No party member can play the maverick with impunity when the speaker can casually call his attention to the fact that the party congressional campaign fund is at the speaker's disposal to finance generously a rival candidate against the intransigent member at the next party nominating primary.[22] Republican party discipline approached an all-time high in the Eightieth Congress. For example, it was no accident that there were only three Republican votes against and 236 Republican votes for the controversial Wolcott Housing Bill or that, on the motion to recommit the Knutson Tax Bill, every one of the 236 Republican votes cast was in the negative. Speaker Cannon could have done no better. There is something to be said for a system like this. It is even an approach again to party government in the House such as enabled President Theodore Roosevelt to deal understandingly with Speaker Cannon as the responsible spokesman of the House majority. The Republican majority could not in the 1948 election dodge responsibility

---

[22] Peter Edson, "Half a Dozen Men Run Show in Boss Ridden House," Syndicated Column, *Lima News,* June 15, 1948.

for its record in the Eightieth Congress, and the electorate passed decisive judgment on the Congress thus disciplined. And time will tell whether some president with qualities of leadership can again effect a workable organic relationship with such a House as Theodore Roosevelt did under similar circumstances.

Formal changes in the mechanics of our government may ameliorate but can never solve the problem of conflict between president and Congress. Least of all can it be solved by adopting a parliamentary system. What many an American enthusiast for such a solution overlooks is the fact that the essential features of the British system consist of a set of usages: the appeal to the country, the resignation of a ministry on an adverse vote, the monarch asking the leader of the victorious party to form a ministry—these are mere English political habits institutionalized by long usage. There are those who seem to believe that we might, by constitutional amendment and formal statute, make legally compulsory in America a set of British governmental usages. Our own peculiar system evolved naturally without conscious planning as indeed did the British parliamentary system. And "the concept of checks and balances can never lack meaning for government in a society of divergent interests."[23]

We will undoubtedly be compelled to develop some better American procedures and habits to displace some unsatisfactory ones. Ever since the Civil War we have from time to time toyed with the plan of seating Cabinet members in Congress oblivious of the fact that legislation is done in the committees. But reliance upon organizational changes alone has proved pretty futile in the past. The overthrow of Czar Cannon in 1910 was hailed as a great reform, but who today can say that Congress was markedly improved by the Revolution of 1910? Joe Martin's and Sam Rayburn's firm grip on the House brought us back to "where we came in" in the first decade of the century and demonstrates the persistence

[23] E. P. Herring, *Presidential Leadership* (1940), p. 14.

of deep-seated tendencies with respect to American speakers that
were rooted originally in the experience of colonial legislatures.
The La Follette-Monroney Act "reforming" the committee system
of Congress was not in effect six months before profound disappointment was being expressed over how much Congress was
still like Congress. It was a scholar-Congressman who expressed
a philosopher's judgment upon this event: "It is those who mag-
nify gadgets and seek to cure the grudges that attend their mal-
functioning who will be disappointed at any and every reorganization of Congress."[24]

Nor need it be assumed that we are in the clutches of inexorable
fate. Improvements must be persistently sought with the understanding always that this is no age of miracles. State legislatures
must be put under the persistent pressure of an enlightened public
opinion to remap congressional districts, give urban population
their fair share of congressmen, and thereby remove the suggestion
of rotten boroughs in rural constituencies. As the urban pressures
approached the point of explosion, the legislature of Illinois in
1947 redistricted congressional constituencies near the end of half
a century without change. The electorate in evenly balanced
congressional districts where the two-party system functions most
healthily may yet become cognizant of how seniority reduces their
share in the councils of the nation to little more than a shadow
and become insistent that this further distortion of representative
power be corrected. The gross injustice due to seniority will ultimately doom it, but the present difficulty is that no feasible
substitute is in sight. Election of chairmen by the committees
would doubtless precipitate demoralizing contests. Public opinion
would scarcely support a return to the method in use before the
introduction of seniority in 1910, that is, appointment of chairmen
by the speaker of the House. However, this would restore a

---

[24] T. V. Smith, "Review of *Congress at the Crossroads*," *Saturday Review of
Literature*, XXIX (1946), 12.

semblance of party government to the House and provide an opportunity for the electorate to pass stern judgment on the party in the majority, which could scarcely dodge responsibility for sins of commission and omission.

Since cutting Gordian knots is out of the question, why not encourage the emerging concept of a legislative-executive council or Cabinet? Professor Corwin suggests that the president so construct his Cabinet as to contain leading members of the two houses, to which would be added from time to time heads of departments and chairmen of independent commissions as issues pertaining to these agencies needed to be dealt with.[25] Such a Cabinet, observed Corwin, "would comprise men whose political fortunes were not identical with his, who could bring presidential whim under an independent scrutiny which today is lacking and yet who by putting the stamp of approval upon his proposals would be able to facilitate their enactment into law." Here is a definite proposal to institutionalize what has hitherto been merely a matter of haphazard improvisation. The structure and formal provisions would be far less important than the usages that would develop in its actual operation. And this is as unpredictable as human conduct. "For most of the things that can be called evils," observed the late Justice Holmes, "the main remedy is for us to grow more civilized." This of course will afford little satisfaction to impetuous souls like the radical abolitionist Theodore Parker. When some one assured him that God in his own good time would end slavery, Parker remarked, "The trouble is God isn't in any hurry and I am."

[25] *The President: Office and Powers* (1957), p. 297.

VIII

The President

as Chief Legislator

* **WHERE CAN ONE FIND** a finer example
of the natural history of our political institutions than the way
in which the dynamic forces of American society have transformed
the chief executive of the written Constitution into the chief
legislator of our unwritten constitution? Apparently the framers
of the former expected the president to be most of all a co-
ordinator of the political organs of the federal government, and
it is by no means certain that they intended him to be even the
administrative chief.[1] In picturesque metaphor the late Samuel P.
Orth probably came close to recovering the conception of the
Founding Fathers as to what the president was intended to be:
"The Fathers' idea of leadership [of the President] was modest,"
Orth wrote. "It was the leadership of an orchestra, every member,
including the conductor, bound to follow the music, the principal
duty of the leader being to insure tempo and harmony, not too
fast, not too slow and all together."[2]

Certainly the contrast is striking between the prescriptions for
the presidency in our fundamental instrument and the functioning
reality of the great office in mid-twentieth century. No matter

---

[1] See Frank J. Goodnow, *Comparative Administrative Law* (1893), I, Chap. II.
[2] "Presidential Leadership," *Yale Review*, April, 1921, p. 454.

what misconceptions the typical American citizen may have picked up in his secondary-school study of government, in due course, when a voter, he seems to sense intuitively the patent realities of the legislative function of the president, as his conduct at the ballot box almost always reveals. In fact the citizen, as a voter, scarcely shows any consciousness whatever of the president's executive function, but instead manifests a quadrennial concern as to the legislation the presidential candidates, if elected, may promote or prevent. "Popular demand for the appearance of the President in lesser parts leaves him little time to star as Chief Executive," observed Professor McBain. "Politics has transformed his minor into his major role."[3]

What will the presidential candidate, if elected, do about taxes, farm support, the welfare of labor, and all the other issues that constitute the subjects of congressional legislation? What can he induce Congress to do or keep it from doing? Look at the dominant issues of presidential campaigns over the decades. In 1884, 1888, and 1892 it was the tariff; in 1896 and 1900, the currency and insular expansion; in 1912, a progressive versus a conservative program; in 1932, depression relief; in 1936, the New Deal policies; in 1940, isolationism versus national defense preparation; in 1948, farm support; in 1952, "creeping socialism," state rights, "Korea, Corruption, and Communism"; and in 1956, "Peace and Prosperity"—but seldom if ever what kind of executive the candidate is or may turn out to be.

Even in the midst of the administration of President McKinley Henry Jones Ford perceived "that the only power which can end party duplicity and define issues in such a way that public opinion can pass upon them decisively is that which emanates from presidential authority. It is the rule of our politics that no vexed question is settled except by executive policy."[4] Then he proceeded to point out that even presidents repudiated by their parties—

[3] Howard Lee McBain, *The Living Constitution* (1927), p. 115.
[4] *The Rise and Growth of American Politics* (1898), p. 284.

Tyler, Johnson and Cleveland—furnished the issues on which party action turned.

The twentieth-century version of the president as chief legislator was consequent upon a revolution as marked in the transformation it effected as the Jeffersonian and the Jacksonian revolutions. The latter-nineteenth-century conception of the presidency that the current one displaced was concisely epitomized in the Wade-Davis Manifesto of 1864 in which the Republican majority leaders of the House and Senate respectively published a furious blast at President Lincoln for his pocket veto of a Reconstruction Bill.

> He must understand . . . *that the authority of Congress is paramount,"* declared the irate congressional leaders, "and must be respected; that the whole body of Union men in Congress will not submit to be impeached by him of rash and unconstitutional legislation, and if he wishes our support [Lincoln was a candidate for re-election then] he must confine himself to his executive duties—to obey and execute, not to make the laws.[5]

As a consequence of the prevailing Republican dogma of presidential subordination to Congress, the typical latter-nineteenth-century presidential message to Congress was so perfunctory that James Bryce in the 1880's observed: "The expression of his [the President's] wishes conveyed to Congress in messages has not necessarily any more effect on Congress than an article in a prominent party newspaper."[6] Presidential messages then tended to be innocuous scissors-and-paste assemblages of departmental reports to the president constituting poorly integrated miscellanies. Customarily, within Congress, various parts of the message were assigned to appropriate committees, where they were likely to be pigeonholed.

When, in the very midst of this era, President Cleveland confined his message of December, 1887, to an earnest plea for tariff

[5] Quoted by Nicolay and Hay, *Abraham Lincoln: A History* (1890), IX, 125–27.
[6] *American Commonwealth* (Commonwealth Edition, 1908), I, 230.

reduction, such a partisan uproar resulted that Cleveland failed to be re-elected, the Democrats lost both houses of Congress, and the new Congress drastically revised the tariff upward instead of downward, as Cleveland had urged. Once when a friendly critic asked President Theodore Roosevelt the reason for the interminably long melange of topics constituting his messages, he got the reply, "Are you aware also of the extreme unwisdom of irritating Congress by fixing the details of a bill concerning which they are very sensitive instead of laying down a general policy?"[7]

Despite his professed precaution as to specific demands in his messages, President Theodore Roosevelt was a pioneer in initiating the twentieth-century trend of presidential leadership in legislation, and in fact he "gave the presidency an organic connection with Congress."[8] "In theory," wrote Roosevelt years after retiring from the presidency, "the Executive has nothing to do with legislation. In practice, as things now are, the Executive is or ought to be peculiarly representative of the people as a whole."[9] With the perceptive eye of the practiced politician, President Roosevelt saw the then well-nigh omnipotent Speaker of the House, Joseph Cannon, as a medium through whom he might exercise his legislative leadership of the House if not of Congress, since, in those days, even the Senate could be bent repeatedly to the will of Speaker Cannon.[10]

No sooner had Joseph Cannon been elected Speaker than President Roosevelt asked him to call at the White House, and their conferences became frequent. Thanks to Roosevelt's own experience as a legislator, he and Cannon came to a working understanding of their respective roles in lawmaking.

[7] J. B. Bishop, *Theodore Roosevelt and His Times* (1920), I, 233.
[8] S. E. Morison, *Oxford History of the United States* (1927), II, 449.
[9] *Autobiography* (1913), p. 292.
[10] See Blair Bolles, *Tyrant from Illinois* (1951), pp. 76, 77.

We did not always agree [admitted Cannon years later], in fact we more often disagreed but seldom on principle and usually as to practical methods. Roosevelt had the outlook of the Executive and the ambition to do things. I had the more confined outlook of the legislator who had to consider ways of meeting the expenditures of new departments and expansions in government.[11]

Since the chairmen of the committees conferred with the Speaker, his office was a clearinghouse of majority opinion to be relayed to the President, who conferred with Speaker Cannon on all important proposed legislation throughout his administration. "He was a good sportsman," said Cannon, "and accepted what he could get so long as legislation conformed even in part to his recommendations."[12] Cannon no doubt idealized the relationship somewhat, but here was the earliest attempt to systematize the function of the chief legislator.

Sometimes President Theodore Roosevelt could resort to audacious stratagems not at all free from considerable guile in accomplishing a legislative objective. Thus in February, 1903, the Elkins Bill forbidding rebates by the railroads was passed without difficulty. But the President was pushing a bill to establish a new Department of Commerce and Labor containing a Bureau of Corporations "to investigate the operations and conduct of interstate corporations." This proposed bureau alarmed big business, and John D. Archbold, who had become the presiding genius of the Standard Oil Company, wrote to a Pennsylvania congressman in opposition to the bureau. Getting wind of this, Roosevelt conveyed to Washington correspondents that he understood six senators had received telegrams from John D. Rockefeller against any antitrust legislation. This proved to be a bombshell, as it was intended, and while none of the six senators was ever identified,

[11] L. W. Busbey, *Uncle Joe Cannon* (1927), pp. 217, 218.
[12] *Ibid.*, p. 219. See G. R. Brown, *The Leadership of Congress* (1922), pp. 122, 123, 127.

the public reaction was effective. "I got the bill through by publishing those telegrams and concentrating public attention on the bill," said the President somewhat later.[13]

President Roosevelt's immediate successor, Taft, had none of the Roosevelt flair for dramatizing presidential leadership. Taft did however astonish conservatives and the constitutional purists by collaborating with his Attorney General, Wickersham, in preparing the draft of the first corporation tax bill, which he sent to Congress along with a message. This was resented as an encroachment upon the legislative function of Congress.[14] And somewhat later Attorney General Wickersham submitted to Congress a bill to extend the authority of the Interstate Commerce Commission, which evolved into the Mann-Elkins Act.[15]

In contrast with President Theodore Roosevelt, whose legislative leadership was that of pragmatic opportunism, Woodrow Wilson brought to the presidency the matured theory of a would-be prime minister.[16] It was Woodrow Wilson's great contribution to the presidency to have made the provision of the Constitution for the presidential message to Congress the basis of dynamic legislative leadership. The extraordinary significance of the State of the Union Message today owes much to the imagination and initiative of the only political scientist to have become Chief Magistrate of the United States. He literally dramatized the presidential message to Congress.

Woodrow Wilson's dogma of presidential initiative in legislation, based on the message to Congress, had been maturing during the long generation since the publication of his first article.[17] One president after another, as the years passed, failed to measure

[13] H. F. Pringle, *Theodore Roosevelt, a Biography* (1931), p. 341.

[14] See H. M. Bowman, "Congress and the Supreme Court," *Political Science Quarterly*, March, 1910, p. 20.

[15] 36 Stat., 539.

[16] Art. 2, sec. 3.

[17] See Woodrow Wilson, "Cabinet Government in the United States," *International Review*, VI (August, 1879), 46–163.

up to Woodrow Wilson's hopes until Theodore Roosevelt, concerning whom he wrote, "We must admit that he is an aggressive leader. He led Congress—he was not driven by Congress." Essential to Wilson's dogma was his conviction that the president must be a party man "who has the personality and initiative to enforce his views upon the people and upon Congress."[18] Persistent in the pattern of Wilson's conception of the presidency is the analogy of the prime ministry he read into the Constitution's provision for the presidential message to Congress. As he conceived it, the president as party leader and quasi prime minister should resign if one of his major legislative proposals to Congress was voted down. Thus he would have resigned if the repeal of the exemption of American vessels from payment of Panama Canal tolls, contrary to a treaty agreement, had been defeated when voted on in the early days of his presidency.[19] "In case of failure in this matter," he had declared, "I shall go to the country, after my resignation is tendered, and ask whether America is to stand before the world as a nation that violates its contracts as mere matters of convenience, upon a basis of .expediency."

The custom of President Wilson to appear dramatically before Congress in person on major proposals for legislation instead of simply following the century-old custom of sending a written message to be read by a clerk was in keeping with his formula of the prime ministry. Under his dynamic leadership the first consistent revision of the tariff since the administration of President Polk was achieved after an effective co-ordination of the parts played by president and congressional committees and a Wilsonian blast at the tariff lobbyists, which sent them scurrying.[20] The grist of the congressional mill became the most consistent since the Hamiltonian program of the first years under the Constitution —a program put through the First Congress by one who also

---

[18] Woodrow Wilson, *Constitutional Government in the United States* (1907), p. 65.

[19] David Lawrence, *The True Story of Woodrow Wilson* (1924), pp. 310, 311.

[20] Ray Stannard Baker, *Woodrow Wilson, Life and Letters* (1927–33), IV, 123, 124.

insisted on being considered the prime minister. In addition to the Underwood Tariff there were such statutory landmarks as the Federal Reserve Banking Act, the Clayton Act, and the Federal Trade Commission Act.

So cordial was the relation of President to his party organization in his first Congress that the considerable opposition to the Federal Reserve Act was overcome, and on the final vote every Democratic Senator voted for the bill.[21] Here was a perfect fulfillment of the Wilson dream of party government under the leadership of a prime minister. Herein was his realization of the full possibility of the Constitution's provision for the presidential message. Circumstances provided the opportunity, but whatever hopes Wilson may have had of institutionalizing this peculiar pattern of presidential leadership were doomed to disappointment.

The three Republican presidents between Woodrow Wilson and Franklin Roosevelt made no contribution to the trend toward the chief legislatorship that Theodore Roosevelt had initiated. Franklin Roosevelt revived the Wilsonian pattern of presidential leadership in legislation. "Without leadership, alert and sensitive to change, we are all bogged up or lose our way," he said only a week after his first election.[22] Not in a dozen years had such a note been struck by a president. Two months later he was the honor guest at the annual dinner of the Harvard Club of New York City. Former President of Harvard A. Lawrence Lowell, an outstanding political scientist under whose tuition the President-elect had studied, was the principal speaker. Discoursing on the presidency, Lowell turned to Roosevelt to say that the most important principle for the chief executive is that he must always take and hold the initiative in his dealings with Congress and with his Cabinet and generally with the public. He declared that if Roosevelt would always apply this principle, there would be little doubt of his success.[23]

[21] *Ibid.*, 174 ff.

[22] *New York Times*, Nov. 13, 1932, Sec. 8, p. 1.

[23] Louis B. Wehle, *Hidden Threads of History* (1953), p. 134.

The crisis of March, 1933, when Franklin Roosevelt was inaugurated, provided the greatest opportunity since the Civil War for exploiting the peculiar political aptitudes and talents of Franklin Roosevelt. Thus he reassured a perplexed and almost despairing people: "In every dark hour of our national life a leadership of frankness and vigor has met with understanding and support of the people themselves which is essential to victory."[24]

Then followed the "hundred days" during which President Roosevelt, avoiding clashes, collaborated with amateur congressmen who, without executive leadership, would have been bewildered by the gargantuan crisis. Confronted by an undisciplined Congress and an inchoate public sentiment, the President nevertheless managed to control the situation. "By great fortune," wrote Pendleton Herring, "a skilful politician was in the White House who knew how to handle the public and how to negotiate with Congress. The President was able to outmaneuver his opponents and to compromise when a clear cut victory was impossible. His leadership supplied the unifying force."[25]

After the "hundred days," leadership became more systematic. Former legislator Roosevelt knew that lawmaking is a tedious process, that committee hearings are required for groups concerned about pending legislation to be heard. Congressmen must estimate the strength of conflicting constituent interests on bills and calculate the balance of social forces on pending measures. In time President Roosevelt developed a procedure of his own for promoting legislation. Preliminary studies of a proposed piece of legislation were made by outstanding specialists in the field. Meanwhile information was disseminated to inform the public and bring constituent pressure to bear on legislators. Roosevelt took pains to have administration bills assigned to favorable committees when possible, and seldom did one reach a hostile

[24] Franklin D. Roosevelt, *On Our Way* (1934), pp. 255–56.

[25] "The First Session of the 73rd Congress," *American Political Science Review,* XXVIII, No. 1 (1934), 82.

committee. When, in the committee stage, hearings were held, the specialists were ready with answers to the questions propounded. A prepared bill usually accompanied the message proposing the legislation.[26]

Congress was surely listening to a disciple of Woodrow Wilson when, in his second State of the Union address, Franklin Roosevelt was saying, "Out of these friendly contacts we are fortunately building a strong and permanent tie between the legislative and executive branches of the government. The letter of the Constitution wisely declared a separation, but the impulse of a common purpose declares a union."[27] Such was the theory implemented frequently by a 9:45 meeting by the Secretary of State, the Budget Director, the Senate majority leader, and the Speaker of the House. "In practice," as E. P. Herring observed of the President, "he evolved a 'master ministry' of congressional leaders, cabinet officers, and executive officials working through the White House,"[28] No doctrinaire President, Roosevelt frankly avowed he employed the play-by-play tactics of the football quarterback.

Pliable though President Roosevelt might have been as to means employed, he was, in his first term, inflexible as to his "must" legislation. The confusion in Congress early in 1935 led to a rumor that the President was in poor health and his leadership seriously impaired, but by the time Congress had adjourned even so critical a commentator as Charles A. Beard concluded that

> the victory of the President was complete all along the line . . . After the democratic processes of debate and confusion were given free rein, leadership emerged in the end. When results

---

[26] See "Congress' Reasons for Delay in Passing the President's Bills," *United States News and World Report,* Jan. 18, 1946. The "Delay" in the title refers to events in the administration of President Truman, who was less systematic in promoting his measures.

[27] F. D. Roosevelt, *On Our Way* (1934), p. 204.

[28] "The Second Session of the 73rd Congress," *American Political Science Review,* XXVIII, No. 5 (1934), 854.

were surveyed at the conclusion of the discussion and uproar, it could be truly said that seldom, if ever, in the long history of Congress had so many striking and vital measures been spread upon the law books in a single session.[29]

How far have we gone since the day when a president sat down at his desk and scribbled out his longhand messages to Congress? The elaborate organization of the Executive Office of the President has now practically institutionalized the preparation of the messages or addresses on the state of the Union, the budget, and the Economic Report. Let us take President Truman's State of the Union Message to the Eighty-first Congress. As early as the preceding July the Budget Bureau had received from various agencies the replies to its requests for the budget estimates for suggested items of legislation. The Legislative Reference Division of the Budget Bureau then prepared from the replies a tentative list of eighty-three items of possible legislation, divided into those considered certain to be recommended and those less certain. Then teams of experts from the White House staff, the Federal agencies, and the Budget Bureau began long-range drafting of tentative legislation and preparing supporting data and arguments. Meanwhile White House staff members sorted out and analyzed the proposed items of legislation and began work on the State of the Union Message. As tentative drafts were completed they were circulated among Cabinet members and other top officials.

President Truman himself laid down the outline of the message before a word was written. The message evolved through several drafts under the supervision of the President's legal counselor and his personal legislative assistant and then went back to the President for comments. President Truman went over the final drafts, sentence by sentence, determining final choice of words and of emphasis. Twenty-five of the eighty-three legislative items gathered

[29] "The Labors of Congress," *Current History,* Oct., 1935, p. 64.

by the Legislative Service of the Budget Bureau appeared in the finished draft of the State of the Union Message.[30]

President Eisenhower's third State of the Union Message illustrates the perennial search for recommendations of legislation that would represent the translation of the aspirations of our complex society into public policies. The list was impressive: higher minimum wages, lower tariffs, reduced draft calls, higher Federal salaries, more irrigation dams, flexible farm price supports, subsidies for medical schools and for health insurance, Taft-Hartley Law changes, relaxing immigration restrictions, votes for eighteen-year-olds, aid for public schools, more public housing, and aid for small-scale farmers.[31] The demands of an interest group lurked in every item.

Concerning almost any recent president's legislative program, would it not be appropriate to recall former Congressmen-Professor T. V. Smith's "principle of plain politics" that "nobody is to get nothing; nobody is to get everything; everybody is to get something."[32] And if, in the practical application of this broad and generous formula, the president hopes to fortify the group combination constituting the majority that elected him with a weather eye on the next election, so much the better. The grist of the legislative mill depends upon the competition of our political parties for the good will of the elements of American society with competent presidents as chief engineers of the process. By and large the better a shrewd State of the Union Message exemplifies the application of the formula, the better for the nation.

The power that the Constitution vests in the president "on extraordinary occasions [to] convene both houses or either of them" is exclusively his power. Congress in recess cannot of its

[30] Stephen K. Bailey and Howard D. Samuel, *Congress at Work* (1952), pp. 84, 85.

[31] "What Eisenhower Wants for Everybody in 1955," *United States News and World Report*, Jan. 21, 1955, pp. 28–29.

[32] "The Political Way of Life." Address delivered at Santa Barbara, California, September 16, 1948.

own volition convene itself, as much as Congressmen from time to time have wished that they might. The president can convene Congress when it does not want to meet, as President Truman certainly did with the Eightieth Congress in the summer of 1948. A resolute president cannot be pressured into convening Congress. President Johnson was under just such pressure during the eight months in 1865 between his assuming the presidency following the assassination of Lincoln and the convening of Congress in the regular session required by the Constitution in December of that year. During those eight months President Johnson was proceeding with reconstruction under the lenient terms initiated by Lincoln.

Meanwhile the congressional leaders who had resisted Lincoln's generous policy were determined to compel Johnson to impose severe terms for restoration of the governments of the states of the late Confederacy. "Is there no way to arrest the insane course of the President in reorganization?" inquired savage old Thaddeus Stevens. "If something is not done the President will be crowned King before Congress meets," declared Senator Sumner.[33] As a precaution against Johnson ever again exercising his power not to call a special session, Congress at its next session passed a law "for the meeting of the Fortieth and all succeeding Congresses immediately after the adjournment of the next preceding one."[34] By this legislative stratagem Congress remained in continuous session throughout the remaining three years of Johnson's presidency.

Congress was not in session when the attack on Ft. Sumter confronted Lincoln with the problem of armed resistance to Federal authority. The experience of presidents who called special sessions of Congress at the beginning of their administration had generally been disastrous. Half a century later President Taft, and still later

---

[33] *Johnson Papers*, quoted by E. P. Oberholtzer, *History of the United States Since the Civil War* (1917–37), I, 41.

[34] *U. S. Statutes at Large*, XIV, 378.

President Hoover, called special sessions early in their administrations to revise the tariff. In both instances it started intraparty
strife that seriously impaired presidential prestige. In Lincoln's
time a special session in May was regarded as symbolic of political
disaster, and Secretary of State Seward warned Lincoln particularly against that month.[35] There was then no telegraph line to
California to notify congressmen there of a special session, and
they could not have traveled quickly to Washington after receiving
notice of the call. As it turned out Lincoln set July 4, eleven weeks
after the fall of Sumter, as the date of the special session. Meanwhile Lincoln had a free hand and exercised half a dozen powers
that the Constitution vests in Congress. Lincoln's and Johnson's
delays in convening Congress underscored the extraordinary
power inherent in the president's exclusive discretion as to
whether or not to call special sessions.

The threat of a special session has been used by a resolute
president to bring a sitting but dilatory Congress back under his
legislative leadership. Thus President Wilson warned his first Congress, which was planning to postpone action on the Federal
Reserve Bank to a later session, that if they adjourned without
action on the bill, he would promptly convene Congress in special
session, which threat produced the desired effect.[36]

President Truman's calling the Eightieth Congress with its Republican majority into special session in the summer of 1948 and
urging it to enact into law some of the just adopted Republican
platform pledges shows how the power to convene a special
session can be used as an instrument of party strategy by a president who has the audacity to do it. In his speech of acceptance
delivered to the Democratic convention that had just nominated
him, Truman reviewed the measures he had recommended to this
Eightieth Congress only to have them rejected. Now the recently
adjourned Republican convention had pledged the party to the

---

[35] James G. Blaine, *Twenty Years of Congress* (1884–86), II, 55.
[36] J. P. Tumulty, *Woodrow Wilson as I Knew Him* (1921), p. 170.

enactment of some of the very measures their own party had turned down in the recent session. In the midst of his acceptance speech, as we have seen, President Truman with unprecedented guile announced he would call Congress into special session and urge it to enact the measures the Republican platform advocated. The power to call special sessions has been used by other presidents to their detriment and even to that of the public. But a president equipped with a shrewd understanding of party strategy and endowed with imagination, sufficient self-assurance, and a sense of timing—when to and when not to—can utilize his discretionary power to call special sessions as a potent instrument of his legislative leadership.

The veto power has developed into a potential instrument of the president's leadership in legislation. It had been the unrestrained conduct of the popular branch of the omnipotent state legislatures of the 1780's that, by and large, had brought together the framers of the Constitution of the United States. Might not the popular branch of a national legislature, Congress itself, also run riot? So the framers adopted the executive veto, lifting the provision from the Constitution of Massachusetts, which contributed so largely to the content of the national constitution. The first half dozen presidents used the veto power sparingly, mainly to strike down legislation they considered unconstitutional.

A change came with the inauguration of Andrew Jackson, the first President to have been elected by virtually universal white manhood suffrage. Thus fortified by what he considered the mandate of the American people, Jackson initiated the practice of the president deliberately passing his independent judgment as to the wisdom, not just the constitutionality, of acts of Congress. Thus he set the trend that, as already noted, has converted the president into a potential, when not actual, one-man third house of the national legislature. Let those who fret over whether what Jackson did was right and proper be reminded that the forces in American society that shape and reshape our unwritten constitution, like the mills of the gods, grind slowly but grind exceeding small—and care not a whit for such ethical abstractions.

Jackson's veto of the legislation rechartering the Bank of the United States, for example, was based upon the assumption that it was bad legislation. The Whigs denounced this as executive usurpation of the legislative power of Congress. The Jacksonians defended it as "the tribunative voice of the people speaking again through their executive."[37] It was during the debate preliminary to the most important mid-nineteenth-century legislation that the supreme significance of the veto power became evident. It was an open secret that President Zachary Taylor was determined to veto the legislation that he dubbed the Omnibus Bill and that constituted the heart of the Compromise of 1850, but his sudden death brought to the presidency Vice-President Fillmore, who represented the Clay faction of the Whig party and was known to be ready to sign the bill, which he did as soon as it was enacted.

Nor should it be overlooked that the veto is also a positive instrument of the legislative leadership of the president. It can be a potential and ever-present threat to pending bills when White House leaks let the president's resolute opinion of them become known—unless a two-thirds majority to pass them over his veto is known to exist. The president's known views in opposition to pending bills can become the means of bargaining between president and Congress for other legislation, "an instrument to be propitiated by timely and obvious surrenders," as Professor Herman Finer put it.

The President's veto power has become extraordinarily important during the present generation, President Franklin Roosevelt having vetoed almost as many acts of Congress as all his predecessors. This recent development can be attributed to the fact that the President and Congress came to represent rather two different constituencies, two opposing sets of electoral power. Organized labor, for example, is weak in Congress because its

---

[37] Levi Woodbury, *Writing* (1852), I, 571.

voting strength tends to be concentrated in relatively few constituencies. Not only labor but certain ethnic and religious groups also are largely concentrated in great metropolitan centers where they can, when so disposed, swing the weight of their voting power in great pivotal states in such a way as to determine which presidential candidate gets a majority in the Electoral College.

Congress on the contrary is heavily weighted with members so distributed in more sparsely settled districts as to overrepresent agrarian, suburban, middle-class interests with property-conscious and entrepreneurial biases. Considerably more than a majority of representatives in Congress represent districts with no city of as many as 50,000 inhabitants. During the Franklin Roosevelt and Harry Truman administrations it is scarcely an exaggeration to say that the president came to be peculiarly the champion of the consumer-conscious urban voters, whose interest they protected more than once with the weapon of the veto and whose votes kept the Democratic party in power until the magic of the formula was broken by the glamor of a candidate who had just doffed a five-star uniform.

The tug-of-war between the congressional and presidential constituencies is illustrated by the Taft-Hartley legislation. The bill was overwhelmingly favored by both houses, 320 to 79 in the House of Representatives and 54 to 17 in the Senate. Two months before its passage Democratic leaders, including National Chairman Ed Flynn, were already urging the President to veto. So was the Executive Committee of the American Federation of Labor, while the C.I.O. was holding rallies to that end in a dozen cities. By June 18 the White House announced the receipt of 157,000 letters, 460,000 cards, and 23,000 telegrams, most of them urging veto. The Democratic National Committee announced that a poll showed Democratic party officers favoring the veto 2 to 1. President Truman vetoed the Taft-Hartley Act, which was promptly passed over his veto, and one year later he was elected to another term after a campaign in which he made the Taft-Hartley Act an issue. But such is the congressional constituency in contrast with the presidential that neither Truman nor Eisenhower, who also was elected pledged to revision of the act, was able to get a single amendment made by Congress.[38]

In the hundred and forty years before the organization of the Executive Office of the President, a president might prepare a veto message in person or ask a Cabinet member to do it. Thus President Johnson asked Secretary of War Stanton to prepare the veto of the Tenure of Office Act in 1867. The establishment of the Executive Office in 1939 literally led to the institutionalizing of the preparation of veto messages. For example, in 1950, Congress passed an act designed to clarify uncertainties in the Federal Trade Commission's duties as affected by a Supreme Court decision.[39] This Basing-Point Bill, as it was called, would have legalized certain price-fixing practices in the cement industry obnoxious to small business and consumer interests. When the Bureau of the Budget received the engrossed bill from the President it turned it over to its Division of Legislative Reference for scrutiny by the staff. The Bureau functions like a congressional committee and holds hearings to get the consensuses of the interests affected by the legislation. In this case it prepared a tentative veto, which President Truman used after the Democratic National Chairman had polled the constituencies of the Truman administration's strength.

Senators who had been unsuccessful in opposing the bill resorted to the White House to urge veto. President Truman's decision to veto the bill signified a choice of the left instead of the right. Had Truman signed the bill, he would have risked alienating the very base of his political power—labor, farmers, and small business. He would thereby have repudiated his own supporters and given aid and comfort to his bitter enemies, the Dixiecrats. It remains for some researcher eventually to ascertain what percentage of vetoes of the last quarter of a century has been

[38] See Bailey and Samuel, *Congress at Work* (1952), pp. 435–38.
[39] Federal Trade Commission *v.* Cement Institute. 333 U. S. 683 (1948).

determined by similar political calculation.[40] In that period, at any rate, the vetoes from time to time reflected the clash of the haves with the have-nots of the urban masses with the agrarians and their largely suburban allies.

To a degree impossible to measure objectively the legislative leadership of the president is a consequence of the usage that has made him the titular, and when he has the capacity and aptitude also the actual, leader of his party. Thomas Jefferson initiated the usage of seeing to it at the very beginning of his presidency that a Jefferson man was chairman of every Congressional committee. No president has ever exceeded Jefferson's feat of putting the extraordinarily drastic Embargo Act through Congress in one day, December 22, 1807. Jefferson, who might be said to have been the first national politician to attain the presidency, was already accustomed to using the press to achieve his purposes and continued that practice as President. During his administration appeared the first newspaper recognized as an adminstration organ, a practice not uncommon with presidents in the generation before the Civil War.

President Jackson held the House of Representatives in the hollow of his hand from the very beginning of his presidency, and insurgent Democratic senators were picked off one by one as their terms expired, and Jackson managed replacement by faithful partisans, which eventually gave him also a Jackson Senate. The erudite Senator George F. Hoar of Massachusetts expressed the opinion that no president except possibly Jackson had such influence over the Senate as McKinley,[41] and another Senator, Shelby M. Cullom of Illinois, wrote: "We have never had a President who had more influence with Congress than McKinley." No one can doubt the actual party leadership of Theodore Roosevelt or his use of it in getting legislation he desired. President Wilson's

[40] See Earl Latham, *The Group Basis of Politics: A Study of Basing Point Legislation* (1952), Chap. VI.
[41] *Autobiography of Seventy Years* (1903), II, 47.

effective party leadership was a corollary of his conception of the president as a prime minister who was implicitly head of the party in power. Franklin Roosevelt's party leadership as an effective instrument of legislation is unparalleled in our party history. The president who in this century isolates himself from Congress and party leadership may have the experience of a Coolidge, whose biographer wrote, "Congress has devoted itself to bloodying the President's nose, boxing his ears, and otherwise maltreating him."[42]

The judicious distribution of patronage among the party faithful was long a potent factor in the legislative leadership of the president. At the peak of the spoils system in 1864 President Lincoln could send Charles A. Dana on a mission to win the support of two obdurate congressmen whose votes were necessary to get Nevada admitted to the Union in order to have the pending Thirteenth Amendment ratified by the one more state still necessary. "Whatever promise you make to them I will do," declared Lincoln, and it turned out eventually just as Lincoln had planned it.[43] President Cleveland, in 1893, resolutely set out to obtain repeal of the Silver Purchasing Act, which was exhausting the "gold reserve" of the Treasury. When a Senator told the President that hell would freeze over before the Purchasing Act would be repealed, he got the President's prompt reply, "Then Hell will freeze over in exactly twenty-four hours." Cleveland knew because he had dispensed the necessary patronage to that end.[44] Thereupon the prolonged filibustering against the repeal came to a sudden end.

President Wilson suspended distribution of patronage during the extra session of his first term until his remarkable legislative program had been enacted into law. During the hundred days of emergency relief legislation President Franklin Roosevelt would

[42] Claude M. Fuess, *Calvin Coolidge* (1940), p. 342.

[43] C. A. Dana, *Recollections of the Civil War* (1898), pp. 174 ff.

[44] Harry Thurston Peck, *Twenty Years of the Republic* (1906), p. 349. James Ford Rhodes, *History of the United States* (1893–1922), VIII, 403; *Historical Essays* (1909), p. 224.

now and then put off an importunate congressman with the excuse, "We haven't got to patronage yet." The result of this coyness led Pendleton Herring to the conclusion: "The session indicated that the consummation of a national program is greatly aided by transmuting, through patronage, the localisms of our politics into support of the Chief Executive."[45] Patronage is a means by which a president may, when it is available, persuade congressmen to risk the displeasure of important constituent interests by strengthening his position among influential and "deserving" party leaders at home.

The Federal patronage available to the president has been declining ever since the Pendleton Civil Service Act became law in 1883 and with extraordinarily accelerated speed in recent years. Nor is this decline altogether regretted by congressmen who feel more than formerly the burden of participating in its distribution. They are increasingly aware of the president's power through patronage to coerce, cajole, and seduce them to support his program of legislation. The first critical shortage of patronage upon the succession of a president of one party to that of another party was experienced by President Eisenhower. So scarce indeed was the unclassified personnel subject to patronage that only a meager number was available for the faithful who had been waiting twenty long years for "the day."

The Eisenhower administration's reduction of the payroll ten per cent even cut out about as many positions without as within the classified service. Only a strong president with the flair of a Roosevelt can utilize the patronage still available to his own advantage. Due to Eisenhower's inexperience in the game of party politics Congressmen sometimes turned patronage accorded them against the administration, one Senator even managing to plant a personal partisan in the State Department, where he was able to embarrass if not harass the administration.

[45] "The First Session of the 73rd Congress," *American Political Science Review* XXVIII, No. 1 (1934), 82, 83.

In the absence of adequate patronage as an instrument of managing passage of party measures, the Eisenhower administration turned to other devices. Thus in 1955 even a Democratic Congress was prevented by the administration from passing a twenty-dollar individual tax reduction despite its extreme attractiveness to members of both parties representing close districts. The trick was turned by mobilizing political and business forces back in the districts to support the administration's pressure on wavering congressmen. It was believed at the time that such tactics would assure almost solid Republican party support on most administration measures except reciprocal trade.[46]

Technology itself seems to be conspiring to publicize the president more and more at the expense of Congress to the frequent frustration of our national legislators. In our day the president's power in shaping policy and getting policy translated into statutes is chiefly the power of publicity rather than the power invested in him by the letter of the Constitution. "His slightest utterance is headline news," wrote Howard Lee McBain long before televised broadcasting had become commonplace and had enabled the president to speak to the people of the nation face to face. Governor Franklin Roosevelt invented the fireside chat which he carried with him to the White House. During the "hundred days" with which his exceptional leadership was ushered in it is said that he had only to glance at the microphone in the presence of a delegation of protesting congressmen to have them drop the matter. They dreaded the flood of letters from constituents that every fireside chat had been bringing.

Today the president has only to make the request that the nation's broadcasting systems be cleared to catch the ear of a listening nation. Every top member of the administration likewise has access to the broadcasting channels at will. President Truman and Eisenhower in turn adopted and adapted the fireside chat with the enhanced advantage of television.

[46] *Newsweek*, March 28, 1955, p. 19.

Congress is always at a disadvantage in its competition for public attention because of its very plurality when pitted against the incomparable singularity of the president. When President Truman broadcast his reason for the veto of the Taft-Hartley Act, Senator Taft followed with his broadcasted reply, but Mr. Republican could never quite be Mr. Congress and could speak only for a fraction of the legislative branch even if a major part. Franklin Roosevelt converted the press conference into a powerful instrument to which Congress had no comparable counter-instrument. Now that the performance is televised to be viewed by the nation, a disconcerted Congress has more reason than ever for frustration with the president's opportunity to make the give and take with the news correspondents extraordinarily effective in his role as chief legislator.

Most significant today is the routinizing and even institutionalizing of the legislative leadership of the president. To prepare his plan of taxation and expenditures for submission to the consideration of Congress he has the Budget Bureau, which includes a well-staffed Office of Legislative Reference providing a clearinghouse for every executive agency's recommendation of legislation enroute to Congress and which office may even prepare his veto messages. White House counsels safeguard his legislative program against constitutional pitfalls. The Council of Economic Advisers and his personal economic adviser provide expert advice on his proposals for keeping the economy on an even keel. The National Security Council performs its appropriate purpose in formulating the president's domestic and foreign policies. Every unit of this elaborate apparatus plays its intended part of program-making for the chief legislator, and not a trace of it existed during the presidency of Woodrow Wilson.[47]

It is a far cry from that day long ago when President Lincoln called together his cabinet to present them with the *fait accompli* of the finished draft of the Emancipation Proclamation and say,

---

[47] See E. S. Corwin, *The President: Office and Powers* (1957), pp. 299–305.

"I have got you together to hear what I have written down. I do not wish your advice about the main matter, for that I have determined for myself." Nothing could be more different than the Eisenhower way. He has come to treat his cabinet as an instrument for collective policy-making, and it is appropriately equipped with a secretariat. This new departure with respect to the cabinet is but part of the process of institutionalizing the policy-determining function of the president. It first stood out in all its astonishing possibilities when the critical illness of President Eisenhower caused scarcely a tremor in the functioning of the government. Fortunately "Congress had adjourned. The President had acted on all bills, requiring his attention. The Big Four Foreign Ministers' meeting was still nearly a month away. Many high officials had just got off on vacation. Preparation of the messages to be submitted to Congress in January was in the early stages."[48] Assistant President Sherman Adams could not perform a single official act of the President, "but by telephone from Denver to Washington he could suggest, 'It is the President's wish that . . . or 'The President hopes you will . . . and so forth.' "[49] What may happen if a president falls ill in a crisis of the Cold War no one can say.

[48] Robert J. Donovan, *Eisenhower: The Inside Story* (1956), p. 370.
[49] *Ibid.*, p. 370.

IX

The Chief

Executive

* **NO DISTINCT** executive organ, on a continental scale, was created when, in 1775, the responsibility for conducting the collective concerns of the thirteen Revolutionary states suddenly fell into the lap of the rather astonished Second Continental Congress, which had convened in May, 1775, for no such purpose. By sheer necessity the Congress assumed charge of the war and the other common concerns of the thirteen colonies still in uncertain transition into states. In so far as any semblance of the executive function was provided for at all, it was at first performed by *ad hoc* executive committees, a new one for each resolution or purpose until there were more than a hundred of them. The extraordinarily able John Adams is said to have served on ninety of these executive committees. Here, in embryo, was what, in due time, evolved into the national executive of the United States. Decade by decade usage, statute, even the personality of energetic presidents have conspired to concentrate executive responsibility at a precise point until President Truman could epitomize the culmination of the trend by the motto on his desk, "The buck stops here."

Within a month of the convening of the Second Continental Congress the transition of some of the executive committees into permanent boards had begun. The first of these, a Board of War and Ordinance, was appointed with John Adams at its head.[1] In December, 1776, Congress appointed a committee "to prepare a plan for the better conducting the executive business of Congress, by boards composed of persons, not members of Congress."[2] By 1778 the Treasury Office of Accounts had evolved out of the Finance Committee of Congress, and a similar transition resulted in several other boards. Then in 1781 Congress carried this evolution from committees to boards one step further to the establishment of four executive departments: Foreign Affairs, War, Finance, and the Marine. The framers of the Constitution eventually crowned this evolving executive system by the creation of the chief executive. The President and the First Congress under the Constitution enacted statutes re-establishing the first three of the four executive departments initiated by Congress under the Articles of Confederation—Foreign Affairs (soon to be renamed Department of State), War, and Treasury.

A fundamental purpose of the framers of the Constitution was the replacing of the feeble system of the Confederation with a vigorous government provided with an adequate executive. The imposing list of powers delegated to Congress in the eighteen clauses of the eighth section of Article One of the Constitution might have been but a futile gesture with only the shadowy executive provided by the Continental Congress. Hamilton expressed the consensus of the framers when he wrote in Article 70 of the *Federalist*,

> Energy in the Executive is a leading character in the definition of good government. It is essential to the protection of the

---

[1] George Bancroft, *History of the United States from the Discovery of the Continent* (1885), IV, 425.

[2] *Journal of the Continental Congress*, VI, 1041.

community against foreign attacks. It is not less essential to the steady administration of the laws. . . .A feeble Executive implies a feeble execution of the government. A feeble executive is but another phrase for bad execution; and a government ill executed, whatever it may be in theory, must be, in practice, a bad government.

There epitomized is the philosophy of the Founding Fathers of the Constitution with respect to the executive, a conceptual pattern certainly not less valid in the atomic age than in the infancy of the republic.

"He shall take care that the laws be faithfully executed"[3] is the characteristic economy of phrase with which the Constitution makes the president the chief executive of the United States. Let it be noted that the president is not directed literally to enforce the law himself. No president has ever done this, although Andrew Jackson may have been preparing to do so just before the Nullification impasse of 1832 was resolved by Clay's Compromise of 1833. The chief executive's responsibility is, of course, to see to it that the execution is done by those invested with that responsibility. The president's authority for seeing to the faithful execution of the laws derives from five sources: first, those powers conferred directly by the second article of the Constitution, which concerns the executive; second, the specific executive powers created by acts of Congress and vested in the president; third, the discretionary powers vested by statute in the numerous executive agencies of the national government; fourth, the power to enforce criminal statutes; fifth, the nondiscretionary or ministerial duties vested in the executive agencies concerning the performance of which the office has no choice and which it is the duty of the president to have faithfully performed.[4]

The executive powers enumerated in the preceding paragraph are all based squarely on specific authorization by the supreme

[3] Art. 2, sec. 3.
[4] E. S. Corwin (ed.) *The Constitution of the United States: Analysis and Interpretation* (1953), pp. 475–76.

law of the land, that is, upon the Constitution, treaties, and Federal statutes. But does the president possess still other executive powers than these? Can it be that the president has executive powers inherent in the very nature of his office, in short, prerogative power, such as an English monarch possesses? Alexander Hamilton evidently thought so and expounded it over the pen name, "Pacificus," in a controversy that arose in 1793 concerning President Washington's Proclamation of Neutrality in the war that had broken out between England and France. American citizens, sympathetic with France, even Jefferson and Madison, condemned the Proclamation as a violation of the Treaty of Alliance with France made during the Revolutionary War and moreover as a usurpation by the President of the legislative power of Congress to declare war.

Hamilton plunged into the constitutional controversy, making much of the argument that the Constitution is quite specific and detailed as to the powers of Congress, limiting them specifically to the "legislative powers herein granted,"[5] whereas it vests the executive power, without qualification, in the president by the sweeping clause, "The executive power shall be vested in a President of the United States of America."[6] "The general doctrine of our Constitution then is," Hamilton argued, "that the executive power is vested in the President, subjected only to the exceptions which are expressed in the instrument." Hamilton also pointed out that the president's oath of office pledges him to "execute the office" not just "the law."[7]

Half a century after Hamilton's investing the president with prerogative power through constitutional exegesis, a keen exponent of the dogma of state rights, Able P. Upshur, President Tyler's Secretary of State, made a similar observation as to presidential

[5] Art. 1, sec. 1, clause 1.
[6] Art. 3, sec. 1, clause 1.
[7] Alexander Hamilton, *Works* (Lodge, ed., 1885), IV, 142–44.

power with the difference that he deplored what Hamilton approved in the vagueness of the Constitution:

> The most defective part of the Constitution beyond all question [wrote Upshur] is that which relates to the executive department. It is impossible to read that instrument without being forcibly struck with the loose and unguarded terms in which the powers and duties of the President are pointed out. So far as the Legislature is concerned, the limitations of the Constitution are perhaps as precise and strict as they could be safely made; but in regard to the Executive, the Convention seems to have studiously selected such loose and general expressions as would enable the President, by implications and construction either to neglect his duties or to enlarge his powers.[8]

More than a century after Hamilton's broad interpretation of executive power, President Theodore Roosevelt, apparently unaware of Hamilton's views on the matter, expounded his "stewardship theory of the executive power" of the president by his "insistence upon the theory that the executive power was limited only by specific restrictions appearing in the Constitution or imposed by Congress under its constitutional powers.... I declined to adopt the view that what was imperatively necessary for the Nation could not be done by the President unless he could find some specific authorization to do it."[9]

The loose interpretations of presidential power by Alexander Hamilton and Theodore Roosevelt may be dismissed as merely expressions of personal opinion rather than authoritative expositions of the law of the land. The courts have never accepted quite so much. In 1916 former President William Howard Taft, then a professor of law at Yale University, attempted to express the then prevailing judicial consensus on the scope of the executive power of the president. "The true view of the Executive functions," he wrote, "is that the President can exercise no power which cannot be fairly and reasonably traced to some specific grant of power

---

[8] *A Brief Enquiry into the True Nature and Character of Our Federal Government*, (1840), pp. 116.

[9] *Autobiography* (1913), p. 389.

or justly implied and included within such grant as proper and necessary."[10] However this did not express Taft's final interpretation, because ten years later in the Myers case he found implied power of the executive in the opening clause of the third article of the Constitution, "The executive power shall be vested in a President of the United States," the very clause from which Hamilton had derived presidential prerogative as early as 1793.

A full decade before Theodore Roosevelt publicized his stewardship theory of the presidency, he had already given a demonstration of it. In May, 1902, the accumulated grievances of the anthracite miners of Pennsylvania culminated in what turned out to be a historic strike. Roosevelt could have dismissed the matter as none of his responsibility until the Governor of Pennsylvania would ask for federal troops to restore order. But before the strike was a month old, he had sent his Commissioner of Labor to investigate and make recommendations, which neither side would accept. The East depended on anthracite coal for heating purposes, and if the strike continued into the autumn and winter, intense suffering would result.

Roosevelt got the operators and labor leaders together in a White House conference, where the conduct of the leading operator was so offensive that the President said later, "If it wasn't for the high office I hold I would have taken him by the seat of his breeches and the nape of the neck and chucked him out the window." Roosevelt was seriously considering sending the army to seize the mines and under it have the miners get out the coal, when he broke the impasse by sending Secretary of War Elihu Root to confer with the New York financial giant, J. P. Morgan, under whose influence the operators agreed to arbitrate. But in order to protect the miners' rights, Roosevelt saw to it that the arbitration board included a Catholic bishop and a union official, whom he palmed off as an "eminent sociologist," which the agreement to arbitrate had required.

[10] *Our Chief Magistrate and his Powers,* (1916), pp. 139–40.

The "stewardship theory" of the presidency proved "prophetic of developments in a field Theodore Roosevelt had staked out for its application—that of industrial relations."[11] Nothing so drastic as Roosevelt's methods in 1902 have been used since, but in the next forty-five years there were 26 instances in which a president intervened in a similar way in industrial crises by other than a purely police capacity, that is instead in an extralegal and extra-constitutional manner, which is the essential nature of the steward-ship theory of the presidency.[12] The stewardship of the presidency must now be considered an established usage of the office.

In 1936 the Supreme Court of the United States decided a case in which it sanctioned an area of executive power inhering in the office of the president. Congress had, by joint resolution, author-ized the President to lay an embargo on the sale of arms and munitions to two South American republics, Bolivia and Para-guay, then at war with each other, if he found that such an em-bargo might contribute to the restoration of peace between them. The act prescribed fine and imprisonment for violators of the President's proclamation. President Franklin Roosevelt, in ac-cordance with the resolution, issued a proclamation laying such an embargo, which a corporation violated by selling machine guns to Bolivia. When prosecuted, the corporation contended that the delegation of authority by Congress to the president had given him "unfettered discretion" and that the delegation was con-trolled by no standard, which the courts had only recently insisted upon in congressional delegation of its power. This defense was rejected by the Supreme Court. Speaking through Justice Suther-land the majority declared that "the investment of the federal government with powers of external sovereignty did not depend upon affirmative grants of the Constitution." As a sovereign nation the United States possesses, with respect to foreign re-lations, all the powers other sovereign nations enjoy, and this power is not dependent on delegations by the clauses of the

[11] E. S. Corwin, *The President: Office and Powers* (1957), p. 153.
[12] *Ibid.*, pp. 408–409.

Constitution. In brief here is an area of inherent national power. Justice Sutherland quoted the dictum of Representative John Marshall uttered in a debate in Congress, March 7, 1800. "The President is the sole organ of the nation in its external relations and its sole representative with foreign nations."[13] This meant that, in delegating the power of the joint resolution of Congress concerned in the case being considered by the Court, Congress needed to prescribe no standard as it must in the domestic field of specified powers of Congress. In the field of foreign relations not only Congress but even the president has inherent powers.[14] In one area then the prerogative dogma of Hamilton had been judicially vindicated.

As a general rule only Congress can authorize or create the offices and agencies available to the president in seeing to the faithful execution of the law. Until late in the nineteenth century it had been generally assumed that there could be no exception to this rule. But in 1889 there occurred a dramatic episode that determined the matter otherwise. Stephen J. Field, whom Lincoln had appointed an Associate Justice of the Supreme Court, had developed a capacity for survival in the turbulent days of the California gold rush, having acquired, among other accomplishments, the subtle art of shooting from the pocket. He had promptly accepted challenges to duels only to have challengers withdraw on second thought. In 1888, Justice Field in the face of a threat of assassination decided a case against Althea Hill, who had filed a will found to be a forgery. For outrageous misconduct in court, she and her attorney, David S. Terry, who soon afterward married her, were held for contempt by Justice Field. Terry declared he would shoot Field if he returned to California for his next session of circuit court. Thereupon President Benjamin Harrison acting through his Attorney General, detailed a United States deputy marshall, Neagle, to accompany and protect Justice Field, to the

[13] *Annals*, 6th Cong., col. 613.
[14] U. S. *v.* Curtis-Wright Export Corp., 299 U. S. 304 (1936).

utter disgust of the latter, who was accustomed to taking care of himself.

Upon Field's return to California on circuit court duty, Terry made a murderous attack upon him, but Marshall Neagle was quicker on the trigger and killed Terry. Neagle was arrested at once by a California sheriff and charged with murder. The California prosecutor argued before the court that, since no act of Congress had authorized the President to appoint Neagle, he was not an officer but merely a private citizen and therefore guilty of murder. When the case, on appeal, reached the Supreme Court of the United States, it was decided that the president, in the exercise of his obligation "to take care that the laws be faithfully executed" may, without statutory authorization, appoint an officer to protect the life of a Federal judge.[15] Thus the president's duty is not restricted to "the enforcement of Acts of Congress or of treaties of the United States according to their express terms," but includes "the rights and obligations growing out of the Constitution itself, our international relations and all the protection implied by the nature of the government under the Constitution." That much authority of the president then inheres in the very nature of the office of chief executive. Hamilton would have applauded the decision of the case *in re* Neagle.

Let no one assume from the outcome of the Neagle case that the president is not limited by statute law. During the undeclared war with France in 1798–1799 Congress enacted a Nonintercourse Act authorizing the seizure of American vessels sailing *to* France or its dependencies. President Adams directed the captains of armed vessels "to be vigilant that vessels really American but covered by Danish or other paper bound to or from French ports be intercepted. Under these orders the *Flying Fish*, a Danish vessel, was captured bound *from* France while the law had authorized interception only of vessels sailing *to* France. The naval captain was sued by the owners of the captured vessel for damages

[15] *In re* Neagle, 135 U. S. 1 (1890).

and plead in defense that he was acting under orders of the President. In due course the Supreme Court of the United States had to answer the question: "Will the orders of the President misconstruing the Act of Congress release from damages the officer obeying them." The Court decided unanimously that "the instructions cannot . . . legalize an act which without the instructions would have been a plain trespass."[16] This principle that the president cannot legalize what is otherwise a violation of law is just as valid today as it was a century and a half ago when Marshall gave the decision of the Court. In fact, Justice Thomas C. Clark based his opinion against the legality of President Truman's "seizure" of the steel mills in 1951 on the very decision of Little v. Barreme[17] just quoted.

Even a more striking decision emphasizing the fact that the president, in his capacity of commander-in-chief, cannot legalize what is not already legal is that of U. S. v. Lee. In the midst of the Civil War, Congress had ordered confiscated the estate of General Robert E. Lee, the present site of Arlington Cemetery, for failure to pay taxes due on it. After General Lee's death his heirs took legal steps to recover the property. Their action took the form of ejection of the military stationed with troops on the estate under orders of the President. The Attorney General of the United States found himself unable to prevent the ejection of the officers despite the fact that they were there under orders of the Commander-in-Chief. The Attorney General endeavored to prevent suit on the ground that the sovereign cannot be sued without its consent. The Supreme Court however chose to consider the action as one against persons. "No man in this country is so high that he is set above the law," said the Court. "No officer may set that Law at defiance with impunity. All officers of the government from the highest to the lowest, are creatures of the law and are bound to obey it."[18] The Attorney General failed also because of

[16] Little v. Barreme, 2 Cranch 170 (1804).
[17] 343 U. S. 579, 660, 661.
[18] U. S. v. Lee (1882).

the constitutional provision, which the act of Congress authorizing the confiscation explicitly recognized, namely that "no attainder of treason shall work corruption of blood except during the life of the person attained."[19] The decision of the Court signified once more that not even the President himself acting in his capacity of commander-in-chief can authorize anyone, in this case an army captain, illegally to occupy private property without the person so directed being subject to penalty for trespass.

In 1952 President Truman, in order to avert a threatened strike of steelworkers, which he believed would interfere with national defense in the midst of the Korean War, issued an executive order to the Secretary of Commerce to seize and operate most of the steel mills of the country. He did this upon the advice of the Attorney General under the assumption that the Constitution and the laws had vested such powers in the president. The President reported his action to Congress conceding at the same time that it had the power to supersede his executive order. In the legal maneuvering that followed, the issue reached the Supreme Court of the United States, which decided by a vote of 6 to 3 against the legality of the President's order. Justice Black, who delivered the opinion of the Court, reasoned that no statute authorized the President to take possession of the property. In framing the Taft-Hartley Act Congress had refused to authorize such action. Such authority, the Court held, could not be derived from the aggregate of the president's executive powers nor his powers as commander-in-chief. The powers the President here sought to exercise in law-making the Constitution vests in Congress alone.[20]

So far as emergency powers of the president are concerned the Supreme Court decision in the steel-seizure case induced about as much controversy as conviction. The so-called "emergency power" of the President apparently constitutes a field of authority he may exercise unless Congress limits it by legislation. Now

[19] Art. 3, sec. 3, clause 2.
[20] 343 U. S. 579.

Congress had, by the Taft-Hartley Act of 1946, prescribed a procedure that President Truman by-passed. In the opinion of Professor Robert Dishman, "Considering the bullheadedness of both sides and the cumbersome administrative machinery which had been set up to handle the stabilization and mobilization problems, I believe that a strike was inevitable and that therefore nothing would have been gained by invoking the Taft-Hartley Act."[21]

Professor Glendon Schubert was convinced that the majority opinion of the Court did not at all challenge Truman's declaration of emergency when he seized the steel mills in 1952 but simply ignored this fact of emergency, which led Schubert to conclude, "In any event that opinion of the Court is *sui generis*."[22] Whether the steel-seizure decision represents finality or not, Professor Corwin observed that it was "unquestionably contradicted by a long succession of presidential pioneering in territory eventually occupied by Congress."[23] The area remains vast in which the president may act in order "to take care that the laws be faithfully executed" and to perform his duties as commander-in-chief.

The "convenient vagueness" of the Constitution has required judicial clarification in scores of court decisions on the executive powers of the president. Some of the prescriptions of the Constitution, however, are so clear as to be self-explanatory. Certainly no one but the president can "grant reprieves and pardons for offenses against the United States."[24] He cannot delegate to anyone else his function as commander-in-chief. It is only he who "shall receive ambassadors and other public ministers and commission all officers of the United States."[25] He alone can veto acts of Congress. It is when the Constitution vests in the president the duty to take care that the laws be faithfully executed and when acts of Congress create and vest in him specific duties that he may

[21] E. S. Corwin, *The President: Office and Powers* (1957), p. 410.

[22] *The Presidency and the Courts* (1957), p. 357 n.

[23] *The President: Office and Powers* (1957), p. 155.

[24] Art. 2, sec. 2, clause 1.

[25] Art. 2, sec. 3.

exercise his authority as chief executive through an appropriate department whose act, if performed within the law, then becomes the president's act.[26] Moreover the president may not, without statutory authority, delegate a discretionary duty so that it will not be his act but that of another.[27]

But if the acts of public officials who directly enforce the law are legally the president's acts, how can he be assured that they are such dependable subordinates that he is willing to be held responsible for their acts? The First Congress wrestled with this very problem in a long debate. It came down to the question as to whether the Constitution intended that the Senate, which by precise prescription shared in appointing, would by implication share likewise in the removal power of officials? No action was taken by Congress on the question then, and that very inaction "produced the *net result* that the President alone has the power to remove at pleasure all superior officers, at least until Congress positively undertook to regulate their tenure."[28] The assumption underlying this conclusion is, as noted above, that the president cannot logically be held responsible for the acts of his appointees unless he has the sole power to remove them.

The first great test of the power of the president to remove his appointees occurred in 1832 when President Andrew Jackson removed Secretary of the Treasury William J. Duane because he would not comply with the President's policy of removing Federal deposits from the Bank of the United States. By removing Duane, Jackson raised the question as to whether this could be legally done in the face of the statute[29] that vested discretion solely in the secretary of the treasury. Jackson stood his ground on the removal in the face of an unprecedented uproar in the Senate and argued "that the entire executive power is vested in the President," that the power to remove those officers who are to aid him in the

---

[26] Wilcox *v.* Jackson ex. dem. McConnel, 13 Peters, 498 (1839).

[27] Williams *v.* U. S., *1 Howard,* 290, 297 (1843).

[28] James Hart, *The American Presidency in Action, 1789* (1948), p. 247.

[29] *U. S. Statutes at Large,* III, p. 274.

execution of the laws is an incident to that power, and that the secretary of the treasury was no exception. Not until nearly a century later was the question judicially settled. President Wilson had removed a postmaster before the end of the four-year term for which he had been appointed under a statute of 1876 that had made removal specifically subject to the consent of the Senate, which President Wilson did not even pretend to seek. Ultimately the question of the legality of the removal reached the Supreme Court, which sustained the President's action, and since then the absolute power of the president to remove executive appointees has not been judicially challenged.[30] Nor need the president give any reason whatever for the removal of such an official.[31]

Under his power to see to the enforcement of the law the president must inevitably interpret law preliminary to its enforcement. It cannot be maintained that the courts only have this power, for they cannot accept jurisdiction until a live case involving a question of law is brought before them by someone who insists he has been hurt by enforcement of the law. Nor is this presidential interpretation of law confined to executive orders and ordinances, that is, executive regulations or rules authorized or required by statute and having the force of law. In addition there are such matters as the order of the Attorney General in the Neagle case directing a United States marshal to accompany and protect the life of a threatened Justice of the Supreme Court. The

[30] Myers v. U. S., 272 U. S. 52 (1926).

[31] It should be noted that when Congress creates an agency to which it, under proper regulation, delegates quasi-legislative or quasi-judicial authority in order to carry out a congressional rather than an executive function, Congress may constitutionally restrict the removal power of the president to certain offenses. Thus when President Franklin Roosevelt removed William E. Humphrey from the Federal Trade Commission, the removal was held to be illegal by a unanimous Supreme Court. In the act creating the commission Congress had confined the President's power of removal to "inefficiency, neglect of duty, or malfeasance in office," none of which was assigned by the President as the reason for Humphrey's removal. Humphrey's Executors v. U. S., 295 U. S. at 602 (1935).

marshal in that mission "got his man." Though no law had authorized the appointment of the marshal, the "order" was nevertheless held by the Supreme Court to be "a law of the land." But long before that the Attorney General had to decide that the appointment was constitutional.

In seeing to the enforcement of the laws the president is not at all limited to employing ordinary personnel of the judicial and executive branches, but may also employ armed forces. The first large-scale challenge of Federal authority was made in 1794 by the whisky rebels of western Pennsylvania, who rioted against collection of the whisky excise. Resistance collapsed when President Washington mobilized and ordered against them 15,000 state militia, which Congress had authorized him to call into Federal service for such a purpose by legislation under the power granted it by the Constitution.[32]

If one of the whisky rebels of 1794 could have reappeared in the midst of the Little Rock desegregation crises of 1957, he would inevitably have wondered what had happened in the intervening 163 years to unsettle the matter apparently so decisively determined then in western Pennsylvania. Washington had taken decisive action in sending the "federalized" militia against the defiers of court orders—that is, the whisky rebels. There had been tarring and feathering then of Federal marshals who attempted to serve court writs on persons refusing to pay the whisky excise. In 1957 the Federal District Court in Arkansas had approved the Little Rock school board's program of gradual integration "with all deliberate speed" as the United States Supreme Court had directed May 31, 1955, and the District Court enjoined all persons from interfering. Nevertheless Governor Orval Faubus called out the Arkansas state militia or National Guard ostensibly to preserve order, but two days later under the Governor's order the militia was deliberately preventing integration. When the Federal judge,

[32] Art. 1, sec. 8, clause 15.

sitting in the district, granted an injunction against interference
with integration, Governor Faubus withdrew the National Guard,
and rioting against integration broke out in Little Rock. President
Eisenhower, following the statutory provision in force since the
Whisky Rebellion, issued the required proclamation commanding
all persons obstructing justice to cease and desist and disperse.
When the mob defied the President's proclamation, he ordered
Federal troops into Little Rock and federalized the Arkansas
National Guard, which deprived Governor Faubus of command
of it. In calling the militia into Federal service no less than in
ordering Federal armed forces to Little Rock the President was
but following in the footsteps of Washington in 1794 and Lincoln
in 1861 when Federal authority had been obstructed.

In 1808 Jefferson issued a proclamation ordering all officers
having authority civil or military who shall be found in the vicinity
of an unruly combination resisting enforcement of the Embargo
Act to assist in suppressing the combination "by all means in their
power, by force of arms and otherwise."[33] What Jefferson ordered
would have constituted a *posse comitatus*, based upon common
law by which a sheriff might summon the inhabitants of a county
to suppress disorder and enforce law. It was a striking comment-
ary of the late Henry Jones Ford on Jefferson's about-face on
utilizing Federal power when his administration instead of
Washington's or Adams' was employing it that "the enforcement
act passed to sustain the embargo was a greater interference with
the ordinary privileges of citizens than would have been necessary
in the exercise of war powers."[34]

Specific statutory authorization of utilizing private citizens in
the chief executive's "taking care that the laws be faithfully
executed" was incorporated in the Fugitive Slave Act of 1850.[35]

---

[33] "Federal Aid in Domestic Disturbances," S. Coc. 209, 59th Cong., 2nd Sess.,
p. 51 (1907).

[34] *The Rise and Growth of American Politics* (1898), p. 132.

[35] *U. S. Statutes at Large*, IX, 453 ff.

The Federal commissioners appointed to apprehend fugitive slaves were authorized "to summon and call to their aid the bystanders, or a *posse comitatus* of the proper county when necessary to ensure faithful observance of the clause of the Constitution referred to, in conformity with the provisions of this act."

It was under his duty to take care that the laws be faithfully executed that Lincoln, in 1861, employed Jefferson's conception of the *posse comitatus* by issuing his call for 75,000 state militia under the authority of the Act of 1795 for calling the militia into the Federal service. As Lincoln conceived it, the entire Union army constituted a gigantic *posse comitatus* summoned to suppress combinations obstructing the enforcement of Federal law. It was an augmented police force, and those who are puzzled because no declaration of war was ever made in 1861 need to be reminded that police are not expected to "declare war" in exercising their duties.

The Constitution provides that the United States shall protect each state "on application of the legislature, or of the executive (when the legislature cannot be convened) against domestic violence."[36] The long and harrowing economic depression of the 1870's led, in time, to railroad strikes so widespread and violent that nine governors called upon President Hayes for assistance. The use of Federal troops for suppressing internal disorder, other than resistance to Federal authority, was then unprecedented. President Hayes proceeded with his characteristic circumspection and, in consultation with his exceptionally competent Cabinet, arrived at judgments that established permanent precedents for similar later episodes. Among these precedents were the conclusions that the president can, when necessary, declare martial law, can insist upon formal constitutional requests from the state for Federal military aid, can issue proclamations in accordance with Federal statutes, and can make judicious use of troops under

[36] Art. 4, sec. 4.

Federal authority to preserve order and protect property but *not to break* the strike.[37]

In 1894 President Cleveland introduced a new pattern of the use of the military in civil disorder, in this instance, using Federal troops ostensibly to maintain the mail service and ensure free flow of interstate commerce but actually to restrain strikers seeking to force arbitration in a dispute with employers. The American Railway Union, acting in sympathy with striking Pullman-car workers, refused to handle trains that included Pullman cars, which action practically tied up passenger traffic in the United States. Without waiting for any application from the state legislature or the state executive of Illinois, as the Constitution requires in cases of domestic violence, and in the face of the vigorous protests of Governor John P. Altgeld of Illinois, President Cleveland dispatched Federal troops to Chicago.

> The actions of the President which were really the actions of his Attorney General Richard Olney [as Professor Rossiter correctly observed] were ill conceived, disconnected and thoroughly effective in breaking the strike.... At every point in the course of the strike and its suppression the wishes of the railroad officials who acted through the General Managers Association, found support in the federal government's action. Like Hayes, Cleveland intervened to restore public order. Unlike Hayes he accomplished this by judicially and physically breaking the strike.[38]

Whatever the merit or demerit of Cleveland's action in the Pullman strike, the issue was eventually resolved by a United States Supreme Court decision that "the entire strength of the nation may be used to enforce, in any part of the land, the full and free exercise of all national powers. The strong arm of national government may be put forth to brush aside all

[37] See Clinton L. Rossiter, "The President and Labor Disputes," *The Presidency in Transition* (The Journal of Politics), February, 1949, p. 97.

[38] *Ibid.*, p. 98.

obstructions."[39] No president since Cleveland has used the military in effect to break a strike, but they all have instead returned to the practice initiated by Hayes. In the anthracite coal strike of 1902 President Theodore Roosevelt resolutely refused the demand of the operators that he follow Cleveland in using troops to break the strike. On the contrary, after months of deadlock, Roosevelt was ready, if the operators had remained obdurate against arbitration, to use troops to seize and operate the mines in order to supply the fuel needed in the approaching winter. In 1907 President Theodore Roosevelt forced an unwilling Governor, who had deceived him into dispatching troops to Goldfield, Nevada, into policing his own state.

By mid-twentieth century the President's role in labor controversies that constituted national emergencies had evolved into an amalgam of legal authority plus sheer usage based upon the accumulating prestige of the presidency. In the Neagle case[40] Justice Miller had declared that there is a "peace of the United States" which is the basis of some of the president's unenumerated powers. This might justify a presidential title of "Protector of the Peace."[41] In his hectic first year as President just after World War II, Harry Truman spent unnumbered hours "writing labor messages to Congress, sponsoring labor management conferences, appointing emergency fact finding boards, sending personal pleas to strike bound union leaders, seeking injunctions from Judge Goldsborough, and seizing plants and whole industries threatened or paralyzed by work stoppages."[42] No wonder President Truman was led to say that "the principal power that the President has is to bring people in and try to persuade them to do what they ought to do without persuasion. That's what I spend most of my time doing. That's what the powers of the President amount to."[43]

[39] *In re* Debs, 158 U. S. 564 (1895).

[40] *In re* Neagle, 135 U. S., 1, 69 (1890).

[41] Rossiter, "The President and Labor Disputes," *The Presidency in Transition,* February, 1949, p. 94.

[42] *Ibid.*

[43] *New York Herald Tribune,* May 7, 1948, p. 16.

Let it be noted that the president not only has the authority to enforce a law but also the discretion not to enforce it. When he chooses not to enforce a law, that settles the matter. No power under heaven could compel President Truman to apply sanctions of the Taft-Hartley Act to strikers when he decided not to do so, and the rage of his political foes against him for failing to do so was just so much wasted energy. Impeachment of the president has been out of the question since the folly of the Radical Republicans in 1868 in turning it against President Johnson. In any case, it is difficult to frame articles of impeachment sufficient to convict any president of "treason, bribery, or other high crimes and misdemeanors"[44] on the basis of his failure to execute his power as chief executive.

Even when the president is ready and eager to enforce the law, he may be frustrated by the inadequate means of enforcement provided by an indifferent Congress. For example, why had the consumers' interest in adequate enforcement of antimonopoly legislation never been quite satisfied? The answer is contained in the Report of the Attorney General of the United States for 1938, in which he reveals:

> It is a well known fact that the anti-trust laws have been ineffective in preventing combinations in restraint of trade... From 1914 to 1923, during which our system of mass production and vast corporative enterprise may almost be said to have come of age, the average of attorneys in the Anti Trust Division was only 18. With such a personnel regardless of what the formula of the law might have been, no practical results were possible.

This condition was typical of the understaffing of other agencies. So handicapped was the Food and Drug Administration by its meager field force that its objective became "A maximum

---

[44] U. S. Constitution, Art. 2, sec. 4.

of enforcement with a minimum of resistance."[45] Congressional jealousy of the presidency is fortified by strong constituent interests in the districts, which exert their influence to prevent maintenance of effective administrative apparatus for uniform enforcement of laws regulating business. Thus it can be said that, with respect to some matters, the power of the chief executive may be but the shadow of his authority. In no case can the hand of the chief executive be stronger than the forces in society that give him whatever support he may possess.

[45] E. P. Herring, *Public Administration and the Public Interest* (1936), Chap. IV.

X

Implementing

the Presidency

* SOMEWHAT MORE than a century ago President James K. Polk could "faithfully execute the office of President of the United States" at the same time that he was managing two or three of the executive departments whose heads had fled from the sweltering summer heat of Washington. Of course this extraordinarily faithful Chief Executive was expending his physical reserves so rapidly that he was to have the shortest ex-presidency of any incumbent of the office—only three months, to be specific. His immediate successor, Zachary Taylor, is said to have managed with two assistants and a few clerks. That presidents in mid-nineteenth century could get along in this manner underscores the overwhelming growth of presidential responsibilities in the last century.

As late as the 1880's President Cleveland is said to have answered all White House telephone calls in person, not so arduous a burden in a city that may have had no more than a few score specimens of that novel gadget. President McKinley was able to maintain contact with the entire executive pyramid with the aid of eight or ten persons, and a small secretarial staff took care of all his personal and official correspondence. On January 1, 1958 that group of immediate presidential staff, the White House Office, had a personnel of 398 busy people.

The framers of the Constitution seem to have introduced somewhat casually into the fundamental instrument the injunction that the president "take care that the laws be faithfully executed." There is no clear indication as to just how they expected him to get this done. The first session of the First Congress ran headlong into the question in the debate as to whether, the Senate, since it shared in the appointment of executive officers, would by implication likewise share in the removal of these officers. They solved the problem for the time being by inaction, assuming it to be self-evident that the president would not be able to "take care that the laws be faithfully executed" unless he had the unhampered power to remove subordinates. This congressional inaction has been designated the Legislative Decision of 1789, and it had indeed, tentatively at least, the force of a Supreme Court decision on the question.[1]

There followed more than a century characterized, by and large, by makeshifts to carry out executive functions devised by those presidents who concerned themselves more than ordinarily with law enforcement. Meanwhile the functions of the Federal government administered through agencies created by Congress for their execution grew from Washington's administration on. Nearly half a century ago Woodrow Wilson wrote, "Men of ordinary physique and discretion cannot be Presidents and live, if the strain be not somehow relieved. We shall be obliged to be picking our chief magistrates from among wise and prudent athletes—a small class." And this was written before the burgeoning of agencies consequent upon two world wars and the Great Depression of the 1930's. It was indeed the fantastic expansion of Federal functions in a single generation that initiated a trend toward disintegration of the executive function, the administration of the Federal government, and thrust the problem of reform of the executive upon the attention of presidents, administrators, and scholars. Thus an observer of Franklin Roosevelt was to remark, "It is a

[1] See James Hart, *The American Presidency in Action, 1789* (1948), pp. 190–214.

mystery to me how each morning he selects the few things he *can* do from the thousands he *should* do." The time had arrived when something would have to be done to prevent the president from becoming so overwhelmed that he might decline into little more than a titular chief of state.

As agencies multiplied over the years, the president was becoming overwhelmed with the signing of papers and making decisions without the pertinent information on which to base his judgments. Presently it began to be suspected that the management of Federal finance might provide the key to a more efficient executive. Before Harding's administration, the Federal budget, if it could be called that, was prepared by the Treasury Department, which was then permitted merely to receive, index, and transmit to Congress a compilation of whatever estimates it had received from the numerous agencies of the government, and one clerk was kept busy doing nothing else. This compilation was designated simply the Treasury Book of Estimates. Franklin McVeagh, President Taft's Secretary of the Treasury, had proposed an executive budget to Congress, and the President appointed the Commission on Economy and Efficiency to study the problem. The commission concluded that no improvement of any consequence in government was possible without an executive budget. But when President Taft had the departments prepare estimates that were submitted to Congress, that jealous body resented the infringement on its prerogatives, and that ended that.

It was the rather sudden increase of the national debt by about 2300 per cent as a consequence of World War I that induced Congress to make an about-face on a budget system. A nation long accustomed to a Federal debt hovering around a billion dollars was confronted with a debt of over twenty-four billion. In 1921 President Harding signed the Budget and Accounting Act, which charged the president with the preparation of a complete budget of estimated revenues and expenditures for the consideration of Congress. The agency created for this purpose was the Bureau of the Budget, housed in the Treasury for eighteen years after which it became the most important element of the Executive Office of the President.[2]

By a stroke of good fortune President Harding appointed Charles A. Dawes, a Chicago banker, as the first Director of the Budget. This extraordinary extrovert made it impossible for the public to ignore the Bureau of the Budget. The first meeting of personnel dealing with the budget estimates, numbering some hundreds of persons, was treated to a dramatic demonstration by the Director falling not far short of a vaudeville performance. Seated on the stage behind the Director were the members of the Harding Cabinet. It must have been breath-taking to see the mercurial Director Dawes rush over in front of the dignified Secretary of State, Charles Evans Hughes, and shaking his menacing index finger in the face of the head of the Cabinet, declare, "Mr. Secretary of State, you must economize," and so on down the line of notables, Herbert Hoover and the rest of them. Tearing into the wing of the stage the Director emerged with a bundle of brooms and announced the bargain price when purchased in quantity. Then disappearing again he came back with a single broom announcing the extravagant price paid for it by a thriftless agency. Such spectacular histrionics could not be ignored by the elated newsmen present and in less than twenty-four hours practically every literate American knew that there was a functioning Bureau of the Budget. The emergence of the bureau turned out to be the first notable step in the evolution of what was in due time to become the Executive Office of the President.

It is a historic truism that in every major crisis the people of the United States have a tendency to turn to the president almost as children to a father. In a crisis of the war to preserve the Union there was the marching song "We are coming, Father Abraham, three hundred thousand more." Fortunately an able leader has usually but not always appeared when needed. Apparently it began finally to dawn on the public consciousness that

[2] See Harold D. Smith, *The Management of Your Government* (1945), Chap. v.

Federal administration had become too vast and complicated to depend solely on the fortuitous concurrence of exceptional presidential leadership with each major crisis. Institutionalizing the presidency had been long overdue when in the nick of time just before the dawn of the Atomic Age the Executive Office of the President was established.[3]

The President's Cabinet never manifested any tendency toward institutionalizing the presidency, and in the last generation it suffered a marked decline. The custom of many presidents of calling on the members in turn at the Cabinet meetings elicited a miscellany of unrelated episodes of the members of a group each engrossed with the matters of his own department and unprepared to give the matters collective consideration. The resulting nature of the meetings created an atmosphere of boredom. The Cabinet persisted by sheer usage. Curiously enough it afforded opportunities for informal transaction of interdepartmental business while members were gathering or leaving. Cynicism developed, and members were likely to resent Cabinet meetings as a waste of time.[4] Less than three weeks before the Armistice of November 11, 1918, Wilson's Secretary of the Interior, Franklin K. Lane, recorded in his "Notes on Cabinet Meetings," that "For some weeks we have spent our time at Cabinet Meetings largely in telling stories."[5] By 1938 George Graham declared that the Cabinet's "contribution to government at present seems to be nil and that it is a bleeding and anemic patient."[6]

The decline of the Cabinet was accelerated by a tendency of presidents, in constructing their Cabinets, to ignore the fundamental distinction between the administrator and the technician

---

[3] It is a curious fact that a proposal for reform of the presidency was made when Washington had been President only four and a half months. Clinton Rossiter, "The American Presidency," *Yale Review*, xxxvii (1948), 631.

[4] Arthur W. MacMahon and John D. Millett, *Federal Administrators* (1939), p. 5.

[5] *The Letters of F. K. Lane* (1922), p. 293.

[6] "Reorganization—A Question of Executive Institutions," *American Political Science Review*, xxxii (1938), 712.

and to appoint specialists of a kind as department heads illustrated strikingly by the Eisenhower Cabinet. Such a cabinet contrasts strikingly with those of the great days of strong Cabinets such as that of President Hayes, of which the late John W. Burgess in 1916 wrote, "Taken altogether, it was the strongest body of men, each best fitted for the place assigned to him, that ever sat around the council-table of the President of the United States."[7] Theodore Roosevelt's Cabinet was such that James Bryce declared that he had "never in any country seen a more eager and efficient set of public servants."[8] In those earlier Cabinets the heads of the executive departments were usually experienced politicians who had learned the art of mediating between Congress, the public, and the specialists in their departments. When a president appoints a Cabinet whose members know only what they think ought to be done instead of how to get it done in the inevitable political milieu, no wonder the president looks elsewhere for advisers who can tell him how to go about getting his policies enacted into law and administered efficiently.

Faint foreshadowing of the institutionalizing of the executive have appeared from time to time in such informal manifestations as the Kitchen Cabinet, Tennis Cabinet, Inner Circle, Men behind the Throne, or even Presidential Cronies. Franklin Roosevelt had gathered about him such an advisory group even before his first inauguration. Rexford Tugwell, A. A. Berle, Jr., Samuel Rosenman, Hugh Johnson, and others came in time to be called the Brain Trust, which drove to fits of rage devotees of the *status quo*.[9] Soon it was being denounced as a palace guard, and the mystery surrounding its extralegal character, the youthfulness of its members and their academic connections induced a deafening uproar of anti-intellectualism. Yet this informal group

---

[7] *The Administration of President Hayes* (1916), p. 65.

[8] Quoted by W. D. Lewis, *The Life of Theodore Roosevelt* (1919), p. 258.

[9] See Raymond Moley, *After Seven Years* (1939), p. 55.

foreshadowed, vaguely, at least, the future Executive Office of the President and may well have been its matrix.

The Office of the Executive, as is usually the case with new institutions, was the child of crisis and circumstance rather than of deliberate design. The setting of its origin was the Great Depression of the 1930's. The inauguration of Franklin Roosevelt in 1933 brought to the presidency an inveterate pragmatist in politics at the very moment that the depression had become most critical. Under his energetic leadership, as he boldly, if somewhat erratically, attacked the pressing problems produced by the depression, new governmental agencies proliferated—the National Recovery Administration, the National Youth Administration, the Civilian Conservation Corps, the Agricultural Adjustment Administration, the Resettlement Administration—to name a few of them. To co-ordinate this maze of multiplying agencies, the President, in his first year, set up an Executive Council, whose functions were soon taken over by a newly created National Emergency Council, which performed temporarily a useful function in broad executive planning and co-ordinating of the functions of the ever-increasing alphabetical agencies. However when this council failed to live up to expectations, the President created in 1934 the Committee on Administrative Management consisting of Louis Brownlow as Chairman, Charles Edward Merriam, and Luther Gulick to study the whole problem of over-all management and to make recommendations.

The report of this Brownlow Committee, as it came to be called, and the legislation consequent upon it constitute one of the landmarks in the evolution of the presidency. The committee, with its highly competent staff, made a study that was searching and thorough. Recognizing the overwhelming burden of the chief executive, the committee epitomized its problem in a four-word statement, "The President needs help." Its outstanding recommendation for the president was a White House staff "to assist him in obtaining quickly and without delay all pertinent information possessed by any executive department so as to guide him in making his responsible decisions" and then "to assist him in seeing to it that every administrative department and agency is promptly informed of his decision along with his directive." This staff was to be no place for an extrovert, but its personnel was to remain in the background. "They should be possessed of high competence, great physical vigor and a passion for anonymity."[10] The committee envisaged the flow upward through the staff of pertinent information from subordinates on which the president could base his decisions and the flow downward of the results of these decisions through the White House staff as directives to the appropriate executive agency. Thus might the president at long last be equipped with the apparatus to fulfill his constitutional duty "to take care that the laws be faithfully executed."

The White House Office was the paramount contribution of the Brownlow Committee to the institutionalizing and implementing of the presidency, but the committee's recommendations covered almost the whole range of the larger emerging Executive Office of the President. "What I am placing before you," declared President Roosevelt in presenting the committee's recommendations to Congress, "is not the request for more power, but for the tools of management and the authority to distribute the work so that the President can effectively discharge those powers which the Constitution now places upon him. Unless we are prepared to abandon this part of the Constitution, we must equip the Presidency with authority commensurate with his responsibilities under the Constitution."[11]

Unfortunately the recommendations of the Brownlow Committee were thrown into the lap of Congress just when its blood was up over the President's drastic proposal for reform of the Supreme Court—the Court-Packing Bill, as his enemies called it.

---

[10] See report of the *President's Committee on Administrative Management,* United States Government Printing Office, Washington, 1937, p. 5.

[11] *Ibid.,* p. v.

The bill to carry out the recommendations of the Brownlow Committee was promptly dubbed the Dictator Bill, a spurious term persistently publicized by antiadministration newspapers throughout the nation, and the issue was thereby sadly confused by irrelevant controversy. There was consequently some watering down of the matured judgments of the committee. However it was under the authority vested in the president by the resulting Reorganization Act of 1937 that President Franklin Roosevelt issued the famous Executive Order Number 8248 allocating the agencies constituting the Executive Office of the President. Concerning the new arrangement Leonard D. White declared, "There can be no doubt that they came just in time to avert a dangerous break down at the top of the Federal System."[12] In a few years it came to be recognized that the Executive Office was a decisive factor in the effective management of our part in World War II. It should be noted that the Executive Office of the President is but one of the many agencies of the vast executive branch of the national government.

President Roosevelt's Executive Order Number 8248 and later ones all prescribing the organization of the Executive Office of the President have determined its present setup. Most immediately important for the president's day-to-day performance of his duties is his staff, the White House Office, which must not be confused with the larger Executive Office of the President of which the staff is only a component part. The personnel of the White House Office in 1957 included among others an Assistant to the President and several assistant assistants, several administrative assistants, numerous special assistants, an economic advisor, a military aide, a naval aide and a physician to the President, a personal secretary to the President and one to his wife, and a chief usher—with a total personnel of 398. This staff provides the medium through which flows inward from the vast executive network information and outward to their appropriate

[12] *An Introduction to the Study of Public Administration* (1948), p. 62.

destinations directives from the President. The staff is somewhat analogous to the human brain, which receives stimuli conveyed along the channels of the nervous system on the basis of which it sends outward the motor impulses that determine human action.

The Executive Office of the President includes the Bureau of the Budget, the Council of Economic Advisers, the National Security Council, the Central Intelligence Agency, and the Office of Defense Mobilization. The gradual development that, after a long generation, culminated in the Executive Office of the President had begun as an economy project to which, in time, was added the goal of efficiency in administration. When the office was at last formally established, the objective had become "to save the Presidency from paralysis and inattention . . . to rescue not merely administration but the Presidency itself from the babel and bedlam of the modern state."[13] It is to be noted that within a single year there had been reorganizations of Congress, the National Judiciary, and the National Executive.

Even as late as 1948, when the Executive Office of the President was several years old, Professor Rossiter could still quite correctly report "that the American Presidency is almost out of hand and that its limits as a one-man job have been reached if not overpassed."[14] Fortunately President Eisenhower's habits as a general contributed to systematizing and toning up the White House Office. Its staff became more than ever the clearinghouse for policy matters. Sherman Adams, Assistant in Chief to the President, would be in and out of the President's private office half a dozen times a day. An assembly of upper staff officers in Adams' office every morning at 8:30 reduced the President's work for the day to essentials, sharpening up issues for discussion with the President. Nearly everything went to him with a one-page synopsis on top besides which he was given oral briefings.

[13] Clinton Rossiter, "The Constitutional Significance of the Executive Office of the President," *American Political Science Review*, XLII, No. 6 (Dec. 1949), 1212.
[14] "The American Presidency," *Yale Review*, XXXVII (1948), 619.

President Eisenhower required precise recommendations from department and agency heads. His closest staff officers after Sherman Adams were Press Secretary Hagerty and Secretary of State John Foster Dulles and his brother Allen, Chief of the Central Intelligence Agency. These could even waken the President at night on a matter of national crisis, which was almost done when the news of Stalin's death came in.[15] President Eisenhower shaped the staff to handle his backbreaking job. It gave him time to talk with congressmen and make contacts with civic groups, even to receive a Thanksgiving turkey presented by the National Turkey Growers Association and have the presentation recorded for nationwide telecasting as indeed it ought to be. "For the first time in history the White House is becoming a self operating institution—more of an institution than a man."[16] Let the person who would object to this institutionalizing of the presidency figure out how else to make the job tolerable to mortal man.

Under President Eisenhower the White House Office underwent a marked reorganization. Roosevelt and Truman had treated the White House Office as a group of informal senior assistants, each with direct access to and operating through the person of the president. But with the advent of General Eisenhower the informal group took on the character of an organized agency with the Assistant to the President cast in the role of Chief of Staff.[17] Sherman Adams consequently presided over an organization with documents moving from one level to another within the White House Office. Adams had "a greater impact on the Presidency during the Eisenhower disability than that of any elective official."[18] It was due to the smoothly functioning staff that

[15] Charles J. Murphy, "Eisenhower's White House," *Fortune,* July, 1953, p. 77.

[16] "The Way Ike Runs His Job," *United States News and World Report,* December 31, 1954, pp. 31–33. See also in the same periodical, "A Day in the Life of the President," March 14, 1958, pp. 35–42.

[17] See J. R. Steelman and H. K. Kreager, "The Executive Office as Administrative Coordinator," *Law and Contemporary Problems,* Autumn, 1956 (Duke University Law School).

[18] E. S. Corwin and L. W. Koenig, *The Presidency Today* (1956), p. 116.

President Eisenhower's illnesses caused no such breaks in the continuity of executive functions as occurred in earlier cases of presidential indisposition.

Whenever Sherman Adams spoke, it was assumed that it represented President Eisenhower's views on a matter. Adams had attempted to grasp Eisenhower's views before backing him as the convention nominee in 1952. As the President's assistant he acquainted himself with his chief's views on many problems. He attended Cabinet meetings, National Security Council meetings, and all important staff conferences and came to learn how Eisenhower's mind worked in detail. Adams was a practical politician and had to break down the prejudices against politicians held by the businessmen with whom Eisenhower packed his Cabinet and he was said to have succeeded in this. When department heads differed with Adams, he talked it over until unanimous consent was obtained if possible, and differences had to yield before the President was told that a decision had been reached. A recalcitrant Cabinet member might be asked to take his objections to the President. The staff worked quite as planned even if it apparently gave the President rather too much opportunity to neglect the initiative in administration policies.[19]

The peculiar structure and functioning of the Eisenhower staff were eminently satisfactory to him. The evidence is overwhelming that President Eisenhower was bored by the operational side of government, and he made no effort to conceal it. In this he contrasted with Truman, to whom every phase of government was interesting. Eisenhower may have been just about the least interested in newspapers of any president since Lincoln, who was an avid and purposeful reader of them. Eisenhower frequently astonished a news conference with the statement "I never heard of that" concerning a matter of common knowledge to the public. Contributing to this strange phenomenon was his rule that he wanted

[19] See the "Presidency: Can One Man Do The Job," *U. S. News and World Report,* November 22, 1957, pp. 50–72.

a part in the administrative process only when the unanimity mentioned above had been attained. This limited his function to ratification or veto of the relatively few matters on which unanimity could be arrived at. Quite understandably a study of the Eisenhower methods by the London *Economist* led to the conclusion: "Amid the mechanical apparatus, the presidency is insulated from information and pressures which stimulate imagination, feed inspiration, foster insight, and develop sensitivity."[20]

Any budget for the ensuing year, whether that of a family, a municipality, or a nation, inevitably includes what the budget-maker believes should be the work program of the next year. More and more the president's budget is looked forward to by the public as a revelation of the administration's legislative program, and incidentally it constitutes his bid for electoral favor no matter how vehemently the arguments for its adoption may be couched in conventional terms of the national welfare. So that branch of the bureau designated the Office of Budget Review receives the estimates and supervises and prepares the budget itself in accordance with the presidential program. This office then is the technical agency for preparation of the president's detailed appeal to the Congress and the nation.

Because the budget inevitably involves the president's legislative program, it is logical that an Office of Legislative Reference should be located in the Bureau of the Budget. It is one more indication of the unplanned nature of emerging political institutions that the earliest forecast of the idea of this Office of Legislative Reference appears in a letter of Chairman Martin B. Madden, of the just-then-created House Appropriations Committee, to Budget Director Dawes in 1921, a month before Harding presented the very first presidential budget to Congress. Madden suggested central clearance of proposed legislation through the Budget Bureau.[21] Here was an observation that

---

[20] See Richard H. Rovere, *The Eisenhower Years* (1956), pp. 353–57.

[21] See Richard E. Neustadt, "Presidency and Legislation, The Growth of Central Clearance," *American Political Science Review*, XLVIII, No. 3 (Sept., 1954), 643.

apparently prompted the earliest presidential effort to assert central, that is presidential, control over the views of any Federal agency on pending legislation. However, the clearance required by Harding, Coolidge, and Hoover was only of charges on the Treasury. It was President Franklin Roosevelt's contribution to the development of central clearance to extend it to all agency proposals for legislation. So rapid was the spread of the area of executive clearance that, as early as 1939, the Legislative Reference Office of the Budget Bureau processed 2448 pending public bills.[22]

As organized today the Legislative Reference Office co-ordinates and clears for conforming with the program of the president all recommendations of Federal agencies on proposed legislation, enrolled bills, and executive orders. Even when a congressional committee requests from any administrative agency information and advice on proposed legislation, the response of the agency must be routed through the Legislative Reference Office back to the Congressional committee. The day is long past when a president hesitates to assume positive leadership in legislation. Indeed the machinery is so set up that the executive can scarcely avoid exercising this function. Even more notable is the fact that Congress has adjusted itself to this species of executive leadership. The President is now formally and literally the spokesman of the administration. Congress tends to be confused by the diverse advice by the experts of the administrative agencies. Functioning through the Legislative Reference Office the president can resolve this confusion at the same time that he can temper the sharp pressures of the lobbies and, if politically expert enough, he can serve as the organ for the expression of national consensuses.

There is another function of the Budget Bureau that marks the far cry from the middle period of our history when the president took the question of a presidential veto to his Cabinet and after due deliberation asked some member to prepare the veto message.

[22] *Ibid.*, p. 653.

Since 1938 the Budget Bureau has been the advisory agency of the President as to the signing or vetoing of bills passed by Congress. The value of this newly institutionalized veto function can be appreciated when the constitutional ten days permitted the president for considering this matter is recalled. A Budget Bureau circular of 1939 gave absolute priority to presidential requests for information on enacted bills, and any Budget Bureau recommendation against the president's signing a bill was to be accompanied by a draft of a tentative veto message or a memorandum of disapproval in case of a possible pocket veto. For example, the Bureau of the Budget obtained facsimile copies of the Taft-Hartley Bill before it reached the engrossed stage and transmitted them to administrative agencies and commissions concerned with the matter of the bill. Two of the agencies claimed no concern and made no recommendation; two pointed out defects but made no recommendations; one recommended that the President sign it; two refrained from recommendations because their representatives were participating in White House conferences on the bill; the Departments of Labor and of the Interior and the National Labor Relations Board advised veto, which advice the Bureau of the Budget forwarded to the President with its approval and recommendation.

President Truman consulted his cabinet members, and those most concerned with labor legislation advised veto. The White House staff with others were completing analyses, and when President Truman returned from an official trip to Canada, a leather brief case on his desk contained a complete analysis of the act. Veto was favored by a majority of the Cabinet, administration leaders in Congress, and the most influential members of the Democratic National Committee and leaders of organized labor. For forty-eight hours the President was closeted with his Counsel, Clark Clifford, Presidential Assistant Charles Murphy, and his Press Secretary, Charles Ross, writing the veto message that, 5500 words in length, was sent to the House on June 20. The Taft-Hartley Act was promptly passed over the President's veto by the two houses, but the reaction against it undoubtedly contributed somewhat to Truman's unanticipated election for a second term a year later.[23] At any rate, of the members of the House defeated for reelection that year all but four had voted to override that veto.

The Republican Eightieth Congress, asking the Budget Bureau for information on pending bills, was thereby sounding out the Truman administration's views on pending legislation. Regardless of party the practice increasingly took hold, providing a growing opportunity for the presidential views to be conveyed to Congress on important bills nearing the committee report stage. Thereby the president finds it possible consistently to make his signature or veto an instrument for shaping administration policies. Before inauguration day, 1953, most of President Eisenhower's Cabinet members designate were being briefed by the Budget Bureau on their work, with the clearance function of the Legislative Reference Office receiving due emphasis. Thanks to this apprenticeship the transition on this matter from the Truman to the Eisenhower administration was made smoothly. The procedure of reference had become stabilized. "Here is the oldest, toughest organism in the presidential orbit," declared Neustadt. "The making of the budget is still the prime general-purpose-decision-and-action forcing process yet institutionalized in the executive."[24]

World War II provided the seedbed of one of the important agencies of the Office of the Executive, the Council of Economic Advisers. As never before that war had required wholesale conversion of our industrial system to the production of the vast apparatus of modern warfare. When victory finally seemed near at hand, public opinion became engrossed with the problem of industrial reconversion to peacetime production. It was almost universally assumed that the interval of reconversion would entail a gigantic total of unemployment of unpredictable millions.

---

[23] Stephen K. Bailey and Howard D. Samuel, *Congress at Work* (1952), pp. 437–39.

[24] Richard E. Neustadt, "Presidency and Legislation, The Growth of Central Clearance," *Amer. Pol. Sci. Rev.,* XLVIII, No. 3 (Sept., 1954), 669.

Gradually there developed a demand for legislation designed to control employment, which culminated in the Employment Act of 1946. The purpose of the act was, through the Federal budget and other means to be recommended by the President, to aim at a balancing of the total public and private national investment with the total public and private national spending to the end that near full employment might be maintained. This would involve a countercyclical stepping-up at one stage and at another stage a deliberate cutting-down of government projects and spending. Since the initiative in this plan was vested in the President, he required expert economic advice on which to base his recommendations to Congress. For this purpose the Employment Act of 1946 created the Council of Economic Advisers to consist of three economists and made it a component agency of the Executive Office of the President. It is indicative of the potentialities of this council that President Eisenhower, apparently on the advice of business interests, at first considered abolishing the Council of Economic Advisers but soon recognized its importance and came to rely heavily upon its advice.

The genealogy of the Council of Economic Advisers appears to have been first the Office of War Mobilization, which was created in 1943 in order to co-ordinate all agencies that played a part in total mobilization in World War II and was to be christened a year later as the Office of War Mobilization and Reconversion. Functionally this was a forerunner of the Council of Economic Advisers of the Employment Act of 1946.[25] Thus a development that had started as an informal group, if not a clique, of advisers of the President had evolved through makeshift *ad hoc* agencies created by executive orders and had culminated in a permanent agency created by Congress, invested with statutory functions and located in the Executive Office of the President.

That the president needed competent economic advisers had been evident ever since President Roosevelt's erroneous prediction

[25] E. G. Nourse, *Economics in the Public Service* (1953), p. 65.

of continuous prosperity in 1936 on the very eve of the recession of the late 1930's. Informal groups had been providing most of the President's economic advice, and Congress in 1946 wanted to make sure that no longer would the source of such important information for the president come from secret sources and smack of palace intrigue. Hence Congress created the council and invested it with statutory authority. While designed to limit the president's freedom in seeking information, its very creation was an unconscious congressional confirmation and further institutionalizing of presidential leadership in legislation to maintain economic stability—then a novel conception of Federal responsibility.

In 1947 Congress created the National Security Council, now consisting of an ex-officio personnel: The president, vice-president, secretary of state, secretary of defense, director for mutual security, and director of the Office of Defense Mobilization. This council's function is to assess and appraise the objectives, commitments, and risks of the United States in respect to actual and potential military power in the interest of national security. This council is and will be what circumstances and the personal qualities of the incumbent of the presidential office make it. Global tensions gave it exceptional importance in the Eisenhower administration. The president's Cabinet, which had been declining in significance for more than a generation, continued this trend for a while under President Eisenhower, who sensed the extraordinary potentialities of the Security Council and presided over its frequent regular and special meetings. How important Eisenhower considered this agency was indicated by the statement of one of his associates: "It is apparent that he has done his homework when you see him preside over National Security Council Meetings."[26]

Institutionalize the presidency however much, the fact still

[26] "The Presidency: Too Big For One Man?" *U. S. News and World Report,* November 22, 1957, pp. 57.

stands that the president himself is indispensable. There are things extraordinarily significant the staff can never do. Professor Richard Neustadt has pointed out that, three days after President Eisenhower's heart attack, Cairo announced its deal for arms with the Czechs, which upset the entire power balance in the Middle East. American diplomacy was not caught by surprise, but under the circumstances of an incapacitated President nothing but futile protests and indecisive conferences took place. The circumstances called for decisive action by the one person with constitutional authority to give the orders. Some have speculated that a Truman might have ordered the Sixth Fleet to the Aegean to prevent shipment of Czech arms by sea or air. No one can say what Eisenhower might have done. This is but a sample of a set of circumstances that reveals the stark limitations of the staff and the absolute indispensability of the president to make decisions no one else on earth has the authority to make and execute.[27]

---

[27] See "The Presidency at Mid-Century," *Law and Contemporary Problems,* Autumn, 1956 (Duke University Law School), pp. 615–16.

I am indebted for some of the material in this chapter to Professor Lester G. Seligman's paper, "Informal Organization, Presidential Leadership, and Institutionalization: A Case Study," read at a panel discussion at the annual American Political Science Association meeting in Chicago, 1954.

* XI

The Commander-
in-Chief

* **IN MAKING** the President commander-in-chief of the armed forces of the nation, the framers of the Constitution were following precisely the model to which they had turned with one accord for the presidential office, that of the state governor, whom twelve of the thirteen state constitutions had made commander-in-chief of the state's military forces. Incidentally, in one sense at least, the Revolutionary state governors were by no means mere ciphers, as they assumed paramount leadership whenever British invasion of their states required mobilization of the state's militia. The placing of the supreme authority over the military in the hands of the chief civilian officer of the nation was in accord with the current development of English constitutional history and, as it turned out, of English-speaking peoples everywhere. More than a century before Premier George Clemenceau declared that "war is too important a business to be entrusted to the soldiers." That very idea had been planted securely in the constitutions of the American Revolutionary states and then carried over into the Constitution of the United States.

The Constitution of the United States prescribes succinctly: "The President shall be Commander-in-Chief of the Army and Navy of the United States and of the militia of the several states

when called into the active service of the United States."[1] A mis-
conception as to the nature of the commander-in-chiefship has
somehow crept into the prevailing pattern of our thinking. It is
not at all an extra office in addition to that of chief executive.
The function of commander-in-chiefship is simply one of the
means to the fundamental purpose of the presidency, that is,
seeing to the execution of the law. "Presidents have been wont
to assert the title (Commander-in-Chief) to eke out a paucity
of statutory power," observed Charles Fairman. He continued,
"But the President does not, in the English phrase, 'wear two
hats.' Being Commander-in-Chief is merely one of the incidents
inseparable from his office."[2]

Did investing the president with the commander-in-chiefship
mean that he might assume command of the army in the field?
"Did the framers expect or intend the President to do this?"
asked the late Charles A. Beard and then proceeded to answer
his question. "I am of the opinion that many of them did. Of this
I am fairly sure." Beard then proceeded to cite the statement of
Luther Martin, who was a delegate in the Constitutional Convention at Philadelphia. Concerning the debates there Martin said,
"It was wished to be so far restrained that he should not command
in person but this could not be obtained. Hamilton and Patterson
likewise proposed the same restraint but it was not adopted."[3]
Since it was universally taken for granted that General Washington, who was presiding over the Convention's deliberations,
would be the first President of the United States, it might have
seemed not quite courteous to have inserted such a restriction in
the Constitution.

President Washington was present at the mobilization of the
15,000 militiamen he sent against the whisky rebels of western
Pennsylvania in 1794, but he did not lead them in the field.

[1] Art. 2, sec. 2, clause 1.
[2] "The President as Commander-in-Chief" in Robert S. Rankin (ed.), *The Presidency in Transition, Journal of Politics*, xi, 1949, p. 145.
[3] C. A. Beard, *The Republic* (1944), p. 101.

Joseph Story in his *Commentaries on the Constitution,* published almost half a century later, thought "it would be dangerous to let him command in person without any restraint as he might make bad use of it."[4] President Jackson's intimate adviser, Martin Van Buren, reveals that Jackson yearned to lead in person the 35,000 troops he was prepared to summon to march against the South Carolina nullificationists in 1833 before the impasse was composed by Clay's Compromise Tariff.[5]

During actual or even expected war the president may delegate command of the nation's armed forces to one person. Thus, in 1798, when preparations were being made for an expected war with France, President Adams appointed Washington lieutenant general and Commander-in-Chief of the army being raised. Lincoln's Attorney General, Bates, contended that "no general-in-chief should be selected but that Lincoln should exercise his constitutional prerogative as Commander-in-Chief and assume personal direction of operations in the field." Lincoln appointed one commander after another over the Army of the Potomac until he discovered Grant's superior ability and appointed him general-in-chief of the Union armies. Lincoln's fatherly letter to General Hooker when, with due diffidence, he appointed him to the command of the Army of the Potomac in 1863 reveals the commander-in-chiefship at high tide. The letter leaves no doubt that Lincoln was no mere titular Commander-in-Chief. (See the copy of this letter at end of this chapter.)

No matter what authority Adams and Lincoln delegated to the sole commander of the nation's armed forces, these presidents were still commanders-in-chief. Lincoln in 1862 issued an order for a general advance against Richmond by the forces under General McClellan. President Wilson in 1918 decided against merging American armed forces in France with those of the Allies

---

[4] *Commentaries on the Constitution of the United States* (3 vols., Boston, 1883), Sec. 1492.

[5] Martin Van Buren, *Autobiography* (John F. Fitzpatrick, ed., 1920), p. 544.

on the Western Front and maintained instead an independent American command. President Truman in 1945 made the momentous decision to order dropping the atomic bombs on Hiroshima and Nagasaki. Not just by constitutional delegation alone but also by the fundamental principles of international law does the president possess all the military power inhering in any supreme commander of a nation. "He may invade the hostile country and subject it to the sovereignty and authority of the United States."[6] If foreign territory is occupied, its government falls under the president's rule until Congress decides otherwise, but annexation of such territory is absolutely beyond his authority. Control of the secret service inheres in the president's commander-in-chiefship. He has authority to suspend hostilities by means of an armistice, the terms of which he may stipulate. As commander-in-chief his is the ultimate tribunal for enforcing the rules and regulations Congress prescribes for the government of the armed forces, which however he may amend at will in time of war.

What then are the limits of the power of the commander-in-chief? The late Charles A. Beard, who, as the dean of American historians and political scientists and especially as an authority on constitutional law and history, had given about as much thought to the question as anyone, concluded that "the war powers of the President are in fact so great and so indefinite that their nature will not be fully known until our Republic has passed through all its trials and ceased to be. The President's war powers are the unexplored 'Dark Continent' of American Government."[7]

The first experience with the commander-in-chiefship in a foreign war was in the War of 1812, and it was an unhappy one. President Madison was not cast for such a role. Washington Irving, writing at the time, considered him "a withered little Applejohn." The country was divided on the issue of war and

---

[6] Fleming v. Page, 9 Howard 603, 615 (1815).
[7] *The Republic* (1944) p. 103.

utterly unprepared for it. It required six months to clear incompetent heads out of the War and Navy Departments and a year more before successful generals such as Andrew Jackson and W. H. Harrison were in high command. The standing army was practically nonexistent so that the President, in June, 1812, sent a call to the governors of the seaboard states for quotas of militia to guard the seacoast. The call was made pursuant to congressional legislation. The Constitution authorizes the Congress "to provide for calling forth the militia to execute the laws of the Union, suppress insurrections, and repel invasions."[8] Unfortunately the Constitution does not designate the authority that is to decide when an emergency justifies summoning the militia into Federal service, and the governors of Massachusetts and Connecticut in 1812 refused to respond to the call arguing that they instead of the President had the authority to decide when the necessity existed for calling the militia into the Federal service.

Indicative of the prevailing confusion as to where the seat of military authority resided in 1812–1815 was the fact that, when the Governor of Vermont in 1813 attempted to recall the Vermont troops in the midst of the war, the troops refused to obey and sent back to the Governor the defiant reply, "We will not obey, but will continue in the service of our country until discharged."[9] The constitutional issue, along with others, was ultimately resolved authoritatively by a decision of the Supreme Court of the United States in 1827. Justice Joseph Story, delivering the opinion of the Court, declared that the president is the sole judge of the existence of the emergency and his judgment is conclusive; the militia when called are subject to the commander-in-chief or any superior officer he appoints.[10] That settled the matter.

The Mexican War taught us that the commander-in-chief can present a *fait accompli* that leaves Congress no choice but to declare war. On January 13, 1846, President Polk ordered

---

[8] Art. 1, sec. 8, clause 15.
[9] A. C. McLaughlin, *Constitutional History of the United States* (1935), p. 350.
[10] Martin *v.* Mott, 12 Wheaton 19 *et seq.* (1827).

American troops to cross the Nueces River into disputed territory claimed by both the United States and Mexico. In May President Polk presented for the consideration of the cabinet his decision to ask Congress for a declaration of war. Fortunately for the President before the day ended came news of the outbreak of hostilities between American and Mexican troops. Polk promptly informed Congress that "now, after reiterated menaces Mexico has invaded our territory and shed American blood on American soil."[11] When the act of Congress of May 13th, 1846, which recognized "a state of war as existing by act of the Republic of Mexico," was passed, the battles of Palo Alto and Resaca de la Palma had been fought and won by General Taylor's army. President Polk had demonstrated the powers of the commander-in-chief to initiate war. But only Congress can legalize a state of war.

It was the Civil War that provided the first great opportunity to experiment with the ability and scope of the commander-in-chiefship. With the bombardment of Ft. Sumter overt armed resistance to Federal authority began. Lincoln promptly issued a call for 75,000 militia, under the Act of 1795, by which Congress had authorized such a call in Washington's administration. Lincoln's proclamation declared that the laws of the United States had been opposed and that the execution thereof had been obstructed by combinations too powerful to be suppressed by the ordinary course of judicial proceedings or by the powers vested in the marshals by law. These state militia, thus called into the service of the United States, became subject to the Commander-in-Chief in accordance with the Constitution's provision to that effect.

Mobilizing the militia was strictly constitutional. But the emergency was great and required prompt action. Congress was not then in session and indeed, in those days, could not have been promptly convened. So it was called to convene July 4, nearly

[11] James D. Richardson, *Messages and Papers of the Presidents* (1927), IV, 442.

three months after the fall of Ft. Sumter. Meanwhile Lincoln, assuming that the emergency justified extraordinary measures on the part of the Commander-in-Chief, executed one move after another, the authority for which the Constitution has explicitly vested in Congress. Thus Lincoln ordered the regular army increased by 22,714 officers and men and the navy by 18,000, and he called for 42,034 volunteers for three years. This could be justified by no interpretation of the powers of the commander-in-chief under the Constitution, which unequivocally vests in Congress the power to "raise and support armies." When Congress convened, Lincoln invited it to grant him retroactive authority for what he had done without authority. "These measures," he informed Congress, "whether strictly legal or not, were ventured upon under what appeared to be a popular demand and a public necessity, trusting then as now, that Congress would ratify them. It is believed that nothing has been done *beyond* the constitutional competence of Congress."[12]

Confronted by what Lincoln had done and by public opinion supporting it, Congress had no choice but to grant Lincoln's request, and the courts did not challenge that ratification. The consequence of such congressional action then and since has been almost incalculable. It has led Professor Clinton Rossiter to conclude that "since we are entitled to assume from past performances that the court regards the war powers of Congress as limited only by the necessities of the case, which are for Congress to ascertain, there is apparently nothing the President cannot do *constitutionally* if war should strike the country."[13]

Lincoln's disregard of constitutional prescriptions continued throughout the Civil War. Despite the Constitution's specific delegation to Congress of the power "to make rules for the government and regulation of the land and naval forces,"[14]

---

[12] *Ibid.,* VI, p. 24.
[13] *The Supreme Court and the Commander-in-Chief* (1951), pp. 101–02.
[14] Art. 1, sec. 8, clause 14.

Lincoln promulgated the elaborate code of rules applicable to armies in the field prepared at his direction by Francis Lieber. Nor can such power be presumed to inhere in the commander-in-chief when the Constitution specifically vests it in Congress. Because Lincoln distrusted certain subordinates, he directed the Secretary of the Treasury to advance without security $2,000,000 of public money to three private citizens for the purpose of paying for certain military and naval measures, and this, despite the Constitution's provision, "No money shall be drawn from the treasury but in consequence of appropriation made by law."[15] All these ultraconstitutional acts Lincoln serenely reported to Congress.[16]

Suspension of the privilege of the writ of habeas corpus may, under certain circumstances, be incidental to the commander-in-chiefship. At the very beginning of the Civil War Federal troops moving through Maryland to Washington were interfered with, and fatal casualties occurred. Lincoln consequently authorized the commanding general of the army to suspend the writ of habeas corpus "at any point or in the vicinity of any military line which is now or should be used between Philadelphia and the city of Washington."[17] Chief Justice Taney nevertheless attempted in vain to have the writ of habeas corpus served in behalf of one Merryman. Upon failure Taney issued in chambers his protest that Lincoln's order was unconstitutional, since the provision authorizing the suspension of the writ is located in the legislative article of the Constitution,[18] and that it could not have been intended that the president possessed the power of suspension.[19] Contrary to Taney's view Lincoln argued that the framers could not have intended to leave the power of suspending the habeas corpus

---

[15] Art. 1, sec. 9, clause 7.
[16] James D. Richardson, *Messages and Papers of the Presidents* (1927), VI, 79.
[17] *Ibid.*, 18.
[18] Art. 1, sec. 9, clause 2.
[19] Ex parte Merryman, 17 Fed. Cas. No. 9487 (1861).

privilege solely to Congress, since that would mean "that in every case the danger should run its course until Congress could be called together, the very assembling of which might be prevented, as was intended in this case," that is, the Merryman case.[20]

At the opening of hostilities in 1861 Lincoln, as Commander-in-Chief, proclaimed a blockade of the belligerent states thereby throwing a perplexing problem into the lap of the courts. Blockade is no power of the president prescribed by the Constitution but instead is derived from international law. How could international law apply in a Civil War, that is, an internal instead of an international war? The Supreme Court, justifying the blockade as an exercise of the president's powers as commander-in-chief, reasoned: "The parties belligerent in a public war are independent nations. But it is not necessary to constitute war, that both parties should be acknowledged as independent or sovereign states. A war may exist where one of the belligerents claims sovereign rights as against the other."[21] Lincoln issued the Emancipation Proclamation as a military order of the Commander-in-Chief designed among other purposes to reduce the labor force of the insurrectionists, and its constitutionality has never been judicially challenged.

The military tribunals established by Lincoln for the trial of civilians were ultimately held to be unconstitutional, but not before hostilities had ended and Lincoln had been assassinated. In September, 1862, the President had issued a proclamation in support of the draft declaring all persons resisting or discouraging voluntary enlistments to be subject to martial law and trial by court martial without the privilege of the writ of habeas corpus. In October, 1864, one Milligan, an alleged major general in the Sons of Liberty, a Copperhead or disloyal organization, was convicted of conspiracy to release rebel prisoners and was sentenced to be hanged on May 9, 1865. By that date the war was over,

[20] E. S. Corwin, *The President: Office and Powers* (1957), p. 230.
[21] Prize Cases, 2 Black 635, 666–667 (1863).

Lincoln was dead, and the case was carried to the Supreme Court, which held that the President had lacked authority to institute the military tribunals outside the actual theater of war where civil courts were functioning. The Court confined the role of president as commander-in-chief to "the command of the forces and the conduct of campaigns."[22] In the hysteria following Lincoln's assassination the decision provoked bitter recrimination against the Court, but the decision has never been judicially reversed. However, it can scarcely be successfully controverted that "the law of the Constitution is what Lincoln did in the crisis not what the Court said later."[23]

President Lincoln's apologia of his extraordinarily broad interpretation of his authority as President and Commander-in-Chief was epitomized in his letter to A. G. Hodges, dated April 4, 1864, in which he wrote:

My oath to preserve the Constitution imposed on me the duty of preserving by every indispensable means that government, that nation, of which the Constitution was the organic law. Was it possible to lose the nation and yet preserve the Constitution? By general law life and limb must be protected, yet often a limb must be amputated to save a life but a life is never wisely given to save a limb. I felt that measures otherwise unconstitutional, might become lawful by becoming indispensable to the preservation of the Constitution through preservation of the nation. Right or wrong, I assumed this ground and now avow it. I could not feel that, to the best of my ability, I had ever tried to preserve the Constitution, if to save slavery or any minor matter, I should permit the wreck of the government, country, and Constitution altogether.[24]

As early as December 20, 1861, Congress was challenging Lincoln's commander-in-chiefship and sought to share the war power through a Joint Committee on the Conduct of the War.

[22] Ex parte Milligan, 4 Wallace 2 (1866).
[23] Clinton Rossiter, *The Supreme Court and the Commander-in-Chief* (1951), p. 39.
[24] Nicolay and Hay, *Works of Abraham Lincoln* (1894), x, 65–68.

Designed ostensibly to assist Congress in the performance of its constitutional war powers, it so far exceeded its constitutional power as to take over partial control of military operations.[25] Their investigating missions at the front undermined army discipline and discouraged competent commanders. The favorites of these "deputies on mission" were Generals Fremont, Butler, and Hooker, three of the less competent commanders in the Union army. Interrogating generals as if they were school boys and advising the President like military experts, the committee sought to intimidate Lincoln by threatening to turn Congress against him.[26] Only Lincoln's extraordinary resourcefulness in outmaneuvering Congress together with his support by loyal public opinion enabled him to maintain unimpaired the authority of the President throughout his incumbency.

No sooner were we in World War I than Congress, quite naturally, turned to the Civil War for precedents and the guidance that the experience then might afford. Three months after the Declaration of War a movement developed in Congress to establish a bipartisan committee of the two houses on the conduct of the war. It was President Wilson's familiarity with our political history that enabled him to counter the move to repeat the strange arrangement that had proved to be such an annoyance to Lincoln, and Wilson's protest promptly scotched the project. Later there was a strong movement for a coalition Cabinet to be headed by ex-President Theodore Roosevelt. Democratic Senator Chamberlain of Oregon led the movement arguing that the military establishment had "broken down and almost stopped functioning because of inefficiency in every bureau and every department of the Government."[27] Just as Asquith's government in England had failed, only to be succeeded by the Lloyd George Coalition cabinet,

[25] G. W. Dimock, *Congressional Investigating Committees* (1929), p. 112.
[26] G. W. Julian, *Political Recollections 1840–1872* (1874), p. 205.
[27] W. E. Dodd, *Woodrow Wilson and his Work* (1922), p. 253; Lindsay Rogers, "Presidential Dictatorship in the United States," *Quarterly Review*, CCXXXI (1919), 141.

so was Theodore Roosevelt heralded as the potential savior of the United States and destined to head a coalition Cabinet.

President Wilson countered this congressional maneuver with neat Lincolnian strategy by sending to Congress a bill asking for a grant to himself of the very powers proposed for the war Cabinet. The result was the Overman Act giving the president practically the powers of a dictator in redistributing the functions, duties, and powers of administrative agencies and personnel of the government as he might deem necessary for the successful prosecution of the war. This move to curb the President in the midst of the war collapsed, and when the clash of arms in France grew furious, the American people gave overwhelming support to the President. An unprecedented hysteria against criticism of the government seized the American people and spread from the people to the Department of Justice and even to the courts, which gave severe sentences for remarks that today would seem to have been no more than legitimate discussion of public issues. However, no civilians were tried by military courts as during the Civil War. Every sentence was given by a civil court after a verdict by a jury, which however also reflected the prevailing hysteria. Official authority, combined with a reign of social terror, drove criticism of the executive under ground. "Senators of sovereign states and leaders of parties groveled in their marble corridors so terrified were they of public opinion."[28]

Confidential information following the Munich debacle in 1938 convinced President Franklin D. Roosevelt that another war in Europe was imminent and that the United States must rearm. When World War II began in Europe, President Roosevelt issued executive orders increasing the army, navy, and marine corps under statutory authority. But he had to await the development of events for the accumulating public opinion that would support rearmament and convert the United States into what he conceived to be the "arsenal of democracy." The fall of France in June, 1940, created an alarm that induced the necessary crystallization of

[28] G. R. Brown, *The Leadership of Congress* (1922), p. 187.

public opinion, and Congress then voted the required appropriations. When Poland fell, the President declared a "limited emergency" based on statutes enacted from time to time during half a
century. When France fell, he declared an "unlimited emergency."
Britain's situation seemed desperate. She had lost most of her military equipment at Dunkerque. She needed destroyers especially
and Roosevelt made a "Yankee horse trade" by which he conveyed
to Britain overage destroyers in return for a ninety-nine-year use
of naval and air bases in west Atlantic islands belonging to Britain.
This deal had violated at least two statutes, and the President had
asserted and exercised a power specifically assigned to Congress
by the Constitution. However his action was defended by Attorney
General Jackson, soon to be an Associate Justice of the Supreme
Court, as resting strangely enough on his power as Commander-
in-Chief to "dispose" the armed forces of the United States. Unlike Lincoln, in similar circumstances, Roosevelt did not ask Congress to ratify his action. So gratified was Roosevelt over the deal
for the air fields that he pronounced it "the most important action
in reinforcing our defense since the Louisiana Purchase."[29]

The arsenal of democracy was enabled freely to supply the foreign armed forces battling the axis through the Lend-Lease statute
enacted by Congress, which authorized the president "to transfer
title, to exchange, lease, lend or otherwise dispose of any defense
article." So sweeping was the authority conferred by this statute
that the venerable John Bassett Moore criticised Congress for ab-
dicating its power "to declare war," "grant letters of marque and
reprisal," "raise armies," "provide and maintain a navy," and
"regulate land and naval forces." Thus congressional powers that
Lincoln cavalierly appropriated, Congress freely turned over to
President Roosevelt, even though the Constitution delegated them
unequivocally to Congress.

One of the strangest episodes in the history of the presidency is
President Franklin Roosevelt's Labor Day address to Congress

---

[29] Roosevelt, *Public Papers* (1940), p. 5.

in 1942 in which he coupled a demand for the repeal of the six-month-old Emergency Price Control Act with the most audacious threat ever delivered by a president face to face with Congress.

> In event that the Congress should fail to act adequately [he declared] I shall accept the responsibility and I will act . . . . I have given the most thoughtful consideration to meeting this issue without further reference to Congress. I have determined in this vital matter to consult with Congress . . . . The American people can be sure that I will use my power with a full sense of responsibility to the Constitution and to my country. The American people can be sure that I shall not hesitate to use every power vested in me to defeat our enemies in any part of the world where our safety demands such defeat. When the war is won, the powers under which I act automatically revert to the people to whom they belong.

Where did the President get this extraordinary power? From the people, he implied, when he said, "When the war is won the powers under which I act automatically revert to the people to whom they belong." How the sovereign conveyed these powers was never revealed. Presumably Roosevelt conceived the powers to be derived from prerogatives of the "Commander-in-Chief in war time." At any rate the Labor Day address to Congress represented the most extreme assertion of the president's war power by Roosevelt.

It may be possible to cover the extralegal and even extraconstitutional acts of Lincoln, Wilson, and the two Roosevelts with the mantle of the "stewardship theory" of the first Roosevelt. Something like this seems necessary in order to rationalize the so-called emergency powers of the president. In time of war it becomes a means of justifying such extraordinary assumption of powers specifically delegated to Congress as Lincoln cavalierly exercised during the four months between the fall of Sumter and the convening of the special session of Congress, July 4, 1861. These acts of Lincoln indubitably went far beyond the mere exercise of the president's commander-in-chiefship. How else can Franklin Roosevelt's "Yankee horse trade" of destroyers in exchange for the lease by Britain of sites for air bases be justified than as an exercise of presidential stewardship of the American people's interest in survival? And Roosevelt's breath-taking assurance to his "children," the Congress, in the preceding paragraph would apparently prove to be classified under "The Stewardship Theory in Total War."[30]

World War II brought an unprecedented instance of wholesale invasion of the civil rights of American citizens. On February 19, 1942, President Roosevelt issued an executive order "by virtue of the authority vested in me as President of the United States and Commander-in-Chief of the Army and Navy," as he expressed it in directing the Secretary of War to take action that excluded Japanese from certain designated areas near the West Coast and removed 112,000 of them from their farms and homes, first to temporary camps, and later to relocation centers, mainly in desert areas of the West. It was apparently the President's intention to base this action on his power as Commander-in-Chief. It was, of course, impossible to legalize the segregation of these Japanese literally as alien enemies since two-thirds of them were citizens of the United States. One Korematsu confessedly violated the order excluding persons of Japanese ancestry from forbidden areas and failed to report to an assembly center. In this case the Supreme Court upheld "the exclusion order as of the time it was made, and when the petitioner (Korematsu) violated it," as the opinion of the majority of the Court was cautiously expressed by Justice Black. He stated further, as justification of the order, "When, under conditions of modern warfare, our shores are threatened by hostile forces, the power to protect must be commensurable with the threatened danger."[31] Dissenting opinions, no less than Justice Black's, revealed how unhappy the Court was over the matter. Four weeks after the President's executive order, Congress enacted a supporting statute that, because of its lack of safeguards of civil rights, was pronounced by E. S. Corwin

[30] See E. S. Corwin, *The President: Office and Powers* (1957), pp. 250–52.
[31] Korematsu *v.* U. S., 323 U. S. 214 (1944).

"just about the most heartless measure ever enacted by the American Congress."[32]

Historically world-policing to protect American citizens and property has been a function of the president as commander-in-chief, with 149 instances between 1798 and 1945 counted by James Grafton Rogers.[33] For example, in 1846 Lieutenant Hollis of *U.S.S. Cyane* bombarded Greytown, Nicaragua, when reparations for the attack of a mob on the United States consul were not forthcoming. President McKinley in 1900 sent 5,000 American troops to join the international military force that went to the relief of foreign legations besieged in Peking by Chinese Boxers, as they were called. The extent to which circumstances determine what the president can do policing the world to protect American citizens is brought into relief by the contrast between how very much President McKinley could do to protect American citizens in China in 1900 and how very little President Eisenhower could do about American airmen held captive by the Chinese in 1955.

On June 24, 1950, a full-scale invasion of South Korea was begun by Communist armies of North Korea. The next day the Security Council of the United Nations Organization denounced the aggression, called for an immediate cease fire, and asked member nations of the United Nations to take action against the invaders. The following day President Truman ordered General MacArthur to aid the South Koreans, which order the Security Council endorsed and then made General MacArthur the United Nations Commander.

Despite the abundant authority under which President Truman acted in resisting Communist aggression in South Korea, he came under a storm of partisan criticism for not having consulted Congress, which alone can declare war. Excited stump speakers during the presidential campaign of 1952 made the most of this by denouncing the Korean conflict as Truman's War. In order

[32] *Total War and the Constitution* (1947), p. 98.
[33] *World Policy and the Constitution* (1945), pp. 92–123.

to forestall another such partisan charge and also to convince Communist China of the essential unity of the American people, President Eisenhower in 1955 asked Congress for a resolution approving in advance military action he might order in defense of Formosa. President Eisenhower frankly stated in his message asking for the resolution his conviction that he already possessed the power. This, thought Richard H. Rovere, "was to act as if the Bricker amendment, which was narrowly defeated in the last Congress and might be narrowly passed in this one, was so sound in principle that its provisions should be honored even without being enacted into law . . . . But any future President who neglects to ask Congress's leave in a matter of this sort will be accused of ignoring the admirable precedent set by Mr. Eisenhower in 1955."[34] While passage of the resolution forestalled calling any resulting hostilities Eisenhower's War, the price paid for that advantage was high in the limitation the precedent set on the freedom of the commander-in-chief in exercising his essential world-policing function in the very midst of the Cold War and with a sudden outburst of nuclear war not impossible.

In January, 1957, in the thick of the Middle East crisis, President Eisenhower again asked Congress for a blank check, this time for authority to provide economic aid and armed support to any Middle East nation requesting it against a Communist threat. Although public opinion, as measured by Gallup polls, appeared to support economic aid 70 per cent for to 19 per cent against and the dispatching of troops 50 per cent for to 34 per cent against, Congress engaged in a prolonged debate and was consequently less prompt than on the Formosa resolution. There were complaints about the cost, the danger of goading Russia into war, and significantly, about Eisenhower "trying to pass the buck to Congress." After two months of debate Congress voted an appropriation of two hundred million dollars for economic-military aid in the Middle East along with the curiously phrased resolution

---

[34] "Letter from Washington," *New Yorker*, Feb. 26, 1955, pp. 88, 89.

that "if the President determines the necessity thereof, the United States is prepared to use armed forces to assist any nation or group of nations requesting assistance against armed aggression from any country controlled by international communism."[35] Thus Congress washed its hands of responsibility for such a move and threw it squarely back in the lap of the President.

What then are the limits of the power of the president as commander-in-chief? In time of war Congress in practice can exercise no restraint as the careers of war presidents Abraham Lincoln and Franklin Roosevelt indubitably demonstrated. Nor can the courts do any better. There is the ominous warning of Justice Jackson, "If the people ever let command of war power fall into irresponsible and unscrupulous hands the courts wield no power equal to restraint."[36] With the legislative and judicial branches incapable of restraining the president's exercise of his power as commander-in-chief, then only the will of the sovereign—the American people functioning through public opinion—can do it if it is to be done at all.

The institutionalizing of the commander-in-chiefship is one of the striking developments of recent years. It is a far cry from the Spanish-American War when, "as his own Chief of Staff, McKinley carried on the war,"[37] to the present elaborate implementation of the office of the commander-in-chief. The most important arm of the commander-in-chief is the National Security Council, consisting of the vice-president of the United States, the secretaries of state and defense, the director of mutual security, and the director of the Office of Defense Mobilization. The Security Council advises the president with respect to the integration of domestic, foreign, and military policies relating to national security. President Eisenhower gave this council such particular emphasis and attention that for a while his Cabinet

[35] See Thomas A. Bailey, *A Diplomatic History of the American People* (1958), pp. 944–45.
[36] Korematsu *v.* U. S., 323 U. S. 214, 248 (1944).
[37] W. H. Taft, *The National McKinley Birthplace Memorial* (1918), p. 78.

seemed to fade into the background. Auxiliary to the Security Council is the Central Intelligence Agency, whose mission is that of co-ordinating the intelligence activities of the departments concerned with the national security. The Office of Defense Mobilization controls and co-ordinates mobilization activities including production, procurement, manpower, stabilization, and transport services. The business aspects of war are administered by the Department of Defense with its three component Departments of the Army, Navy, and Air Force.

No matter how elaborate the apparatus set up to institutionalize the office, the president still remains *the* commander-in-chief. Never could that have been more decisively manifested than in the Formosan crisis of 1955. That the Joint Chiefs of Staff, important as they are, are purely advisory and possess not a spark of authority—with the president perfectly free, with respect to their advice, to take it or leave it—was demonstrated absolutely. Admiral Bradley, Chairman of the Joint Chiefs of Staff, insisted in vain on a blockade of Communist China. Richard H. Rovere observed that "in almost every case the President has pursued the exact opposite of the course recommended by the Joint Chiefs."[38] Despite all the apparatus the president is still as much of a commander-in-chief as he has the capacity and will to be.

[38] *The Eisenhower Years* (1956), p. 249.

LINCOLN'S LETTER TO
GENERAL JOSEPH HOOKER
JANUARY 26, 1863

Executive Mansion
Washington, January 26, 1863.

Major General Hooker:

General.

I have placed you at the head of the Army of the Potomac. Of course I have done this upon what appear to me to be sufficient reasons. And yet I think it best for you to know that there are some things in regard to which, I am not quite satisfied with you. I believe you to be a brave and skilful soldier, which, of course, I like. I also believe you do not mix politics with your profession, in which you are right. You have confidence in yourself, which is a valuable, if not an indispensable quality. You are ambitious, which, within reasonable bounds, does good rather than harm. But I think that during Gen. Burnside's command of the army, you have taken counsel of your ambition, and thwarted him as much as you could, in which you did a great wrong to the country, and to a most meritorious and honorable brother officer. I have heard, in such a way as to believe it, of your recently saying that both the Army and the Government needed a Dictator. Of course it was not for this, but in spite of it, that I have given you the command. Only those generals who gain successes, can set up dictators. What I now ask of you is military success, and I will risk the dictatorship. The government will support you to the utmost of it's ability, which is neither more or less than it has done and will do for all commanders. I much fear that the spirit which you have aided to infuse into the Army, of criticizing their Commander, and withholding confidence from him, will now turn upon you. I shall assist you as far as I can, to put it down. Neither you, nor Napoleon, if he were alive again, could get any good out of an army, while such a spirit prevails in it.

And now, beware of rashness. Beware of rashness, but with energy, and sleepless vigilance, go forward, and give us victories.

Yours very truly

A. Lincoln.

The President

as Chief Diplomat

* "O U R   P R O C E D U R E S for the democratic
review and execution of international engagements are . . . in an
unholy mess,"[1] declared President Dickey of Dartmouth College
several years ago. It should be emphasized that this stricture was
on procedure and not on policy. That the management of foreign
relations is difficult enough for any self-governing people was
demonstrated, for example, by the acrimonious debate in Britain's
Parliament on the Egyptian debacle of 1956, but for the people
of the United States it is complicated by the inflexible prescriptions of the written Constitution only somewhat less than by per-
during usages of the unwritten constitution. In mid-twentieth
century the strain consequent upon our peculiar system for the
determination and execution of foreign policies has been intensified by the fact that the leadership of the free world suddenly
fell into the lap of the United States. The sudden realization in
1957 that we could no longer negotiate as the master power created a crisis.

It is in the management of foreign relations as nowhere else in
the American system of government that except in crisis there is

[1]Quoted by Hans J. Morgenthau in "Conduct of American Foreign Policy,"
Parliamentary Affairs, III, No. 1 (Winter, 1949), 158.

such a dilemma as between what, on the one hand, it seems ought to be done and on the other hand what the oracle of public opinion will permit. Here is where president and secretary of state must, from time to time, consider whether to sacrifice apparently sound policy to the prejudices of a perverse public opinion, aggravated often enough by an irresponsible demagoguery, or seek to promote sound policy by a legerdemain that leaves the public wondering where the rabbit came from. In a critical era it may call for the cultivation of the delicate art of walking on eggs.

Nobody can tell just what the framers of the Constitution intended by the provision that the president "shall have power, by and with the advice and consent of the Senate, to make treaties, provided that two-thirds of the Senators present concur." It is a curious if not significant fact that the semifinal draft of the Constitution, that is, the report of the Committee of Eleven in the Constitutional Convention when it was near the end of its three months of deliberations, provided that "the Senate of the United States shall have the power to make treaties and appoint ambassadors." This was changed to the final form quoted in the opening sentence of this paragraph only ten days before adjournment of the Convention *sine die*. This provision, which would have vested management of foreign affairs exclusively in the Senate, was a natural one since all treaties of the United States then in force had been made by the Continental Congress when there was no chief executive to share the power. It was the Father of the Constitution, Madison himself, who rose in the Constitutional Convention to protest against vesting the treaty power solely in the Senate. That body, he observed, represented the states alone, and for this and other reasons he thought the president as representing the nation should also be an agent in making treaties. An inconclusive debate ensued, and the final arrangement as to treaty-making was determined by the Committee of Five that gave the Constitution its final form and phrasing.

Presumably vesting exclusive treaty power in the president might have jeopardized the rights of the states, of which the

Senate was to be the guardian. However, inclusion of the Senate in treaty-making introduced an element of discord in the formulation of foreign policy, which the very growth of the Senate in numbers has intensified. Statistically inclined commentators have calculated that senators representing considerably less than 10 per cent of the total population of the United States could veto the painfully negotiated work of the executive. The Supreme Court has held that not only does a treaty repeal a statute repugnant to it, but a statute likewise repeals a standing treaty. Since that puts the two on a par as to validity, it has been plausibly argued that treaties be negotiated by the president and submitted to Congress and validated like statutes by simple majority votes of the two houses. But since this would require an amendment to the Constitution, it is inconceivable that the Senate would, in the foreseeable future, give the two-thirds vote for a constitutional amendment surrendering the tremendous treaty power it now wields. Thus it was not until the accumulation of the overwhelming pressures of powerful interest groups that the long-delayed ratification of the St. Lawrence Seaway treaty was effected.

The government under the Constitution was only four months old when President Washington, confronted with the negotiation of a treaty, had to attempt a practical interpretation of the treaty clause of the Constitution. He knew that the governor's council of the colonial and the succeeding state governments was the prototype of the United States Senate. There was as yet no thought of a president's Cabinet and Washington quite naturally assumed that the Senate, which then consisted of only 22 members,[2] would be his advisory council. He confidently expected oral communication with the Senate preparatory to the negotiation of treaties. It has already been related[3] how he came to the Senate in August 22, 1789, and took the chair of the vice-president just as a state governor had customarily taken the chair of the lieutenant governor whenever he came to the council. In the words of

[2] North Carolina and Rhode Island had not yet ratified the Constitution.
[3] See p. 10.

querulous Senator Maclay, Washington "told us bluntly that he had called on us for our advice and consent to some propositions respecting the treaty to be held with the Southern Indians."[4] What Washington desired and confidently expected was the advice of his council, that is, the Senate, to guide him in the negotiations, but such expectations were dashed by Senator Maclay's objection to answering the questions without more information. Senator Maclay spoke up because he was certain if he did not no one else would "and we should have these advice and consents rushed in a degree from us."[5]

It became evident that the Senate would not give "advice and consent" on plans for treaties with the President looking on and, as some senators feared, overawing them. The uniqueness of the episode just related lay in the President's consulting the Senate in person prior to negotiating the treaty. Later in the ensuing three years Washington consulted the Senate by written message instead of in person, and this kind of prior consultation of the Senate did not cease until Washington's drafting of instructions to John Jay preliminary to the negotiating of Jay's Treaty in 1794. "So a practice which Washington seems clearly to have expected to be established as a matter of course was still-born on the very threshold of our constitutional history and the failure of the method was a first step in terminating prior consultation in any form as the normal practice, and hence in reducing the term 'advice' in the constitutional phrase 'advice and consent' to a formalism as meaningless or unreal as it now is in the enacting clause of English statutes."[6]

[4] William Maclay, *Sketches of Debates in the First Senate* (1880), p. 122.

[5] Minor incidents sometimes turn out to be landmarks in constitutional development. Washington had inadvertently failed to invite Senator Maclay to dine with him prior to the incident in the Senate, and when he bethought himself of doing so, it was too late. But it is doubtful whether the dinner invitation would have made any difference.

[6] James Hart, *The American Presidency in Action, 1789* (1948), pp. 94–95. The enacting clause of an English statute is "Be it enacted by the King's Most Excellent Majesty, by and with the advice and consent of the Lords, Spiritual and Temporal and Commons in Parliament assembled and by the authority of the same as follows."

In time the settled practice became that negotiation is solely the responsibility of the president. Though it originated as sheer usage of the unwritten constitution, it has been sanctified as supreme law of the land by the fiat of the Supreme Court. "He alone negotiates," declared the late Associate Justice Sutherland, speaking for the Court. "Into the field of negotiation the Senate cannot intrude and Congress itself is powerless to invade it."[7] Moreover the Senate cannot compel the president to divulge a particle of information concerning the negotiations or anything else he chooses to withhold. However, there is nothing to prevent the Senate from offering the president advice informally through its leaders concerning planned or pending negotiations, and it would be an imprudent president who would spurn or ignore such advice. But, whatever the part played by the Senate, actually ratification of a treaty for the United States is the president's act, dependent for validation of the treaty upon the two-thirds vote of a quorum of the Senate.[8] The Senate may, by a sufficient vote, consent conditionally or unconditionally or not consent at all. Even after the Senate has given its two-thirds vote, the treaty is not the law of the land until the president "promulgates," that is, makes public the treaty. He can decide not to promulgate, which is equivalent to a veto, and unlike the veto of acts of Congress this one is absolute and not merely suspensive, that is, it cannot be overthrown by a two-thirds vote of both houses of Congress.

The president's foreign policy may have to run the gauntlet of the inquisitorial powers of congressional committees with some congressmen giving vent to feelings of frustration over their inability to snatch from the executive the initiative in foreign policy. Such is the division of power in this matter that the president dare not alienate the Foreign Relations Committee of the Senate or the Foreign Affairs Committee of the House or even the Appropriations Committee if expenditures are necessary to execute a foreign

[7] U. S. v. Curtis-Wright Export Corp., 299 U. S. 304, 319 (1936).
[8] See E. S. Corwin, *The President: Office and Powers* (1957), p. 211.

policy. Congress' paring of budget proposals for aid to western Europe and for the Voice of America, as well as the guerilla tactics of the late Senator McCarthy's roving agents among our diplomatic staffs in Europe, illustrate how Congress can modify, emasculate, or even nullify the president's administration of his foreign policy. Congress has used resolutions of either house or joint resolutions of the two houses to warn the president that a proposed foreign policy had better be slanted to placate dissident legislators. That the attitude of congressional leaders can be crucial is illustrated by the intransigence of Republican floor leader Senator Knowland with respect to any Far East policy President Eisenhower might have planned different from the Senator's views. One authority has concluded that

> the issue of the ultimate responsibility for the conduct of American foreign policy is being decided, on each individual occasion by a running battle between the Senate or the two Houses of Congress on one side and the executive branch on the other . . . It can be safely said that, in a period of international relations dominated by the psychology and technique of the 'cold war', the executive branch of the government of the United States must make a greater effort to maintain friendly relations with the United States Congress than with the Soviet Union.[9]

It need not be assumed that internal conflict is an inevitable feature of the theory and practice of formulating American foreign policy. Some administrations are quite free from difficulties in this field. When President Johnson's politician-statesman William H. Seward undertook to acquire Alaska—a hair-brained project, as it then seemed to most Americans—he took the precaution to ensure first the support of Senator Charles Sumner, Chairman of the Committee on Foreign Relations, who vigorously championed the treaty of acquisition on the floor of the Senate. Since the debacle of President Wilson's handling of the Covenant

[9] Hans J. Morgenthau, "Conduct of American Foreign Policy," *Parliamentary Affairs,* VIII (Winter, 1949), 149, 155.

of the League of Nations in the Senate, presidents have developed a technique for co-ordinating treaty formulation with the Senate characterized by considerable finesse. It is axiomatic that a treaty is doomed if ratification becomes a party issue, and there has consequently emerged the practice of a bipartisan foreign policy. A president cultivates the good will of the party of the opposition in support of his foreign policies by conferences and the appointment of senators and representatives to international conferences and organizations—the United Nations, for example. The maintenance of cordial relations with the legislative branch has even been institutionalized in the office of the Assistant Secretary of State for Congressional Relations located in the State Department.

Despite all the difficulties due to constitutional provisions plus the vagaries of our political usages, the president as chief executive and commander-in-chief possesses authority in the area of foreign relations that the Supreme Court has denominated "the very delicate, plenary, and executive power of the President as the sole organ of the federal government in the field of international relations"[10] and in no sense is this a delegated power. It inheres in the presidential office as a consequence of the existence of the United States as a sovereign nation. The Continental Congress promptly became the organ of international relations, and the Articles of Confederation formally vested in it "the sole and exclusive right and power of sending and receiving ambassadors and entering into treaties and alliances." The Constitution continued these powers, and the president has all the powers that international intercourse require that the Constitution does not vest elsewhere. Moreover, international law is law of the land, to which also applies the president's obligation to "take care that the laws be faithfully executed."

Charged with extraordinary power in the determination of foreign policy and exclusive power at that is the prescription of the constitution, "He shall receive ambassadors and other public

[10] U. S. v. Curtis-Wright Export Corp., 299 U. S. 304 (1936).

ministers." Here is a presidential function that Congress rarely presumes to invade. Until the dawn of the twentieth century such recognition of a foreign government by receiving ambassadors was almost automatically given to the government of any nation that appeared to be stable and willing to fulfill international obligations. Presidents Theodore Roosevelt and William Howard Taft did, of course, refuse recognition to the governments of the Dominican Republic, Nicaragua, Haiti, and Portugal until assured protection of American investments there. President Wilson however introduced a striking new departure by withholding recognition of governments in Mexico, Costa Rica, Peru, and Bolivia on the ground that they were not "constitutional governments." The Kerensky government of Russia in 1917 satisfied Wilson and was recognized, but the succeeding Bolshevik government was refused recognition by Wilson and ensuing presidents till 1933.

President Washington had just begun his second term when he had to decide upon the policy of the United States with respect to the war that had broken out between England and Revolutionary France. The problem was complicated by the standing Treaty of Alliance with France under which that nation had aided us by land and by sea in our war for independence, and the antiadministration party was insisting that we repay our ally by a declaration of war against England.[11] In the face of the threat of mob violence by the Francophiles against him, Washington issued the first Proclamation of Neutrality in 1793.

Because the Constitution did not, in as many words, authorize it, the opposition denounced this first presidential proclamation of neutrality as a usurpation of congressional power. Did not Congress have the power to declare war and by inference then to determine peace?[12] The controversy provided Hamilton with an

[11] John Adams, *Works* (1850–56), x, 47, 48.

[12] Even Secretary of State Jefferson in a letter to Madison expressed the opinion that Washington's proclamation that the nation was at peace was equivalent to declaring it would not go to war, which took on the character of encroachment on the legislature. Moreover, had not the President set at naught one treaty of alliance with France and broken our plighted faith?

appropriate opportunity to set forth, over the pen name of Pacificus, a startling interpretation of presidential power, startling at any rate to the already emerging cult of states rights. After enumerating the specified constitutional powers of the president and asserting that it would be unreasonable to assume that his powers were confined to these alone, Hamilton continued:

> The different modes of expression employed in the Constitution in regard to the two powers of the legislature and executive, serves to confirm this inference. In the article which gives the legislative power of the government the expressions are 'all legislative power herein granted shall be vested in a Congress of the United States'. In that which grants the executive power the expressions are 'the executive power shall be vested in a President of the United States. . . .' The general doctrine of our Constitution then is that the executive power of the nation is vested in the President subject only to the exceptions and qualifications which are expressed in the instrument.[13]

Although Hamilton's theory of presidential prerogative did not become established interpretation with respect to domestic matters, it has become accepted judicial interpretation as to the president's power in the conduct of foreign relations. Presidential proclamations of neutrality in due time became an unchallenged exercise of executive power.

If the appropriation of money by Congress for executing foreign policy, the declaration of war by Congress, and the consent of two-thirds of the Senate in validating treaties are excepted, the president's power in the field of foreign relations is plenary. He can declare a policy that in effect has virtually the permanent effect of a major statute, as did Monroe in proclaiming his Monroe Doctrine in 1823 merely by means of a presidential message to Congress, or as Cleveland did in his belligerent message on the Venezuela boundary dispute in 1896 or as Truman did in the Truman Doctrine of the containment of communism in 1947. He can recognize or refuse to recognize a foreign government.

---

[13] Hamilton's *Works* (Lodge edition 1904), IV, 142–44.

There is no legal or constitutional limitation on his authority to direct troops anywhere and leave Congress no choice but a formal declaration of the existence of a state of war as could have happened if President Truman had chosen to order armed resistance to the Berlin blockade in 1948 when he chose instead the airlift to circumvent the seige. No one can doubt President Franklin Roosevelt's imperious mastery in the conducting of foreign policy preceding the outbreak of war with Japan and Germany. His international understandings from the destroyer deal to Yalta were executive agreements consummated as such transactions are without the advice and consent of the Senate.

The growing use of the executive agreement in making compacts with foreign nations is a natural consequence of the Senate's overplaying its veto power of one-third plus one in disposing of treaties negotiated by the president. If an international engagement requires no supplementary legislation or an appropriation, the president can effect it with an executive agreement achieving the same purpose as with a treaty. In the 1940's this device came to be virtually the normal means for effecting international agreements. Significant indeed is the ratio of treaties to executive agreements in a seven-year period: 1939, 10 to 26; 1940, 12 to 20; 1941, 15 to 39; 1942, 6 to 52; 1943, 4 to 71; 1944, 1 to 74; 1945, 6 to 54. Many of these were, of course, then made under the president's power as commander-in-chief.

From early in our history executive agreements have been authorized by treaty or statute with respect to postal, trade-mark, and reciprocal-trade agreements with foreign nations. Such agreements are used in handling day-to-day diplomatic matters such, for example, as territorial or boundary adjustments, policing boundaries, regulating fishing rights, and private claims against foreign governments. This *modus vivendi* can be a temporary substitute for a formal treaty. In time of war temporary virtual alliances have been effected by executive agreements of the commander-in-chief. The naval limitations on the Great Lakes originated in 1817 as an executive agreement, which President

Monroe then submitted to the Senate, where it was approved by a two-thirds vote without formal exchange of ratification with Great Britain.

President McKinley terminated hostilities of the Spanish War in 1898 with an executive agreement on conditions that practically determined the terms of the ensuing Treaty of Peace ending the state of war. In 1901 President McKinley accepted the protocol by the terms of which China agreed to indemnify for losses of our citizens due to the Boxer Rebellion in China, and McKinley never submitted the agreement to the Senate. In 1900 President McKinley's Secretary of State, John Hay, negotiated and consummated his Open Door agreements as to China's trade and territorial integrity, which were never submitted to the Senate. President Theodore Roosevelt in 1905 simply by-passed the Senate by an executive agreement with Santo Domingo for the collection of customs in order to repay creditors who had made loans to that nation after the Senate had refused Roosevelt a treaty to that effect. Then there was the Taft-Katsura Memorandum of 1905 in Theodore Roosevelt's administration permitting Japan a free hand in Korea and in the same administration the Root-Takahira Agreement carrying still further the terms of the Taft-Katsura Memorandum. President Theodore Roosevelt's gentleman's agreement with Japan in 1907 to curb Japanese immigration to the United States was also merely an executive agreement. The House-Gray Memorandum of 1916 pledged probable American assistance to the Allies and the Lansing-Ishi agreement of the following year recognizing Japan's special interest in China was but another executive agreement firm enough that it took two formal treaties to terminate it.

President Franklin Roosevelt's 1933 agreement with Russia's Foreign Minister recognizing the Soviet government in return for its agreement to restrain persons or organizations from fomenting internal disturbances in the United States was, of course, merely an executive agreement. The Supreme Court held this to be an international compact that the President "as the sole organ" of international relations of the United States was authorized to enter into without consulting the Senate and that it superseded contrary state statutes.[14] Evidently this signified that the executive agreement was supreme law of the land. The rise of the executive agreement to such a peak of significance constitutes a notable landmark in our constitutional development. No method of restricting this development is possible short of a constitutional amendment such as Senator John Bricker aimed to achieve.

The Cold War converted the president into the international leader of the free world. If the threat of Soviet world domination was to be countered, the strength of the United States in population, resources, economic productivity, and military potential made it the logical mobilizer of the free world if the president would only provide the leadership. But this required his obtaining agreement of divergent groups at home. It meant readiness to employ military force where needed and an occasional audacious stroke such as Truman's appearance before Congress to ask for four hundred million dollars for economic and military aid to Greece and Turkey, confronted by Soviet threat. World leadership of the president meant such moves as sending the fleet into Formosa Straits, the Berlin airlift, and intervention in Korea. It required formulas flexible enough to cover with the mantle of foreign aid allies as divergent as Communist Tito and Fascist Franco.[15]

The leader of the free world dare not neglect leadership in promoting or enforcing civil-rights legislation at home. The eyes of the free world were upon President Eisenhower throughout the Little Rock crisis. Neither can the president neglect counteracting recession. Let him lead feebly, and Congress seizes the reins thereby impairing his prestige before the world.[16] Moreover, since World War II, leadership of the free world has become institu-

---

[14] U. S. v. Belmont, 301 U. S. 324 (1937).

[15] See Richard P. Longaker, "The President as International Leader," *Law and Contemporary Problems*, Autumn, 1956 (Duke University Law School).

[16] *Ibid,.* pp. 747–52.

tionalized by such organizations as ANZUS, SEATO, NATO, Latin-American pacts, and above everything else the United Nations, which the president addresses from time to time.

No matter if the Supreme Court has declared that "in its vast external realm [of foreign relations] with its important, complicated, delicate, and manifold problems the President alone has the power to speak or listen as the representative of the nation,"[17] his voice is sometimes almost lost by the confusion of tongues in the maze of agencies constituting the executive branch of our government. No technique has yet been devised to ensure avoidance of inter- if not even intradepartmental clashes as to foreign policies. A frustrated congressman may look with ill-concealed glee at the baffled executive branch and sometimes even fan the flames of controversy! There is the instance of Senator McCarthy even planting virtually a personal agent in the State Department to create confusion therein and a near reign of terror in the entire diplomatic service. The State Department is even organizationally divided against itself due to the cleavage between the geographical agencies of Inter-American, European, Near Eastern, and Far Eastern affairs on the one hand and the functional agencies on the other. Furthermore, as Hans Morgenthau has pointed out, "Certain Ambassadors, such as Dodd in Berlin and Kennedy in London in the 1930's and Hayes in Madrid, during the Second World War, were able for months to pursue policies at variance with the policies of the State Department."[18] The Hoover Commission on the Organization of the Executive Branch counted nearly forty-five executive agencies *outside the State Department* concerned with some phase of foreign policy. More than thirty interdepartmental committees and boards were struggling to resolve their conflicting views on foreign policies with the results reaching the president through the National Security Council.

---

[17] U. S. *v.* Curtis-Wright Export Corp. 299 U. S. 304 (1936).

[18] "Conduct of American Foreign Policy," *Parliamentary Affairs,* VIII (Winter, 1949), 158.

There is the picture of President Woodrow Wilson so distrustful of Secretary of State Bryan that he would retire to the privacy of his office with his typewriter and peck out a solemn note to the German Foreign Minister protesting the submarine torpedoing of neutral shipping. Or he would send his *alter ego*, as he called him, his quasi ambassador, Colonal Ed. M. House, abroad to sound out foreign ministries in casual disregard of the regular diplomatic service, quite as Wilson's protégé Franklin Roosevelt used his own roving ambassador, Harry Hopkins, on similar missions two decades later. President Truman had W. Averill Harriman as an informal diplomat whose function became formalized as Foreign Affairs Advisor to the President. But this title expressed precisely what the Secretary of State was intended to be, and the time came when Secretary of State Cordell Hull was to say that the use of presidential envoys "tended in many instances to create havoc with our ambassadors and ministers in the capitals they visited, even though the envoys themselves had no such intentions."[19]

Sometimes a president sends up a trial balloon or has his secretary of state or even the vice-president do it for him in order to test public sentiment as to a contemplated foreign policy. For example Franklin Roosevelt sought to alert an indifferent public to the peril due to the Japanese invasion of China in his Chicago speech in 1937 urging an international quarantine of aggressors as the only means of preserving peace but promptly discovered that he had ventured ahead of current public opinion. But a year later when he boldly declared at Kingston, Ontario, that the United States would help defend Canada against invasion, the Gallup Poll soon revealed public approval. Then there was Vice-President Nixon's off-the-record speech to the American Society of Newspaper Editors in 1954 concerning the Communist aggression in Indo-China. If his startling statement that the United States could not afford further retreat in Asia and that the administration

---

[19] Cordell Hull; *Memoirs* (1948), I, 200. See Felix Morley, *The Foreign Policy of the United States* (1951), pp. 117–19.

should face up to the dispatching of troops to Indo-China was a trial balloon, it was one that did not stay up. There have been times when the president is left in no doubt as to what the public wants, and the country forces a foreign policy on the administration as it did in the 1930's when the enactment of neutrality legislation was virtually forced upon an unwilling President.

No president wants to commit political hara-kiri and consequently inevitably has his eye on the next election and the effect of his foreign policy on it. The very nature of representative government practically compels this practice, and the alternative is dictatorship more or less. A United States Senator once observed that unusual activity in the room of the Committee on Foreign Relations indicated that a presidential election was in the offing.[20] Perhaps no secretary of state was more adept in practical politics than William H. Seward of Lincoln's Cabinet. When an impetuous American naval captain boarded a British mail steamer and captured two Confederate commissioners assigned to Britain, the public in the North was ecstatic over the defiance of the traditional enemy. But the Lincoln administration, harassed by secession and armed rebellion dared not risk a threatened foreign war with England also, and after popular passion had cooled somewhat, the captured commissioners were released. Nor did Seward miss the opportunity to mollify somewhat his public by congratulating the British on having at long last accepted, even insisted on, the principle of freedom of the seas for which we had fought them in 1812. By a narrow margin the Lincoln administration had avoided committing hara-kiri.

The fear of what Congress might do to their policies has become a veritable obsession to many members of the executive departments. And Congress in its turn is susceptible to the pressures of constituent interests that affect foreign policy—the sugar and oil lobbies, the American Legion, and certain ethnic and religious groups. Resolving the consequent confusion of opinion

[20] T. Bailey, *The Man in the Street* (1948), p. 88.

as to what foreign policy shall be depends mainly upon whether the president reasserts the historic role of the chief executive as the initiator and formulator of foreign policy as, for example, for better or for worse, it was played in the presidency of Theodore Roosevelt.

President Eisenhower attempted to utilize the National Security Council in order to co-ordinate and integrate foreign policy as administrative agencies might contribute to it. Here, presided over by the President, convened each week the Secretaries of State and Defense, the Vice-President, the Director of Foreign Operations Administration, and the Director of the Office of Defense Mobilization with the frequent unofficial presence of the Secretary of the Treasury and the Director of the Budget. Inevitably there is difficulty in arriving at an enforceable consensus. "With the exception of the President and the Vice President each member [of the Council] is the ambassador of a significant power complex within the administration, so he can hardly act as a free agent at the N. S. C. meetings."[21] The council affords opportunities for composing intra-administration differences, but if decisions arrived at are to be valid, that is, enforceable, they would have to reflect bargaining power of the several agencies represented, instead of abstract considerations of national security. The various agencies can put their cards on the table, but that does not change the weight the holders of them command, and "it is doubtful whether any magical institution can be devised that will, for example, transform the Secretary of State's cards into aces."[22]

The handicap of the State Department is that it is the orphan child among the great administrative agencies of the Federal government. No matter which political party is in power, it is under attack while the other departments are usually relatively immune. It is "the one major administrative division that *has no*

[21] John P. Roche and Murray S. Stedman, Jr., *The Dynamics of Democratic Government* (1954), p. 394.
[22] *Ibid.*, p. 395.

constituency, no *constellation of interest groups* to look after its interests in the way the Farm Bureau protects the Department of Agriculture. When an appropriation is cut by Congress the protests pour in from indignant farmers."[23] But the Department of State has no farmers. Under both Truman and Eisenhower Secretaries of State Acheson and Dulles in turn became sitting ducks for congressional and public marksmanship without a single powerful interest group ready to fly to their defense. As a consequence the prestige of the Department of State declined in the very era of the Cold War when it most of all needed increased prestige and power, and its essential functions were transferred to the Economic Co-operation Administration, which administered the Marshall Plan aid, to the Mutual Security Agency, now the Foreign Operations Administration, which handles both military and economic aid, and even to the Department of Defense, which has a powerful constituency that can give its officers support and protection while an official of the State Department is "fair game for any Congressman seeking notoriety." "Gradually the State Department has been stripped of its operating functions and left with the hopeless job of formulating policy without being in a position to enforce its decision."[24] In the play of social forces it is apparently the victim of a process of reverse natural selection.[25]

[23] *Ibid.,* p. 80. Italics mine. W. E. B.

[24] *Ibid.,* p. 386.

[25] Henry Adams, distressed by the frustrating experiences of his friend John Hay as Secretary of State under Presidents William McKinley and Theodore Roosevelt at the turn of the present century, dipped his pen in vitriol and wrote: "The Secretary of State exists only to recognize the existence of a world which Congress repudiates whenever it can; of bargains which Congress distrusts and tries to turn to its advantage or to reject. Since the first day the Senate existed, it has always intrigued against the Secretary of State whenever the Secretary has been obliged to extend his functions beyond the appointment of Consuls in Senators' service." *The Education of Henry Adams* (1931), p. 422.

XIII

The Vice-Presidency and
Succession to the Presidency

* **THE VICE-PRESIDENCY** appears to have crept into the Constitution with a curious casualness. Its first mention therein is in the provision that the vice-president shall preside over the Senate and, when necessary, vote to break a tie, but there is no intimation of just how such an office came to be. So it pops up here and there in our fundamental instrument with a happy-go-lucky nonchalance as if it were just something to be taken for granted. The legislative power "shall be vested in a Congress of the United States, which shall consist of a Senate and House of Representatives," "the executive power shall be vested in a President of the United States," and "the judicial power . . . shall be vested in one Supreme Court, and in such inferior Courts as the Congress may from time to time ordain and establish," but nowhere is there any specific authorization of the vice-presidency. It has all the appearance of having been an afterthought of the framers, and such indeed it was.

The problem of the creation of the office of vice-president did not arise until the Constitutional Convention had almost completed its deliberations. The seventh resolution of the so-called Virginia Plan, which practically provided the initial agenda of the Convention, proposed "that a national executive be instituted to be chosen by the National Legislature."[1] No less than five times did the Convention vote in favor of election of the executive by the legislature, that is, by Congress, before finally rejecting that method.[2] The point to be noted is that as long as the Convention adhered to the election of the president by Congress, no distinct stand-by officer to serve when necessary in his stead, such as the vice-president, was made necessary by the Constitution.

The tenth article of the preliminary draft of the Constitution submitted by the Committee of Detail on August 6 provided:

> The Executive Power of the United States shall be vested in a single person . . . . He shall be elected by the Legislature. He shall hold his office during a term of seven years; but shall not be elected a second time . . . . He shall be removed from his office on impeachment by the House, and conviction in the Supreme Court, of treason, bribery or corruption. In case of removal as aforesaid, death, resignation, or disability to discharge the powers and duties of his office, the President of the Senate shall exercise those powers, until another President of the United States be chosen, or until the disability of the President be removed.[3]

Clearly this arrangement required no vice-president. The Senate could not function without a president so that it would have been easy virtually always to have available the one to act as president until Congress, either in regular or special session, could elect a president.

This method of electing the president was abandoned by the Committee of Eleven, and two weeks before adjournment they astonished the delegates with their substitution, which was the proposal of what has come to be called the Electoral College. It provided that the president "shall hold his office during the term

---

[1] C. C. Tansill (ed.), *Documents Illustrative of the Formation of the American Union*, 69th Cong., 1st Sess., House Document, No. 398, p. 117.

[2] Max Farrand, "Compromises of the Constitution," *American Historical Review*, IX (1904), 479 ff.

[3] C. C. Tansill, *op. cit.* (above, Chap. XIII, note 1), pp. 478, 479.

of four years, and together with the Vice President, chosen for the same term, be elected as follows: Each state shall appoint in such manner as the legislature may direct, a number of electors, equal to the whole number of Senators and Representatives to which the State may be entitled in the Congress." It was provided that these electors, meeting in their respective states, would vote by ballot for two persons without designation of the office for which each was intended. When these ballots had been assembled and counted before a joint session of the two houses of Congress, the one receiving the greatest number of votes would be president if such number was a majority of the whole number of votes. The person having the next greatest number of votes would be vice-president.[4]

The history of the vice-presidency since the Constitutional Convention reveals a succession of phenomena suggestive of biological evolution. The germ of the office is to be found in the lieutenant governor of the English colonies. The royal governor, appointed by the king, was sometimes little more than a royal pensioner who remained in England enjoying the emoluments of the office while a lieutenant governor, present in the colony, performed the duties of the office. When the English colonies, in the 1770's, became American states, the office carried over, and in four states that gave their chief executive the title of president his lieutenant became vice-president, and this title was adopted by the framers of the Constitution. "The exact prototype of the office of Vice President is to be found in that of the lieutenant governor of New York (in 1787). He was to preside in the Senate, without a vote, except in case of a tie, was to succeed the governor, when succession was necessary, and was to be succeeded by the President *pro tempore* of the Senate."[5]

Nothing did more to ensure the high quality of our earliest vice-presidents than the provision of the framers that each presidential

[4] *Ibid.*, p. 660.
[5] Alexander Johnson, "What the Federal Constitution Owes to the Constitutions of the Several States," *New Princeton Review*, September, 1887.

elector was to vote for two persons without designating the office for which either ballot was to count. Since, in this blind voting, either ballot might contribute to the election of a president, the elector dared not cast either one for a second-rater. The effect of making the runner-up for the presidency the vice-president had the effect of starting off the vice-presidency with incumbents of very high quality—indeed the office got off to a fine start. In electing John Adams the first Vice-President the system selected probably the second ablest statesman in the country at that time, Thomas Jefferson then being still in France. When the third election promoted Adams to the presidency, Jefferson, receiving the next highest vote of the Electoral College, became Adams' Vice-President. But political parties were getting pretty well established by this time with the consequence that in 1800 every Republican elector cast one vote for Jefferson and the other for Burr with a resulting tie resolved eventually in the balloting of the House of Representatives by electing Jefferson President and leaving the vice-presidency to Burr. By this time the precedents made each vice-president heir-apparent to the presidency. When Aaron Burr in 1800 obtained endorsement of his candidacy for Vice-President by the New York legislature, it must have been with the confident expectation that election to that office, following the established precedent, would make him in due course the successor of Jefferson in the presidency.[6]

In electing to the vice-presidency Adams, Jefferson, and Burr, the Electoral College, functioning as the framers intended, had chosen men of presidential caliber. It can be said that during the vice-presidency of Burr the office had a high prestige it was not to attain again for a century and a quarter. Whatever else can be said of Burr, he served as President of the Senate with exemplary propriety. At the end of his presiding over the impeachment trial

[6] *American Historical Review*, VIII (1903), 512.

of Associate Justice Samuel Chase of the Supreme Court his bitterest opponents commended his rulings. Following his impressive valedictory address (at the end of his term), which reduced some of the senators to tears, the Senate gave him a vote of appreciation for the "impartiality, dignity, and ability with which he had presided over their deliberations."[7]

Because the blind voting for two persons without designation of the office for which each ballot was intended led to the tie vote of 1800 and could have led to an indefinite number of similar ties in future presidential elections, the Twelfth Amendment to the Constitution was adopted. This required the presidential electors to indicate which office each ballot was intended for. The consequence was almost disastrous to the quality of later incumbents and to the prestige of the vice-presidency through the nineteenth century. It stopped promptly the established custom of promotion of vice-presidents to the presidency. Since 1800 only one Vice-President, Martin Van Buren, has succeeded directly by election to the presidency. Nor was the effect of the Twelfth Amendment on the vice-presidency unforeseen when its adoption was pending. For example, as early as 1802 Gouverneur Morris, an active framer of the Constitution, warned that separate balloting for the two offices as such would make the vice-presidential nomination a "bait to catch state gudgeons"—that is, an office to be obtained without skill or merit. Never was a shrewder or more accurate prophecy made by an American statesman. Political parties promptly began nominating vice-presidential candidates selected for no other purpose than to capture the electoral votes of pivotal states, which is precisely what Morris meant by "state gudgeons."

The presidential election of 1804, only a matter of weeks after the adoption of the Twelfth Amendment had been proclaimed, revealed its almost catastrophic effect on the vice-presidency. The exigency of party politics brought to that office George Clinton, than whom "a worse choice...could scarcely have been made,"

[7] Isaac J. Cox, "Aaron Burr," *Dictionary of American Biography*, III, 317.

according to Senator John Quincy Adams. So ignorant was he of parliamentary law that the senators were relieved when he was absent, and absenteeism of the Vice-President came to be almost habitual.[8] Though Clinton's faculties were quite evidently failing, so inconsequential was the office now considered that he was even renominated and served during Madison's presidency until he died at the age of seventy-three. Elbridge Gerry was elected Vice-President in 1812 and began presiding over the Senate frail in health and in his seventieth year. The vice-presidency had become a refuge for aged and ailing statesmen too old for the presidency. Daniel Tompkins, the next Vice-President, was simply absent from his post most of his four-year term.

In 1824 an unusual set of circumstances elevated to the vice-presidency the first incumbent of presidential caliber in almost a quarter of a century. The managers of Andrew Jackson's presidential candidacy needed to dispose of his strong southern competitor, John C. Calhoun. Jackson, aged sixty-one, kept insisting that he was a very old man, in poor health, and not expecting to live very long. He was persuaded to let it be rumored that he practically had one foot in the grave and in no case would consider serving more than a single term. Under such circumstances the vice-presidency proved effective bait for Calhoun. So Calhoun was elected Vice-President, although Jackson was not elected President until four years later when Calhoun was re-elected Vice-President, to be followed by Martin Van Buren. Next came John Tyler, the first Vice-President to succeed to the presidency.

It fell to the first Vice-President, John Adams, to set the pattern of the office's chief function, that of presiding over the Senate. In the absence of an elaborate set of rules, Adams exerted a control over the proceedings of the Senate that its later rules made impossible.[9] He broke twenty-nine ties, the record to this day. Thus he had the opportunity to cast the vote deciding the

---

[8] See Irving G. Williams, *The Rise of the Vice Presidency* (1956), pp. 32–34.
[9] Edward S. Corwin, *The President, Office and Powers* (1957), pp. 60, 61.

president's power of removal of his appointees without consent of the Senate, commercial reprisals on Great Britain, neutrality, and Hamilton's financial policies.[10] Vice-President Jefferson distinguished himself by preparing his *Manual of Parliamentary Practice* for guidance in presiding over the Senate. Since the vice-president was inevitably the runner-up in the balloting of the Electoral College before adoption of the Twelfth Amendment, he tended to become an opposition leader, and Jefferson was an outstanding critic of Adams' administration as indeed Burr was of Jefferson's administration. Calhoun's rulings in 1826 that the vice-president could not call a senator to order set a precedent tending toward the Senate's present-day individualism.[11] Moreover, despite the Twelfth Amendment's insuring that president and vice-president belong to the same party, Jackson's antinullification policy converted Calhoun into a critic of the administration. Calhoun's resignation to become a Senator did not lift the prestige of the vice-presidency, since it implied that a seat on the floor was more significant than presiding over the Senate.

The death of President Harrison in 1841, a month after his inauguration, and the succession of John Tyler mark the greatest landmark in the history of the vice-presidency. During the first fifty-two years under the Constitution there had been no vacancy in the presidency, and the public seemed to assume that there never would be. Immediately upon Harrison's death the five Cabinet members announced the President's death and dispatched Fletcher Webster with a message to Williamsburg, Virginia, addressed to "John Tyler, Vice President of the United States."[12] Returning to Washington, John Tyler was administered the presidential oath only fifty-three hours after the death of Harrison.

The preponderance of evidence seems to indicate that giving Tyler the presidential oath was one of the major errors of our

[10] Worthington Chauncey Ford, "John Adams," *Dictionary of American Biography*, I, 77.

[11] E. S. Corwin, *The President: Office and Powers* (1957), p. 61.

[12] James D. Richardson, *Messages and Papers of the Presidents* (1927), IV, 22, 23.

constitutional history. Ex-President John Quincy Adams, then a Representative in Congress, confided to his diary his dissent to this succession with the entry that Vice-President John Tyler "styled himself President of the United States and not Vice-President, acting as President, in direct violation both of the grammar and context of the Constitution which confers upon the Vice-President on the decease of the President, not the office but the powers and duties of the office."[13] The ambiguity in the Constitution from which the controversy derives was due to an imperfect merging of two Convention resolutions by the Committee of Style of the Constitutional Convention. One resolution provided that in case of a vacancy in the office of president or his "inability to discharge the powers and duties of his office the Vice President shall exercise those powers and duties until another be chosen or until the inability of the President be removed."[14] The other resolution authorized Congress to "declare by law what officer . . . shall act as President in case of vacancy in both the presidency and the vice presidency or the inability of both to perform the duties of the office of President."[15] It is crystal clear that both resolutions intended that no one was ever to be president who had not been elected to that office but others might "perform the duties of the office." In consolidating the two resolutions the Committee of Style produced Article Two, section one of the Constitution in which, in case of vacancy in the office of president "or inability to discharge the powers and duties of said office, the same shall devolve on the vice president." What is the antecedent of "the same"? is the question that plagues us to this day.

Tyler took the oath as President April 6 and three days later published his Inaugural Address,[16] and began promptly to sign official papers, "John Tyler, President of the United States." Whether or not the cabinet made the decision that Vice-President Tyler should become President, they found him to be a resolute

---

[13] Entry of April 16, 1841.
[14] Max Farrand, *The Records of the Federal Convention of 1787* (1911), II, 575.
[15] *Ibid.*, 573.
[16] Richardson, *Messages and Papers of the Presidents,* IV, 36–39.

incumbent. Tyler's son Robert related that when his father confronted the Cabinet at the first meeting following Harrison's death, the Secretary of State, Webster, said, "Mr. President, I suppose you intend to carry out the ideas and customs of your predecessor, and that this administration, inaugurated by President Harrison, will continue in the same line of policy." Seeing that Tyler assented, Mr. Webster continued, "Mr. President, it was the custom of our cabinet meetings of President Harrison that he should preside over them. All measures relating to the administration were to be brought before the Cabinet and their settlement was to be decided by a majority vote, each member of the Cabinet having but one vote." To Webster's suggestion Tyler replied to the effect that he could never consent to being dictated to. "I am President," said he, "and I shall be held responsible for my administration."[17] These are by no means sentiments of an acting president.

Some contemporary newspapers insisted that Tyler was only acting President.[18] However, the controversy subsided, and even John Quincy Adams was soon speaking of "President John Tyler." When, nine years after President Harrison's death, President Taylor died, his Cabinet communicated the information to Vice-President Fillmore by a note addressed to the "President of the United States," and Fillmore took the presidential oath the following day before a joint session of the two houses of Congress. Senator Webster introduced the resolution providing for the administration of the oath to Fillmore as President. Professor Ruth Silva found no evidence of objections to this procedure in either house and considered it significant that the resolution passed unanimously.[19] Although the bitter critics of President Andrew Johnson persistently referred to him as merely "Acting President," their articles of impeachment arraigned him as

[17] John Tyler, Jr., quoted by John Fiske in J. G. Wilson, *The Presidents of the United States* (4 vols., 1914), II, 73 n.
[18] See Ruth Silva, *Presidential Succession* (1951), pp. 18, 19.
[19] *Ibid.*, p. 25.

President of the United States. The usage had settled down into firmly established constitutional law.

From 1840 to the end of the century it seemed to be impossible for the American people to learn from experience the danger of treating the vice-presidency as "bait to catch state gudgeons." Tyler, who never was a genuine Whig but rather an anti-Jackson Democrat, had been put on the ticket with Harrison to gather votes, and his nearly four years as President was a continuous war with Whig Congresses. Fillmore belonged to the conservative wing of the Whig party, and his succession to the presidency brought prompt reversal of presidential policies as to the pending Compromise of 1850. Andrew Johnson was a Union Democrat whom Lincoln selected to be his running mate in 1864 as pure campaign strategy. In 1880 Chester A. Arthur was nominated to placate the Stalwarts or conservative Republicans, who were disgruntled over Garfield's nomination. Even today it still remains to be seen whether the American people have yet learned the serious responsibility resting upon them to select for vice-president candidates who have every qualification requisite in a president of the United States. How far this has been missed is evident from the fact that very few of our vice-presidents have had much else to distinguish them than that they were once incumbents of the office or succeeded from it to the presidency. Even to the reasonably well-informed citizen the role of vice-presidents has the semblance of a list of almost total strangers.

In spite of the serious indifference of party management and of the electorate to the importance of the vice-presidency, the turn of the present century marked the end of an era. President McKinley's first Vice-President, Garret A. Hobart, came to be called the "assistant President," since McKinley frequently consulted him on affairs of state, and he presided over the Senate with such satisfaction that Senator Henry Cabot Lodge declared that he had "restored the Vice Presidency to its proper position."[20] An

[20] *Congressional Record,* 59th Cong., 1st Sess., p. 743.

important factor in the change of the vice-presidency in the present century has been the personality of the incumbents of the office. Contrasting with the frequent nonentities who were vice-presidents in the nineteenth century are such twentieth-century notables as Theodore Roosevelt, Thomas R. Marshall, Calvin Coolidge, Charles Dawes, John Garner, Harry Truman, and Richard Nixon. Theodore Roosevelt had no opportunity to distinguish himself as Vice-President, but he did manage to break the hex that had hitherto prevented any vice-president succeeding to the presidency from getting elected president and thereby serving a second term.

Woodrow Wilson's two-term Vice-President, Thomas R. Marshall, was the first in that office in eighty-eight years to be re-elected. He mastered the rules of the Senate and distinguished himself at first as an impartial moderator until he fell under criticism for not using his office to promote administration policies. By Wilson's second term he functioned as a party man and thereby practically initiated the present-day vice-president's function as the president's principal liaison with the Senate. He presided at Cabinet meetings while Wilson was at the Paris Peace Conference. His most trying experience was during Wilson's long illness, when he was pressured to assume the duties of the presidency, which he resolutely refused to do. Marshall was probably the most popular of all the vice-presidents.

Vice-President Coolidge sat in the Cabinet meetings of President Harding at the President's request and consequently when Harding died assumed the duties of the presidency familiar with the administration's plans. We have William Allen White's judgment that Coolidge "came out of the Cabinet sessions a well equipped man for the job Fate held in store for him."[21] He was a competent presiding officer of the Senate, where he "demonstrated the power of the chair by planned absence and passivity rather than by affirmative action."[22] Thus, after agreeing to

[21] Calvin Coolidge, *The Man Who is President* (1925), pp. 114, 115.
[22] Irvin G. Williams, *The Rise of the Vice Presidency* (1956), p. 125.

recognize a certain Senator to introduce a farm-relief measure, he deliberately left the Chamber at the critical moment after calling to the chair one who refused to recognize the agreed-upon Senator. No wonder Coolidge is on record as declaring that the vice-president's power to recognize "often means that he decides what business is to be taken up and who is to have the floor at a specific time for debate."[23] He had no sympathy with agriculture.

Coolidge's Vice-President, Charles A. Dawes, got off to a bad start by lecturing the senators on their archaic rules only to see filibustering go on as usual. Then, accepting the inevitable, he settled down to presiding so satisfactorily as to win the respect and confidence of the Senate. Coolidge was unable to persuade Dawes to follow his own precedent of sitting in with the President's Cabinet. Dawes provided no legislative liaison whatever for Coolidge but, on the contrary, proceeded to promote whatever legislation he chose regardless of the President. Thus he facilitated passage of the McNary-Haugen Bill for farm relief which anti-agrarian President Coolidge knocked out with a vigorous veto message. No wonder Coolidge felt impelled to comment that "the President of the Senate can and does exercise a good deal of influence over its deliberations." Dawes's successor, Vice-President Charles Curtis, had stood up in the convention that nominated Herbert Hoover and spoken against his nomination on the ground of his doubtful Republican party affiliation. He could consequently provide no legislative liaison and was in fact the last Vice-President nominated without attention to his acceptability as running mate of the presidential candidate.

Franklin Roosevelt is responsible for initiating the modern vice-presidency. Vice-President John N. Garner had been Speaker of the House of Representatives and as President of the Senate he was in a position to be the most expert co-ordinator of the legislative functions of president and Congress in our history. He was adept in dealing with House leaders, and in the Senate he could

[23] *Ibid.*, p. 125.

call someone to the chair while he lobbied on the floor. He would "wander around the Senate during a zig zaggy debate...and sit down in a seat next to a wavering Senator at exactly the right time to come up with that Senator's vote on the subsequent roll call."[24] During the "hundred days" of the New Deal era he would counsel a freshman Congressman: "...the South has been mighty proud to have a Democratic President. They want you to support him ...to yield something.... If I were you I would vote with the President on this and everything else I could.... You are young enough to be my son If I had to campaign I would stake my chances on supporting the President."[25] There were times when President Roosevelt would even telephone Garner at his Texas home seeking his advice. But in the end when Garner broke with the President on the New Deal, he dragged his feet as President of the Senate slowing down if not resisting administration measures.

That leadership of the vice-president depends very much upon personality was demonstrated by the experience of Franklin Roosevelt's second Vice-President, Henry Wallace. In contrast with Garner, Wallace and the senators are said to have been scarcely acquainted with each other even at the end of his four years of presiding over the Senate. The vice-presidency stood still if it did not retrograde during Wallace's term. So indifferent was he said to be that Jesse Jones, though scarcely an unbiased witness, swore that Wallace "usually dozed...often sleeping fifteen or twenty minutes at a stretch."[26] After Wallace, senators were chosen as vice-presidents partly with a view to their functioning as legislative liaison for the president. Vice-President Wallace was far less inept in the diplomatic and administrative duties assigned to him by President Roosevelt during his vice-presidency than in his constitutional function of presiding over the Senate.

[24] Bascom N. Timmons, *Garner of Texas: A Personal History* (1948), p. 229.
[25] *Ibid.*, pp. 180–88.
[26] Quoted by Irving Williams, *The American Vice Presidency* (1954), p. 32.

The weakness of Vice-President Wallace as legislative liaison is believed to have been a factor in the turn to the Senate for the next Vice-President, Harry S. Truman. Three vice-presidents in succession—Truman, Barkley, and Nixon—have come from the Senate. Moreover, Senator Nixon was elected Vice-President in 1952 in competition with Senator John Sparkman, the Democratic candidate for the office. In 1956 Vice-President Nixon was pitted against Senator Estes Kefauver, who won his candidacy in the Democratic convention by a breath-taking victory for that nomination over Senator John Kennedy. For the time being the Senate has become the recruiting ground for vice-presidents.

No vice-president demonstrated more promptly his competence as liaison between president and Senate than Harry Truman. No sooner had he been inaugurated as Vice-President than there fell to him the almost impossible job of getting the Senate to confirm President Roosevelt's nomination of Henry Wallace as Secretary of Commerce. Only once in more than a century had the Senate broken the well-established usage of confirming a president's nomination of a member of his official family and that was when Vice-President Dawes was awakened from a nap too late and did not reach the Capitol in time to break the tie that would have confirmed President Coolidge's nomination of Charles B. Warren as Attorney General. As it was, Vice-President Truman overcame the intense antipathy of the senators to Wallace and persuaded them by personal appeal to his recent colleagues to confirm the nomination. As Jesse Jones put it, "Truman . . . lobbied among the Senators. . . . Otherwise he [Wallace] would not have been confirmed."[27]

Personality, combined with rich experience in both houses of Congress, made Truman's Vice-President, Alben Barkley, seem something like the realization of an ideal with respect to the office. Evidently the era of nonentities in the office was becoming ancient

[27] Jesse H. Jones with Edward Angly, *Fifty Billion Dollars: My Thirteen Years with the R. F. C.* (1951), p. 510.

history. Never had there been a pair that got along so well in office, thought President Truman in 1951. In 1949 upon Truman's recommendation the vice-president was made a permanent member of the National Security Council, whereupon that office acquired its first statutory duties. However, Truman kept the N. S. C. within bounds, fearful, it seems, that it might develop into a supercabinet for supervising other agencies.[28] The vice-president through membership of the council became party to the most secret affairs of state and was obligated to participate in the formulation of policies of national defense and indeed of all the activities of American policy. No longer did the vice-presidency outside the Senate depend upon mere custom and the caprice of the president.

The vice-presidency of Richard Nixon marked the culmination of a trend in the office. From the day of his inauguration he became the busiest of all our vice-presidents, bearing readily the multifarious responsibilities assigned him by President Eisenhower. Never was an amateur politician president more fortunate than Eisenhower in having a trusted expert at hand to brief him on the mysteries of doings at the other end of Pennsylvania Avenue and at the same time to serve as legislative liaison. The death of Senator Taft in the middle of Eisenhower's first year as President increased his dependence on Nixon. The Vice-President proved a good administration lobbyist in the Senate as, from time to time, he called someone to the chair and circulated among the senators. He became a member of the Big Four, a group consisting of the Vice-President, the Speaker of the House, and the majority leaders of the House and of the Senate, who conferred with the President on administration bills.

When President Eisenhower's tax program was threatened in the congressional election year of 1954 by the Democrats' strategy of proposing to increase the income-tax exemption for all taxpayers, the President decided on an all-out opposition. To Vice-President Nixon was assigned the job of reasoning with

[28] H. Truman, *Years of Trial and Hope* (1955), p. 60.

sixty key Republican Representatives from close Congressional districts.... Nixon warned that it was up to the Republicans in the House to back up the President.... He Knew, Nixon said, how tough it was to stand up to the Democrats on such an issue in an election year. But it was often good politics to fight on a seemingly unpopular side of an issue expecially if the voters sensed in their hearts that it was the right side.... Those who heard Nixon were much impressed.[29]

Young Vice-President Nixon was practically catapulted into a key position in the Eisenhower administration. Despite his youth he was probably the most adept politician in the Republican party not excepting the veteran Senator Taft. Someone was needed to explain the black magic of politics to the raw amateurs in the Eisenhower team, particularly the Cabinet of businessmen. "Get to know personally and promptly the key committeemen for your unit," he advised. "Don't take with you, or send to represent you at the Capitol aides prominently associated with the Truman Administration. If you get a formal tough letter from a Member of Congress (and try to prevent such a situation from arising) answer it verbally and in a very friendly way." There never was a president's Cabinet that got sounder advice or needed it more. On the other hand the Vice-President "smoothed ruffled congressional feathers" when businessmen officials acted maladroitly. The death of Senator Taft in August, 1953 increased the importance of Nixon as a mediator between congressmen and the amateurs toward the other end of Pennsylvania Avenue.[30]

It was indicative of the new look of the vice-presidency when Nixon remarked that presiding over the Senate required only about 10 per cent of his time. By having him frequently preside over the Cabinet and the National Security Council, President Eisenhower unconsciously gave the once-neglected vice-presidency a status superior to both Secretary of State and Secretary of

[29] Joseph and Stewart Alsop, "Matter of Fact," *New York Herald Tribune,* March 8, 1954. Quoted by Irving G. Williams, *The Rise of the Vice Presidency* (1956), p. 23.

[30] Irving G. Williams, *The Rise of the Vice Presidency* (1956), p. 247.

Defense. No wonder Nixon's remarks came to be considered as representing administration's policies. He even sent up a trial balloon now and then as when he indicated at a news conference that armed intervention by the United States might be required in the Indo-China crisis. Unless there is a reversal of the trend, the time need never come again when a vice-president will succeed to the presidency unfamiliar with his new duties. The vice-presidency was at long last providing an apprenticeship for the presidency.

President Franklin Roosevelt initiated the vice-president into the field of diplomacy. In 1936 John N. Garner was sent as a sort of good-will ambassador at the head of a senatorial delegation to the inauguration of Manuel Quezon, the first Philippine President, and to Mexico representing the President at the dedication of Laredo Bridge on the Inter-American Highway. Vice-President Wallace was sent on a high diplomatic mission to China from which he returned with some decisions and recommendations that shaped the controversial China policy. Wallace, who spoke Spanish, was sent repeatedly to South America, where he became more popular than at home. Vice-President Barkley flew to the front lines in Korea, had Thanksgiving dinner with the soldiers in 1951, and had conferences at Seoul and Tokyo. Even more extensive and numerous were the well-nigh habitual diplomatic missions of Vice-President Nixon, the most spectacular of which was that of May, 1958, when he encountered riotous anti-American demonstrations in South America that seemed to threaten his very life. If it is objected that this is disconcerting to the State Department, it can be pointed out that this diplomatic function of the vice-president together with his membership on the National Security Council are appropriate preparation in the field of foreign relations for the stand-by president of the United States. At any rate it has become a firmly established usage to assign diplomatic missions as a part of the work of the vice-president.[31]

[31] See Williams, *ibid.*, pp. 25, 26.

Certainly the time is now long past when the only duty a vice-president is certain of having to carry out is that of presiding over the Senate. By statute a member of the National Security Council and by established custom even vice-chairman of the council and of the Cabinet, he is now important in the formulation of administration policy. In the closely divided Senate of the present day he is a frequent voter, although in the breaking of ties his vote is only affirmatively effective, since the tie vote defeats the matter under consideration, which his added negative vote only emphasized. Now that the president becomes more and more certainly the chief legislator, it is increasingly important that the vice-president be his legislative liaison officer. It has turned out that, in considering what it takes to make a good vice-president, the least important of all his qualifications are those that prepare him for the one duty the Constitution prescribes for him while he is vice-president, that is, his presiding over the Senate.

It was not until President Garfield had been shot by a disappointed office-seeker and disabled for eighty days before his death, that the American people became acutely aware of the most enigmatic passage of the Constitution. The essential words of the puzzling passage are: "In case of the . . . inability (of the President) to discharge the powers and duties of said office, the same shall devolve on the Vice President." The poignant problem is how and by whom is the "inability" to be determined. In the perfect babel of opinions on the passage, even by the most competent commentators, no consensus has ever emerged. In the summer of 1881 Secretary of State James G. Blaine and indeed Garfield's Cabinet as a whole were said to have asked Vice-President Arthur to act as President.[32] Arthur was deterred by the fact that he had been nominated as Vice-President to appease the "Stalwart" faction of the Republican party, and at the time of the assassination he was in Albany lobbying to persuade the New York legislature to vindicate by re-election the two New York senators Conkling and

---

[32] Report in *Boston Evening Transcript*, August 24, 1881, cited by Ruth Silva, *Presidential Succession* (1951), p. 54 n.

Platt, who had resigned in protest against an appointment made by President Garfield subject to confirmation by the Senate. Under the extremely embarrassing circumstances Arthur bore himself with dignity and propriety. He came to Washington promptly, standing by for the eventuality of the President's death, and received daily reports from Secretary of State Blaine but made no move to assume the duties of the presidential office. When, late in August, Garfield seemed on the way to recovery Arthur returned to his New York City home, where he remained until the President's death. He never saw Garfield during the President's inability, and, incredible as it seems, apparently no vice-president was ever permitted to see a president at such a time before 1955.

The inherent difficulty of determining just what condition constitutes the "inability" of a president "to discharge the powers and duties of said office" has been intensified by the fact that John Tyler, the first Vice-President, confronted with a vacancy in the presidency, deliberately succeeded to the office of President despite the almost certain intention of the framers that in such a case the vice-president would only "act as President." By the time Garfield was invalided, the error of Tyler had been sanctified as established constitutional usage by the succession of three vice-presidents to vacancies in the president's office. This usage had created the potential corollary implication that no vice-president could ever merely "act as President" but would become irrevocably president upon assuming the duties of a president even during a temporary inability of the latter. No matter how able the displaced president might later become, he would be only an ex-president. Here is another consideration that gave pause to Vice-President Arthur if he was ever inclined to step into Garfield's shoes. When Arthur finally succeeded to the presidency, his urging upon Congress legislation to solve the problem led to debate but not legislation.

Wilson's inability created a much more critical problem than Garfield's, whose illness was not so prolonged and came in a period of relative calm, when Congress was not in session. Wilson's stroke occurred when he was on a tour of the country appealing to the people to pressure Senate ratification of the Covenant of the League of Nations and at the very time that the Senate was in the midst of the debate on the controversial issue. In the eyes of many the President was incapacitated in the midst of an international crisis of which he was the key personality. Since Mrs. Wilson determined, after consulting the President's doctor, what matters were to be brought to the sick President's attention, she became a sort of *de facto* President—at any rate the disposition of momentous issues depended on her judgment as to whether they would be brought to the attention of the only person with authority to pass judgment upon them.

Because of Wilson's inability, twenty-eight acts of Congress, then in session, became law due to the failure of the President to sign them within the ten days prescribed by the Constitution. For three weeks he passed on only one of sixteen acts presented to him. Viscount Edward Grey spent four months in Washington unable to see the President, whom alone the Constitution invests with the duty of receiving representatives of foreign nations. So secluded in fact was the President that the rumor, plausible under such circumstances, that he was dead circulated. Another rumor was that he was insane.[33] Meanwhile Vice-President Marshall was left in complete ignorance as to Wilson's condition.

Under the prevailing circumstances Secretary of State Lansing called twenty-one Cabinet meetings to keep executive business going. This almost certainly forestalled congressional action to establish Wilson's inability. Only after these meetings had been going on for four months did Wilson hear of them and then he angrily denounced Lansing for what he had done and demanded his resignation, which was promptly submitted. "Under our constitutional law and practice, as developed hitherto," wrote Wilson to Lansing, "no one but the President has the right to summon the heads of the executive departments into conference, and no one

---

[33] See Ruth Silva, *Presidential Succession* (1951), pp. 58, 59.

but the President and the Congress has the right to ask their views or the views of any one of them on any public question."[34] An editorial in the *New York Times* promptly observed, "If Congress had accepted the theory which Mr. Wilson now proposed that the Cabinet could do nothing without his presence, and consequently that the government was at a standstill, Congress might have felt it to be its duty to ascertain whether, in respect to the President, the condition described in Article II of the Constitution as 'inability to discharge the powers and duties of said office' actually existed."[35]

When President Wilson was first stricken, those nearest him believed death near, and they refrained from informing Vice-President Marshall lest he assume power too soon. Democrats in Congress made no suggestion to Marshall lest it publicize the President's condition. Republicans did nothing, believing that the *status quo* was embarrassing the Democrats. It was doubted whether Congress had constitutional authority for action on the matter. The language of the Constitution devolves the power specifically on the vice-president in case of the president's inability. Marshall might, on his own volition, have assumed the power, but he refused to do so as resolutely as Vice-President Arthur had thirty-eight years earlier. There was even a story published in the *Christian Science Monitor* that the Chief Justice conveyed through a friend of the Vice-President the message, "Tell Tom Marshall he can have his writ whenever he asks for it" to which Marshall replied he would never do it in a thousand years.[36] The net result of the confusion of opinion and advice in 1919 was exactly nothing, and not an inch of progress has been made on the matter to this day.

Perhaps the shrewdest suggestion yet made is that, whenever there is evidently inability of a president to perform his duties, Congress pass a concurrent resolution asking the vice-president to

[34] *New York Times*, Feb. 14, 1920.
[35] Feb. 15, 1920.
[36] See Ruth Silva, *Presidential Succession* (1951), p. 64 n.

act as president during the period of the president's disability. Fortunately a concurrent resolution does not require a president's signature, and no president would be available under the circumstance. Nor does such a resolution have the force of law but is rather a strong expression of congressional opinion. It would however give the vice-president enormous moral support in the decision to act, which would nevertheless have to be his decision. The concurrent resolution could declare that the vice-president should act as president only until the inability of the president be removed. This would leave undisturbed the long-established usage that the vice-president succeeds to the presidency when there is a vacancy. Sometime the Gordian knot will have to be cut. The concurrent resolution might be the means to the end.

On February 26, 1958, President Eisenhower revealed to the press that he and Vice-President Nixon had arrived at a clear "verbal" understanding as to what was to be done in case of a temporary illness that would take the President away from his desk. The Vice-President and the White House staff would carry on the government so far as constitutionally possible. The Vice-President would hold Cabinet meetings and make policy decisions with the aid of the President's staff. Of course everything would still be subject to the President's approval. This, of course, would be only a make-shift, since the Vice-President would not possess one iota of the President's constitutional or statutory authority. He would have no authoritative control of the administrative system, since he could have none of the President's power to appoint and remove upon which depends executive command of administration. The Cabinet heads would still be Eisenhower's, not Nixon's. It would be Eisenhower's staff in its entire personnel headed by the resolute chief of staff, Sherman Adams, still Eisenhower's Sherman Adams, loyal to his disabled chief. Whatever the Vice-President's conception of foreign policy, he would have Eisenhower's John Foster Dulles, the titular head man of the Cabinet, whom President Eisenhower had even pronounced one of the greatest secretaries of state in our history. Inasmuch as the

President might recover, the Vice-President would be no more than the shadow of a President. Even if, by some means, presumably a constitutional amendment, the Vice-President could be invested temporarily with all presidential powers, the uncertainty of his tenure would impair seriously his determination and administration of policy. In the absence of crisis we would doubtless get by, and even in a crisis the traditional high political morality of the American people could be counted on to help the Acting President. But the uncertainty of the legality of the acts of an acting president will persist until the obscurity of the Constitution at this point is decisively clarified.

The clause of the Constitution concerned with vacancies in the presidency is free from all obscurity where it authorizes Congress "to provide for the case of removal, death, resignation, or inability, both of the President and Vice-President declaring what officer shall then act as President, and such officer shall act accordingly, until the disability be removed, or a President shall be elected." Here the Constitution permits Congress no choice but to provide that whoever they designate can only "act as President" and not succeed to the office unless later elected to it. Congress passed the first law under this clause in 1792. James Madison, then a member of the House of Representatives, had proposed that the secretary of state be designated to act as president, but this was countered promptly by the influence of Secretary of the Treasury Alexander Hamilton, who tended to dominate Congress then as "prime minister," which he asked his friends to call him, and who wanted no arrangement that would devolve the President's duties upon Secretary of State Thomas Jefferson. It is significant that Washington had been so ill with pneumonia in his first year as President that he was not expected to recover.

This first Succession Act, as it has been somewhat erroneously called, provided that in the case of neither president nor vice-president being in office or able to function then the president of the Senate and the speaker of the House of Representatives in turn were to succeed to the duties of the president, that is, "act as

President." The statute further provided that in case of a vacancy in both these latter offices the secretary of state was to call a special presidential election—that is, for the choosing of electors to elect a president. The Whigs, who in 1841 contemplated impeachment proceedings against President Tyler, looked forward to utilizing this provision for a special election in order to elect a satisfactory Whig president. Concerning this first Succession Act Edward S. Corwin has observed:

> It is unlikely that Congress ever passed a more ill-considered law. As Madison pointed out at the time it violated the principle of separation of powers and flouted the probability that neither the President *pro tempore* nor the Speaker is an 'officer' in the sense of the paragraph of the Constitution. It thus contemplated the possibility of there being nobody to exercise the powers of the President for an indefinite period, and at the same time set at naught, by the provision made for an interim presidential election, the synchrony evidently contemplated by the Constitution in the choice of a President with a new House of Representatives and a new one-third of the Senate. Yet this inadequate enactment remained on the statute book for nearly one hundred years becoming all the time more and more unworkable from obsolescence. [37]

Time and again during the ninety-four years that the first Presidential Succession Law was in force there was neither a president *pro tempore* of the Senate nor a speaker of the House of Representatives. During the invalidism of President Garfield, Vice-President Arthur became seriously ill while neither of the two offices, president *pro tempore* of the Senate and speaker of the House, had an incumbent. Four years later President Cleveland did not travel to Indianapolis to attend the funeral of Vice-President Hendricks lest something happen that might incapacitate him when the two offices were again vacant. Almost a year later Congress enacted the second Presidential Succession Law, which

[37] E. S. Corwin (ed.), *The Constitution of the United States of America: Analysis and Interpretation* (1953), pp. 387, 388. Corwin's reference to upsetting the "synchrony" refers to the fact that a president elected by this special election would have to be for the four-year term prescribed by the Constitution.

had been on its way through the congressional mill for some time. It provided that, in case of the disqualification of both the president and vice-president, the members of the president's Cabinet should succeed to the duties of the office, that is, act as president, following one another in the chronological order of the creation of the executive departments of which they were the respective heads, provided they had the qualifications for the president prescribed by the Constitution. The act seemed to imply that the Cabinet member acting as president retained his Cabinet office.

On May 9, 1945, James A. Farley in a speech delivered at Hazelton, Pennsylvania, pointed out that the Succession Act enabled President Truman, in the absence of a vice-president, to appoint his own successor, which he considered undemocratic. This was surely not the first time this had been possible under the sixty-year-old statute. Politically minded Farley may have left unrevealed a partisan concern over the fact that the heir-apparent just then, Secretary of State Edward R. Stettinius, was suspected of being a Republican. At any rate, the point that the president's successor by statute ought to be an elected officer took hold of the public, and President Truman sent a message to Congress recommending that the speaker of the House and the president *pro tempore* of the Senate should in turn be made immediate successors instead of the Cabinet. Congress after some time took to the idea of one of their number rather than the members of the Cabinet, and in 1947 Truman's recommendation became law. The Cabinet members follow in the order of the Act of 1886, but the new act provides specifically that any officer succeeding to the powers of the president must resign the office he held.

The present Succession Law revived the old question as to whether the first two offices in the succession are offices within the meaning of the Constitution. It also makes possible a change of party in the presidential office in the midst of a term by the succession of the speaker. It should be noted that the point that the speaker is a popularly elected official is watered down considerably by the fact that the electorate that selected him is inevitably atypical, not at all analogous to the national electorate. Speakers become eligible only after prolonged seniority due to persistent election by one-party districts and are consequently not intimately in touch with anything like our national multigroup society. This raises the question as to just how impressive might be the popular mandate of a speaker who succeeds to the powers of the president. Presidents *pro tempore* of the Senate have been, on the whole, rather less significant than the speaker, while a long line of notable secretaries of state have presented a claim to statesmanship scarcely less than that of our presidents.

XIV

The President as

a National Symbol

* **IN A FLASH** of intuitive insight the late Henry Jones Ford perceived "that in the Presidential office as it has been constituted since Jackson's time, American democracy has revived the oldest political institution of the race, the elective kingship. It is all there: the prerecognition of the notables, and the tumultuous choice of the freemen, only conformed to modern conditions."[1] Had he chosen to give details, Ford might have mentioned the elaborate ritual of the inauguration, suggestive of the coronation, the twenty-one-gun salute on arrival and departure of the president, and the throngs that gather to see and hear him. A long generation before Ford made his observation, Lincoln's Secretary of State, William H. Seward, had answered an inquisitive English newspaper correspondent, "We elect a king for four years and give him absolute power within certain limits, which after all he can interpret for himself."[2] It is all significant of a deep-seated human longing for symbolism. However, this was not just the work of the Founding Fathers. Their efforts were frustrated by a long generation of resolute resistance of the Jeffersonians to the investing of the office of president with any trace of symbolism.

[1] *The Rise and Growth of American Politics* (1898), p. 293.
[2] *Ibid.*, p. 291.

Whoever has observed the behavior of Britons with respect to their monarch will have some conception of the profound significance they attach to the "oldest political institution of the race"; nor is this significance confined to the unthinking masses. The English monarch is busy enough with ceremonials to kill a horse, but at the point where the sovereign exhausted stops for the day, the president of the United States in addition to such ceremonials starts his practical duties. No wonder two internationally known Oxford dons expressed to the writer their sober conviction that the United States ought to establish a monarchy. Imperturbable and indomitable as the British are, one can only wonder what might be the effect of the sudden loss of the myth of royalty, especially when incarnate in the lovely personality of Elizabeth II. That is something we shall never know, but it is conceivable that the blasting of London by the *Luftwaffe* was but a mosquito bite in comparison. Sir Ivor Jennings writes:

> Certain it is that democratic government is not merely a matter of cold reason and prosaic policies. There must be some display of colour, and there is nothing more vivid than royal purple and imperial scarlet. During the present century, therefore, we have placed almost intolerable burdens on the royal family. They must not only head subscription lists and appear on State occasions; they must, also, inspect this and that, open this and that, lay this stone and that, and undertake a thousand other dull tasks in a blaze of publicity. We can hardly blame Edward VIII if he preferred to make toffee in the kitchen.[3]

Of course, the Queen does not have to open a baseball season by tossing out the first ball or shake hands with interminable lines of people. But the fact that custom has imposed upon the president extraofficial burdens similar to those of royalty is indicative of the symbolism of the president. By and large, he symbolizes the American government to the American people. According to Professor Rossiter, "The American President is the one-man distillation of the American people just as surely as the Crown is

[3] *The British Constitution* (1950), p. 116.

of the British Commonwealth." To William H. Taft he was "the personal embodiment and representative of their dignity and majesty."[4] His voice and only his can be that of the American people whether it be Lincoln at Gettysburg or delivering the incomparable second inaugural. Franklin Roosevelt declaring "The only thing we have to fear is fear itself" was the spokesman of a distressed nation. How many Americans proudly declared, "The President shook this hand of mine." President Hoover reported that after these daily ordeals his hand would be so swollen that for days he could not write.[5]

So our elective king no less than a hereditary monarch goes a breathless ceremonial pace. He awards medals of honor to uncomfortable military heroes, buys the first poppy at the annual V. F. W. sale, broadcasts the opening of the annual March of Dimes, greets delegations of firemen, Boy Scouts, Elks, Eagles, and such, issues the Thanksgiving Proclamation, lays a wreath on the tomb of the Unknown Soldier even as the Queen at the base of the Cenotaph on Whitehall on Remembrance Day, lights the White House Christmas tree, opens distant expositions by pressing a button at the White House, receives monarchs, foreign prime ministers, and delegations of awestruck school children, sponsors the Easter egg rolling on the White House lawn, to mention but a few. Then there are addresses on this, that, and other occasions. Nor can it be doubted that this symbolism serves to strengthen the practical powers of the presidential office.

When Washington was inaugurated in 1789, all adult native Americans had been subjects of George III; and they did not suddenly, on a particular day, cease to be such subjects. The transition was somewhat gradual. For months after Bunker Hill, American chaplains were reverently remembering the King in their prayers. Even as late as January, 1776, and not so many months before the Declaration of Independence, the King's health

---

[4] Clinton Rossiter, "The American President," *Yale Review*, XXXVII (1948), 622.
[5] *The Memoirs of Herbert Hoover, 1920–1933* (1952), p. 323.

was still being toasted nightly in the officers' mess presided over by General Washington.⁶ Fortunately there was no Un-American Activities Committee in that day.

Nor were these professions of loyalty to the King inconsistent. The grievances of the patriots were over ministerial policies, and Washington was battling the "ministerial troops," as his letters then expressed it. So professions of loyalty to the King persisted for nearly a year after the first shot had been fired at Lexington.

Loyalty to the King evaporated rapidly in the spring of 1776. The shift in the attitude of patriots toward King George found expression in a pamphlet published with perfect timing. In Thomas Paine's *Common Sense* not only was King George denounced with savage ferocity, but the symbolism of royalty was covered with obloquy. The Norman Conquest as a foundation stone of British monarchy was given a breath-taking reinterpretation.

A French bastard, landing with an armed banditti, and establishing himself king of England against the consent of the natives, is in plain terms, a very paltry, rascally original. It certainly hath no divinity in it.... Let them promiscuously worship the Ass and the Lion, and welcome. I shall neither copy their humility nor disturb their devotion.... The plain truth is that English monarchy will not bear looking into.

Nearly every literate patriot read *Common Sense* while the ink was still fresh, and its ideas struck a responsive chord. Thomas Jefferson's indictments in the Declaration of Independence were consequently directed against the King, not Parliament.

Undoubtedly the destruction of the symbolism of the King created a psychological vacuum. However, it scarcely mattered, since there was then little sentiment of American nationality that needed to be symbolized. It was state independence, not national, that had apparently been declared. The Continental Congress was an assembly of ambassadors lacking in prestige, and at its best a

⁶ S. E. Morison and H. S. Commager, *The Growth of the American Republic* (1937), I, 77.

congress can scarcely constitute an impressive national symbol. When the Constitution of 1787 invested Congress with specific legislative powers, the opponents of ratification cried out, "We did not dethrone King George only to enthrone King Congress."

The inauguration of President Washington, as well as the later procedures and etiquette introduced by the Federalists, precipitated a controversy over appropriate symbolism of the president. Vice-President John Adams declared, "Take away thrones and crowns from among men and there will be an end of all dominion and justice."[7] Accordingly, while presiding over the Senate, Adams was urging an elaborate and high-sounding title for President Washington and was horrified when the simple title prescribed by the Constitution was retained precisely as set down. "What," he demanded, "will the common people of foreign countries, what will the sailors and soldiers say, 'George Washington, President of the United States'? *They will despise him to all eternity.*"[8]

In the Constitutional Convention Hamilton had avowed a preference for monarchy. Soon President Washington was being maneuvered into something of the separateness of a monarch under the management of public affairs by his energetic Secretary of the Treasury. Hamilton assumed the role (secretly even the title) of prime minister, recommended measures to Congress, and pressured Congressmen to enact them, with the consequence that the legislative program of the first administration still stands as Hamilton's, not Washington's. If the precedent then set had not been battered to bits by the opposition, the president might never have become, as he did in the twentieth century, a combination of king and prime minister.

Adams' and Hamilton's "aping of monarchy" brought about a strong emotional reaction on the part of the inland agrarians. The symbol-smashing French Revolution, which produced an

---

[7] *Gazette of the United States,* March, 1790; quoted in V. L. Parrington, *Main Currents of American Thought* (1927, 1930), I, 311.

[8] James Hart, *The American Presidency in Action, 1789* (1948), p. 36.

epidemic of Jacobin Clubs in the United States, re-enforced the reaction. Jefferson coined a word "monocrats," and, to the glee of his partisans, applied it to the Federalists.[9] Even Washington's inauguration, thought Jefferson, had been "not at all in character with the simplicity of republican government and looking, as if wistfully, to those of European courts." So when the time came for Jefferson's inauguration in 1801, he walked unostentatiously from his boarding house over to the Capitol to deliver his inaugural address to the two houses assembled in the Senate Chamber. The Puritans had not been one whit more determined to eradicate popish symbols from their churches than were the Jeffersonians to divest the president of the trappings of royalty. Deprived of its symbolism, the office of president was to be nothing more than a purely utilitarian agency of government, merely a means to an end.

During the twenty-four years of the Virginia dynasty, not only did the president lose his symbolism, but the very prestige of the office sank to its nadir. Congress took charge of the executive, nominating the candidate for the presidency by congressional caucus, and, under the then prevailing one-party system, nomination was equivalent to election. Madison, for example, was so completely the prisoner of Congress that he could scarcely have been less a factor in the government if he had spent the eight years of his presidency at home on his plantation.[10]

It was the upsurge of the recently enfranchised masses and their election of Andrew Jackson to the presidency as their champion in 1828 that terminated the purely utilitarian conception of the presidency and made the president peculiarly the symbol of the national government. State legislatures had in the main been selecting presidential electors, but this ceased in 1828, and Jackson was practically the first popularly elected President. His unequivocal denunciation of nullification in 1833 and readiness to use

[9] See *The Oxford Dictionary* and Jefferson's *Writings* (1859), III, 494.
[10] See R. V. Harlow, *The History of Legislative Methods in the Period before 1825* (1917), p. 196.

armed force in order to "take care that the laws be faithfully executed" enhanced the prestige and symbolism of the presidency. As a "tribune of the people" Jackson used the veto against special privilege such as the bill to renew the Bank charter in 1832. To this day, a presidential veto tends to strengthen the prestige of a president. The idea of the tribuneship persists, no matter what congressmen may think of it.

The acclaim with which President Andrew Jackson was greeted by the populace heralded a revival of the symbolism of the presidency. His journey to New England in 1833 illustrates the point. Entering Philadelphia on a white charger, provided for the occasion, the aging warrior accepted the obeisances of the crowds for five hours as they filled streets, windows, and roofs, and the reception continued for four days and nights. From New York City Jackson wrote, "I have bowed to upward of two hundred thousand people today." His passage through Connecticut was a continuous ovation. "Across Rhode Island cannon boomed from town to town as if New England were a battle line," and receptions overlapped each other. In Boston he was "received with all the show of honor which we paid to Lafayette," wrote an astonished citizen. And Harvard outdid itself in conferring upon Jackson the degree of Doctor of Laws.[11]

A generation after Jackson's election, so exalted had the president become as the symbol of the Federal government that the symbolism became a major factor in the secession movement. Secession could scarcely have been based on a cool calculation of the results of the election of 1860. The fact is generally overlooked that, although the Republicans had elected Lincoln (with a popular plurality of about 40 per cent), they had nevertheless lost both houses of Congress. They had only 31 of the 66 senators and 105 of the 237 representatives. Had the southern senators and representatives retained their seats, Lincoln could not have made one important appointment—not even of his Cabinet members—

[11] Marquis James, *The Life of Andrew Jackson* (1938), pp. 639–44.

with the consent of only Republican senators. When the southern senators and representatives walked out, they turned the government over to Lincoln and thus paid an unconscious tribute to the symbolism and authority that had become attached to the office of president.

Day after day English newspapers and periodicals must feed the insatiable public appetite for pictures of the Queen and her family. This has its counterpart in the president and his family. Since the first Roosevelt, the White House family has belonged to the nation as an essential element in the symbol of the presidency. Theodore Roosevelt's children running bareheaded out of the White House on their way to school, Quentin riding his pony into the White House and getting it on the elevator, the vivacious young Alice keeping Washington agog with her quips and her unconventional and unpredictable ways, were all part of the first Roosevelt regime. The death of Coolidge's son touched the heart of every American parent. As the barometer registering Truman's popularity struck a new low, one wondered how much more it might have fallen if Bess and Margaret had been out of the picture. How many points of Ike's score depend on Mamie? What might have happened to the presidency if Chief Justice Warren and his bevy of daughters had moved into the White House? The president's family is part of the national symbol that constitutes the presidency.

Never was the symbolism of the presidency more dramatically demonstrated than in the sudden translation of diffident Vice-President Harry Ş. Truman into President, Chief Executive, and Commander-in-Chief in the command of our far-flung battle line in a global war.

> Harry, as the clock under the portrait of Woodrow Wilson in the Cabinet room passed 7:09, suddenly ceased to be 'Harry' and became Mr. President. Then within the time it takes for the clicking of cameras, he was the almost superstitiously honored man symbol of America who can still after our pattern of reverence, be described in the native argument in the American language as one angry truck driver might describe another....

He was not Harry Truman any longer; he never would be again. The prison of the presidency dropped around him. The Secret Service scurried beside him as he moved. The personages shook his hands and fell away.[12]

Even the history of presidential elections emphasizes the symbolism of the presidency. How often has the electorate turned to the candidate who captivated the voters as a symbol rather than as one eminently qualified for the difficult job? If preparation for statesmanship by scholarship, accumulated knowledge, and long practical political experience qualifies for the presidency, few incumbents of the great office were more entitled to a second term than John Quincy Adams. Instead the hysterical populace turned to their idol General Andrew Jackson, whom Adams in a pardonable hyperbole declared to be "a barbarian who could . . . hardly spell his own name." There was scarcely an abler President in the generation preceding the Civil War than Martin Van Buren, but instead of re-electing him the still more hysterical electorate turned to the victor of the battle of the Thames, General William Henry Harrison. In 1848 ignoring the receptive statesmen, Clay and Webster, the perverse electorate preferred instead one whom the latter had pronounced "an ignorant frontier colonel," Zachary Taylor, the hero of Buena Vista.

How could the voters in 1869 turn so decisively from the politically experienced Governor Horatio Seymour to the utterly politically inexperienced General Grant except as he symbolized the salvation of the Union? And in our own day, if he the electorate had been thinking of political experience and demonstrated executive competence, would it have turned so decisively from Governor Adlai Stevenson to a general confessedly unfamiliar with politics and compelled consequently to learn the perplexing art gradually after inauguration? Curiously enough it is when the electorate is most thoroughly aroused that it usually elects a symbol rather

---

[12] Jonathan Daniels, *Frontier on the Potomac* (1946), pp. 9, 12, quoted by D. W. Brogan, *Politics in America* (1954), p. 274.

than a candidate distinguished by demonstrated competence for the presidency.

If anyone asks for conclusive evidence of the symbolism of the president, let him recall the extraordinary demonstrations of personal grief manifested by ordinary people when President Franklin Roosevelt died. Unforgettable are the pictures of these people with streaming tears as they looked at the passing funeral procession. It is conceivable that multitudes of Americans mourned more profoundly the passing of President Franklin Roosevelt than the English people did the death of King George VI.

Nor is such grief anything new. The writer can never forget how he found his father, just after the news of McKinley's assassination had arrived, weeping as bitterly as if he had lost a child. So it was to others when Lincoln, Garfield, and Harding died in office. The son who protested to his foreign-born mother Harding's lack of merit when he found her weeping over news of the President's death got this significant response: *"Ach, aber er ist doch der President."*[13] Here we have the essence of the symbolism. No matter what hard-boiled public officials and politicians may think of such conduct, it is the feeling of the rank and file of Americans, their emotional reaction, that determines the matter of the president as a symbol of the nation.

[13] Henry Reiff, "We Live by Symbols," *The Social Studies*, XXXI, No. 3 (1940), 103. The sentence in German can be translated, "Ah, but he is still the President."

Bibliography

Abbott, Lawrence F. *Impressions of Theodore Roosevelt*. Garden City, 1919.

Adams, George Burton. *An Outline Sketch of English Constitutional History*. New Haven, 1918.

Adams, Henry. *The Education of Henry Adams* (The Modern Library). New York, 1931.

———. *John Randolph*. Boston, 1882.

Adams, John. *Works*. 10 vols., Boston, 1850–56.

Adams, J. Q., *Memoirs*. 12 vols. Philadelphia, 1874–79.

Angle, Paul M. *The Lincoln Reader*. New Brunswick, 1947.

Bailey, Stephen K., and Samuel, Howard D. *Congress at Work*. New York, 1952.

Bailey, Thomas A. *A Diplomatic History of the American People*. New York, 1958.

———. *The Man in the Street*. New York, 1948.

Baker, Ray Stannard. *Woodrow Wilson, Life and Letters*. 6 vols. Garden City, 1927.

Bancroft, George. *History of the United States from the Discovery of the Continent*. 6 vols. New York, 1883–85.

Basler, Roy P. *Abraham Lincoln: His Speeches and Writings*. Cleveland, 1946.

Beard, Charles A. *The Republic.* New York, 1944.

————, and Beard, Mary. *The Rise of American Civilization.* 2 vols. New York, 1927.

Beer, Thomas. *Hanna.* New York, 1929.

Bellush, Bernard. *Franklin Roosevelt, Governor of New York.* New York, 1955.

Bemis, Samuel Flagg. *John Quincy Adams and the Union.* New York, 1956.

Beveridge, Albert J. *Abraham Lincoln.* 4 vols. Boston and New York, 1928.

————. *Life of John Marshall.* 4 vols. Boston, 1916–19.

Binkley, Wilfred F. *American Political Parties: Their Natural History.* New York, 1947.

————. *Powers of the President.* Garden City, 1937.

————. *President and Congress.* New York, 1947.

Bishop, J. B. *Theodore Roosevelt and his Times.* 2 vols. New York, 1920.

Blaine, James G. *Twenty Years of Congress.* 2 vols. Norwich, 1884–86.

Blair, Niles. *The James.* New York, 1939.

Bolles, Blair. *Uncle Joe Cannon.* New York, 1951.

Bowers, Claude. *The Tragic Era.* Boston, 1929.

Brogan, D. W. *Politics in America.* New York, 1954.

Brown, George Rothwell. *The Leadership of Congress.* Indianapolis 1922.

Browning, O. H. *Diary of Orville Hicks Browning.* 2 vols. Springfield, 1925, 1933.

Brownlow, Louis, *et al. The President's Committee on Administrative Management.* United States Government Printing Office, Washington, 1937.

Bryce, James. *The American Commonwealth* (Commonwealth Edition). New York, 1908.

Burgess, John W. *The Administration of President Hayes.* New York, 1916.

Busbey, L. W. *Uncle Joe Cannon.* New York, 1927.

Carroll, E. M., *Origins of the Whig Party.* Durham, N. C., 1925.

Chamberlain, Lawrence H., *The President, Congress, and Legislation.* New York, 1946.

Cole, G. H. D. and Postgate, Raymond. *The British Common People, 1746–1938.* New York, 1939.

Coolidge, Calvin. *Autobiography.* New York, 1929.

Corwin, E. S. (editor). *The Constitution of the United States: Analysis and Interpretation.* United States Government Printing Office, Washington, 1953.

————. *The President: Office and Powers.* New York, 1957.

————. *Total War and the Constitution.* New York, 1947.

Corwin, E. S., and Koenig, L. W. *The Presidency Today.* New York, 1956.

Croly, Herbert. *Marcus Alonzo Hanna.* New York, 1913.

Dana, C. A. *Recollections of the Civil War.* New York, 1898.

David, Paul, Moos, Malcolm, and Goldman, Ralph. *Presidential Nominating Politics.* 5 vols. Baltimore, 1954.

Dawes, Charles G. *A Journal of the McKinley Years.* La Grange, Ill., 1950.

Dennett, Tyler. *John Hay.* New York, 1933.

Dimock, G. W. *Congressional Investigating Committees.* Baltimore, 1929.

Dodd, W. E. *Expansion and Conflict.* Boston, 1915.

Donovan, Robert J. *Eisenhower: The Inside Story.* New York, 1956.

Elliott, Jonathan (editor). *Debates, Resolutions, and Other Proceedings in Convention on the Adoption of the Federal Constitution.* 6 vols. Washington, 1827–46.

Farley, James A. *Jim Farley's Story, The Roosevelt Years.* New York, 1948.

Farrand, Max. *The Records of the Federal Convention of 1787.* 3 vols. New Haven, 1911.

Flynn, Edward J. *You're the Boss.* New York, 1947.

Ford, H. J. *The Rise and Growth of American Politics.* New York, 1898.

————. *Woodrow Wilson, the Man and his Work.* New York, 1916.

Fuess, Claude M. *Calvin Coolidge.* Boston, 1940.

Galloway, George B. *Congress at the Crossroads.* New York, 1947.

Gauss, Christian. *Democracy Today: An Interpretation.* New York, 1919.

Gompers, Samuel. *Seventy Years of Life and Labor.* 2 vols. New York, 1925.

Goodnow, Frank J. *Comparative Administrative Law.* 2 vols. New York, 1893.

Gunther, John. *Roosevelt in Retrospect: a Profile in History.* New York, 1950.

Hamilton, Alexander (H. C. Lodge, editor). *Works.* 12 vols. New York, 1904.

Hamilton, John C. *History of the Republic of the United States of America as Traced in the Writings of Alexander Hamilton.* 7 vols. New York, 1850–51.

Harlow, R. V. *The History of Legislative Methods in the Period before 1825.* New Haven, 1917.

Hart, James. *The American Presidency in Action, 1789.* New York, 1948.

Hayes, Rutherford B. *Diary and Letters of Rutherford B. Hayes.* (C. S. Williams, editor.) 5 vols. Columbus, 1922.

Herring, E. P. *Presidential Leadership.* New York, 1940.

———. *Public Administration and the Public Interest.* New York, 1936.

Hertz, E. *The Hidden Lincoln.* New York, 1940.

Hicks, John D. *The American Nation.* 2 vols. Boston, 1941.

Hoar, George F. *Autobiography of Seventy Years.* 2 vols. New York, 1903.

Hoover, Herbert. *The Challenge to Liberty.* New York, 1935.

———. *The Memoirs of Herbert Hoover, 1920–33.* New York, 1952.

House, E. M. *Intimate Papers.* 4 vols. Boston, 1926–28.

Hull, Cordell. *Memoirs.* 2 vols. New York, 1948.

Hyman, Sidney. *The American President.* New York, 1954.

James, Marquis. *The Life of Andrew Jackson.* New York, 1938.

Jefferson, Thomas. *Notes on the State of Virginia.* Williamsburg, 1782.

———. *The Writings of Thomas Jefferson.* (P. L. Ford, editor.) 10 vols. New York, 1892–99.

Jennings, Ivor. *The British Constitution.* Cambridge, England, 1950.

Johnson, Allen. *Jefferson and his Colleagues.* New Haven, 1921.

Jones, Jesse H., and Angly, Edward. *Fifty Billion Dollars: My Thirteen Years with the R. F. C.* New York, 1951.

Julian, G. W. *Political Recollections, 1840–1872.* Chicago, 1874.

Kerney, James. *The Political Education of Woodrow Wilson.* New York, 1926.

Key, V. O. *Southern Politics.* New York, 1949.

Lane, Franklin K. *The Letters of Franklin K. Lane.* Boston, 1922.

Laski, Harold J. *The American Presidency: An Interpretation.* New York, 1940.

Latham, Earl. *The Group Basis of Politics: A Study of Basing Point Legislation.* New York, 1952.

Lawrence, David. *The True Story of Woodrow Wilson.* New York, 1924.

Learned, H. B. *The President's Cabinet.* New Haven, 1912.

Lewis, W. D. *The Life of Theodore Roosevelt.* New York, 1919.

Link, Arthur S. *Wilson: the Road to the White House.* Princeton, 1947.

Luce, Robert. *Legislative Problems.* Boston and New York, 1935.

McBain, Howard L. *The Living Constitution.* New York, 1927.

McLaughlin, A. C. *Constitutional History of the United States.* New York, 1935.

Maclay, William. *Sketches of Debates in the First Senate.* Harrisburg, 1880.

MacMahon, Arthur W., and Millett, John D. *Federal Administrators.* New York, 1939.

Macy, Jesse. *Political Parties in the United States, 1846-1861.* New York, 1900.

Merriam, Charles E. *A History of American Political Theories.* New York, 1926.

―――. *Four Political Leaders.* New York, 1926.

Moley, Raymond. *After Seven Years.* New York, 1939.

Moos, Malcolm. *The Republicans.* New York, 1956.

Morison, Samuel E. *By Land and By Sea.* New York, 1953.

―――. *Oxford History of the United States.* 2 vols. London, 1927.

―――, and Commager, H. S. *The Growth of the American Republic.* 2 vols. New York, 1937. Revised, 1950.

Morley, Felix. *The Foreign Policy of the United States.* New York, 1951.

Nevins, Allan. *The Emergence of Lincoln.* 2 vols. New York, 1951.

―――. *Ordeal of the Union.* 2 vols. New York, 1947.

Nicolay, John G., and Hay, John. *Abraham Lincoln: a History.* 10 vols. New York, 1890.

―――. *Works of Abraham Lincoln.* 10 vols. New York, 1894.

Nourse, E. G. *Economics in the Public Service.* New York, 1953.

Oberholtzer, E. P. *History of the United States Since the Civil War.* 5 vols. New York, 1917-37.

Olcott, Charles S. *The Life of William McKinley.* 2 vols. Boston, 1916.

Ostrogorski, M. *Democracy and the Party System.* New York, 1910.

Parrington, Vernon L. *Main Currents of American Thought.* 3 vols. New York, 1927, 1930.

Peck, Harry Thurston. *Twenty Years of the Republic.* New York, 1906.

Pringle, H. F. *Theodore Roosevelt, a Biography.* New York, 1931.

Putnam, G. H., and Lapsby, A. B. (editors). *Complete Works of Abraham Lincoln.* New York, 1888–96.

Richardson, James D. *Messages and Papers of the Presidents.* 10 vols. Washington, 1927.

Rock, John P., and Stedman, Murray, S., Jr. *The Dynamics of Democratic Government.* New York, 1954.

Rogers, James Grafton. *World Policy and the Constitution.* World Peace Foundation, Boston, 1945.

Roosevelt, Franklin D. *On Our Way.* New York, 1934.

Roosevelt, Theodore. *Autobiography.* New York, 1913.

Rossiter, Clinton. *The American Presidency.* New York, 1956.

———. *The Supreme Court and the Commander-in-Chief.* Ithaca, 1951.

Rovere, Richard H. *The Eisenhower Years.* New York, 1956.

Sait, Edward M. *American Political Parties.* New York, 1839.

Sandburg, Carl. *Lincoln: the Prairie Years.* 2 vols. New York, 1926.

———. *Lincoln: The War Years.* 4 vols. New York, 1939.

Schouler, James. *History of the United States Under the Constitution.* 6 vols. New York, 1880–1913.

Schubert, Glendon A., Jr. *The Presidency and the Courts.* Minneapolis, 1957.

Sherman, John. *Recollections of Forty Years in House, Senate, and Cabinet.* 2 vols. Chicago, 1895.

Silva, Ruth. *Presidential Succession.* Ann Arbor, 1951.

Smith, Harold D. *The Management of Your Government.* New York, 1945.

Swisher, Carl. *American Constitutional Development.* Boston, 1954.

Taft, W. H. *Our Chief Magistrate and His Powers.* New York, 1916.

Tansill, Charles C. (editor). *Documents Illustrative of the Formation of the American Union.* 69th Congress, 1st Session, House Document, No. 398, 1st Session.

Thomas, Benjamin P. *Abraham Lincoln.* New York, 1952.

Timmons, Bascom N. *Garner of Texas: A Personal History.* New York, 1948.

Truman, Harry S. *Memoirs.* 2 vols. New York, 1955.

Tumulty, J. P. *Woodrow Wilson as I Knew Him.* New York, 1921.

Turner, Frederick Jackson. *The United States: 1830-1850.* New York, 1935.

Underwood, Oscar W. *Drifting Sands of Party Politics.* New York, 1931.

Upshur, Able P. *A Brief Inquiry into the True Nature and Character of Our Federal Government.* Petersburg, Va., 1840.

Van Buren, Martin. *Autobiography.* (John P. Fitzpatrick, editor.) American Historical Association Report, 1918.

Walker, Francis A. *Making of the Nation.* New York, 1895.

Washington, George. *Writings of George Washington.* (Worthington C. Ford, editor). 14 vols. New York, 1889.

Weed, H. A. *Life of Thurlow Weed.* Boston, 1884.

Wehle, Louis B. *Hidden Threads of History.* New York, 1953.

West, Willis M. *History of the American People.* Boston, 1918.

White, Leonard D. *An Introduction to the Study of Public Administration.* New York, 1926. Revised editions, 1939, 1948, 1955.

White, William Allen. *Calvin Coolidge, the Man Who is President.* New York, 1925.

Whitman, Walt. *Complete Prose Works.* New York, 1914.

Williams, Irving G. *The Rise of the Vice Presidency.* Washington, 1956.

Wilson, James Grant. *The Presidents of the United States.* 4 vols. New York, 1914.

Wilson, Woodrow. *Constitutional Government in the United States.* New York, 1907.

Wise, Henry A. *Seven Decades of the Union.* Philadelphia, 1871.

Woodbury, Levi. *Writings.* Boston, 1852.

Index